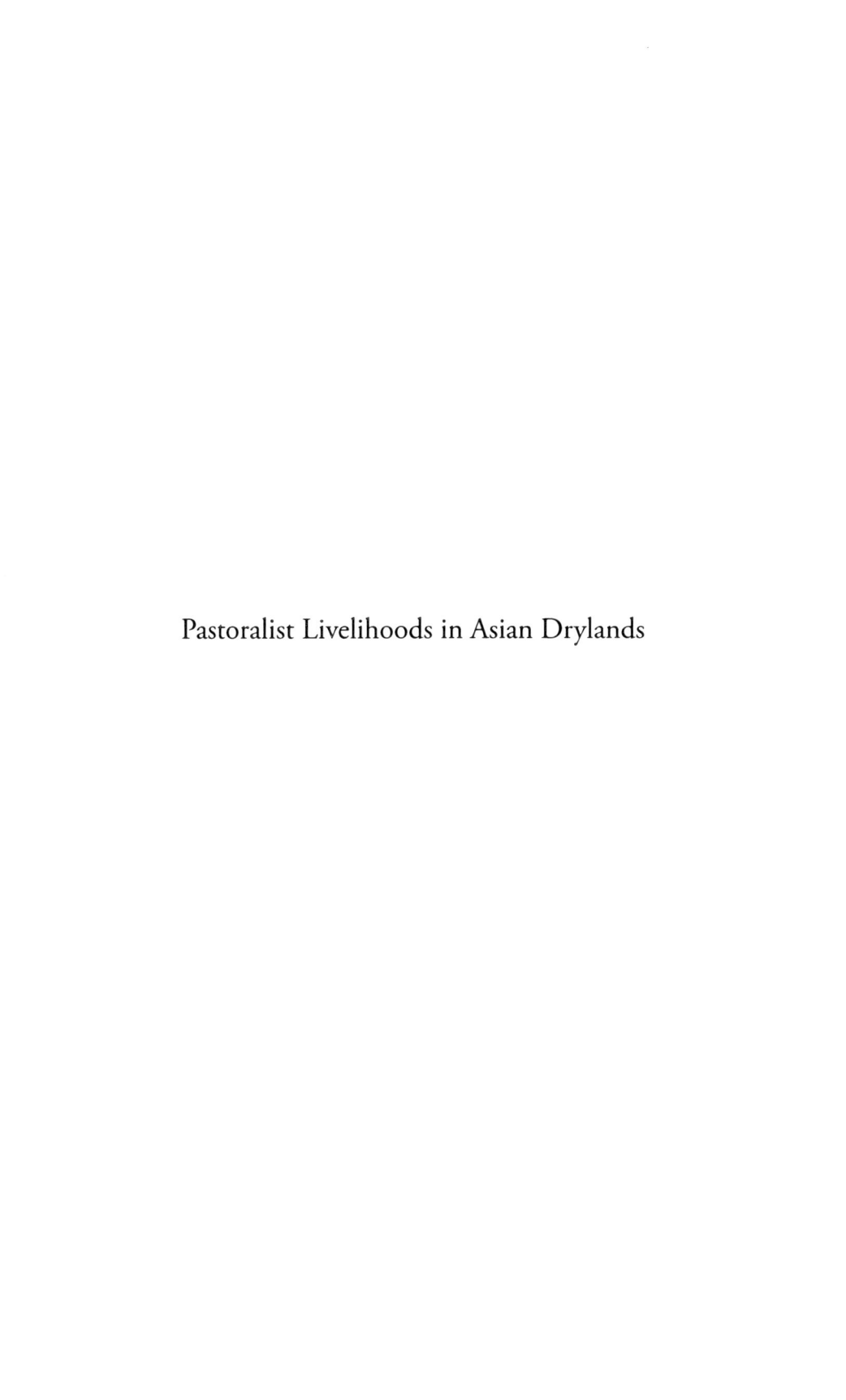

Pastoralist Livelihoods in Asian Drylands

Pastoralist Livelihoods in Asian Drylands

Environment, Governance and Risk

edited by

Ariell Ahearn and Troy Sternberg

with

Allison Hahn

Copyright © 2017
The White Horse Press,
The Old Vicarage, Winwick, Cambridgeshire, PE28 5PN, UK

Set in 11 point Adobe Garamond Pro
Printed by Lightning Source

All rights reserved. Except for the quotation of short passages for the purpose of criticism or review, no part of this book may be reprinted or reproduced or utilised in any form or by any electronic, mechanical or other means, including photocopying or recording, or in any information storage or retrieval system.

British Library Cataloguing in Publication Data
A catalogue record for this book is available from the British Library

ISBN   978-1-874267-98-0 (HB); 978-1-912186-07-5 (ebook)

CONTENTS

Notes on Contributors vii

List of Illustrations and Tables x

1. Introduction
          Ariell Ahearn and Allison Hahn 1

RESEARCH ARTICLES

2. The Afterlife of Nomadism:
   Pastoralism, environmentalism, civilisation and identity in Mongolia and China
          D. Bumochir 17

3. Environment as Commodity and Shield:
   Reshaping Herders' Collective Identity in Mongolia
          Byambabaatar Ichinkhorloo 41

4. From Reform to Revolt:
   Bashar al-Assad and the Arab Tribes in Syria
          Haian Dukhan 71

5. Herder participation in modern markets:
   The issues of the credit loan trap
          Gongbuzeren 91

6. Indigenous Systems of Ecological Knowledge and Conservation Initiatives in Jabal Akhdar Mountain, Oman
          Salah al Mazrui 109

REPORTS FROM THE FIELD

7. Afghan/Pakistan Border Politics:
   What Future for Kuchi Nomads?
          Inam ur Rahim 129

8. Transhumance and Change Among the Rungs
   of Uttarakhand Himalayas
              Nisthasri Awasthi 153
9. From Stewards to Trespassers:
   Pastoralist Management of Forest Resources . . . .
              Aman Singh 177
10. Conservation of Tangible and Intangible Properties
    of the Tent in Jordanian Badia
              Wassef Al Sekhaneh 200
Index   215

NOTES ON CONTRIBUTORS

Ariell Ahearn is an ESRC postdoctoral fellow at the School for Geography and the Environment at the University of Oxford. She holds an M.P.A. from Cornell University and a D.Phil. from the University of Oxford. She has worked with rural pastoralists in Mongolia since 2004 with research focusing on land tenure, local governance, gendered divisions of labour and social organisation. She is particularily interested in understanding social hierarchies and how these map onto institutions and government administrations.

Wassef Al Sekhaneh is an Assistant Professor at the Faculty of Archaeology and Anthropology at Yarmouk University in Jordan. He received the Ph.D. degree in cultural Anthropology from Münster University in Germany in 2005 and another Ph.D. in Nuclear Physics from Duisburg-Essen University in Germany in 2008. His research in social anthropology as a scientific discipline has been characterised as 'the science of the culturally strange', referring to bridging the cultural distance between a particular Bedouin society studied and that of the social anthropologist engaged in research. He is a member of the Jordanian Bedouin society.

Nisthasri Awasthi has a doctoral degree in social anthropology from JNU. She specialises in social and cultural ecology studies. She works as an independent research consultant for various research organisations.

D. Bumochir is a professor of anthropology at the National University of Mongolia. He is currently working as a postdoctoral research associate at University College London funded by ERC. His earlier works focused on shamanism and ritual and he completed a Ph.D. in philology at the Mongolian Academy of Sciences. Later, he obtained another Ph.D. at the University of Cambridge in the field of social anthropology. He has conducted fieldwork in Mongolia and China and his work discusses pastoralism, environment, movement, mining, ethnic politics and state.

Haian Dukhan is a Ph.D. Candidate at the School of International Relations/ Centre for Syrian Studies in St Andrews University. His research interests deal with tribal political systems and social and political exclusion of tribal people in Syria. He is also a disability rights activist who has led different disability campaigns in Syria and the UK. Dukhan's fieldwork experience has been largely done in Palmyra, a world heritage city in Syria, where he originally comes from. During the past four years of Dukhan's work on his Ph.D., he has published many papers, cited in different media outlets; for example, 'Tribes and Tribalism in the Syrian Uprising – The Islamic State and the Arab Tribes in Eastern Syria'. He has also presented his research in different universities and research centres worldwide.

Gongbuzeren is an assistant professor at Southwestern University of Finance and Economics in China. He completed his M.A in ecology and Ph.D. in natural resource management and policy. In the past few years, his research has focused on ecological conservation and rural development in the pastoral regions of China, especially in the pastoral regions of the Qinghai-Tibet Plateau. His studies have focused on community-based rangeland management and innovative adaptations to marketisation and climate change; the relationship between Tibetan culture and ecological conservation; and management of nature reserves and community-based ecotourism development.

Allison Hahn is an Assistant Professor in the Department of Communication Studies at Baruch College, CUNY. She earned a B.A. in African Studies, Anthropology, and Political Science at the University of Pittsburgh. She was then a Fulbright Research Fellow at the National University of Mongolia, Department of Political Science. After returning to the United States, she earned a Masters of International Development (M.I.D.) in Development Planning and Environmental Sustainability and a Ph.D. in Communication from the University of Pittsburgh. Professor Hahn's research investigates the argumentation and protest strategies used in environmental controversies by pastoral-nomadic communities in Kenya, Tanzania, Mongolia and China.

Byambabaatar Ichinkhorloo is a Ph.D. candidate in the Department of Anthropology and Archeology, National University of Mongolia (NUM). His research focuses on pastoralism, political ecology, identity, Development intervention and natural resource management. He has published articles on spatiality and politics in rangeland intervention, government meat reserve programmes and *zud* risk management. Recently he has conducted research on Mongolia's diverse economies and survival assemblages that emerged from socio-political and economic transformation from socialism to capitalism and he is working on local people's participation in decision-making, local perception about corruption and impacts of civil society building projects in Mongolia.

Salah al Mazrui is an independent scholar based in Oman. After completing his Masters in Anthropology (Cambridge, UK) Salah has interfaced between pastoralists and rural communities and the forces of resource extraction in Oman.

His current work addresses issues around indigenous pastoralist knowledge and land use as it relates to national conservation efforts.

Inam ur Rahim is Professor and Chair of the Department of Climate Change and Livestock at the University of Veterinary and Animal Sciences, Lahore. His earlier works focused on the extensive livestock production systems of arid and semi-arid mountain regions in traditional social and political set-ups, in the context of global and climate change. He conducted fieldwork in Pakistan, Afghanistan, Central Asia and West Africa. He worked extensively with the University of Bern and Geneva University, Switzerland for research focusing on the process of urbanisation in the mountain environment and pastoralism.

Aman Singh, based in India, is founder of 'Krishi Avam Paristhitiki Vikas Sansthan' (KRAPAVIS), and Steering Committee Member of the ICCA Consortium. Aman has overseen the regeneration of over 125 Orans (community conserved areas) in Rajasthan (India). Working on documentation about Orans, Aman has written on community-conserved areas, ecology and pastoralism, recently publishing a book entitled *'Orans': Indigenous Community Conserved Areas of Rajasthan*. He has received numerous awards and much recognition in India and abroad. Among his current initiatives are organisation of *Sodhyatra* (customary travelling for the documentation of traditional knowledge for conservation and sustainable livelihoods) and setting up an Oran Resource Centre.

Troy Sternberg is a researcher at the School for Geography and the Environment at the University of Oxford, where he works on pastoral environments in the Gobi Desert. His focus is on natural hazards, environmental processes, the effectiveness of traditional nomadic strategies and the comparative ecological impact of livelihoods across the Asian steppe. In Mongolia his interest is in developing rural water access, quantifying drought and degradation and placing Mongolian pastoralism and the Gobi environment in a broader global context.

LIST OF ILLUSTRATIONS AND TABLES

CHAPTER 1

Figure 1. Map of study areas. 4

Figure 2. Herder prepares for Naadam. Tov Aimag, Mongolia.. 7

CHAPTER 2

Figure 1. Qaidam Basin, Qinghai Province. 18

CHAPTER 3

Figure 1. Research sites: Tes in Western Mongolia, Tariat in Central Mongolia and Bayanjargalan in Southern Mongolia; Survey sites: Uvs, Khovd, Zavkhan, Dornogovi and Bayankhongor *aimags*. 44

Figure 2. Comparison of livestock sector production to Gross Domestic Product of Mongolia (at current prices; NSO, 2014b).. 47

Figure 3. Number of herder households in Mongolia by herd size. Source: Livestock Censuses 1994–2013. 49

Figure 4. Total livestock in Mongolia by household herd size. 49

Figure 5. Herder family in seasonal movement to autumn encampment in Tes, Uvs *aimag*. Some herders, often senior, instruct youths to practice cultural traditions threatened by modernity while keeping camels in use. 52

Figure 6. Senior herder at the one of local horse races at Ovoonii naadam, where people extend their social networks and gain prestige. The herder is being interviewed by Byambabaatar Ichinkhorloo in Bayanjargalan, Dundgovi *aimag*. 52

xi

Figure 7. Private pasture enclosure for livestock emergency grazing during dust and snow blizzard in Bayanjargalan, Dundgovi *aimag*. The fencing supported by development and environmental agencies encourages informal ownership of pasture and resource competition.. 55

Figure 8. Abandoned vegetable field enclosed with support from donor project to motivate collective action of herders who are busy with livestock all year round in Tariat *sum*. 62

Figure 9. Winter fuel wood collection in the Tes river basin in autumn that is often practiced through formal permission from local government or informal *nutag* identity access.. 62

CHAPTER 4

Figure 1. Tribes' Presence in Syria.. 72

CHAPTER 5

Figure 1. Map of Ruoergai County, Sichuan Province, China. 94

Figure 2. Percentage of herders taking different sizes of credit loan among the household samples. 97

Table 1. Analyses of percentage of credit loan from household total annual income.. 97

Figure 3. Sources of credit loan among the interviewed samples in AX Village.. 98

Figure 4. Ways of returning credit loans in AX Village.. 99

Figure 5. Purposes for which herders take credit loans in AX Village.. 100

Figure 6. Factors that limit herders' participation in markets.. . . . 102

CHAPTER 6

Figure 1. Map of Jabal Akhdar region.. 113

CHAPTER 7

Figure 1. Distribution of ethnic communities in Afghanistan. . . . 132

Figure 2. Mobility pattern of Kuchi nomads and distribution of their summer and winter areas in Afghanistan. 137

Table 1. Kuchi flocks and families crossing the Durand line during the annual migratory cycle, Spring 2015.. 139

Figure 3. Kuchi family on the move with their animals. 139

Figure 4. Herders on the way to high pastures in Buner Pakistan. 140

Figure 5. Mobility corridors across Durand line. 141

Figure 6. Map showing significant routes and destinations referred to in Figure 5. 142

Figure 7. The Kuchi herders, finding limited forage at winter lowlands, now increasingly purchase green forage for zero grazing.. 145

Figure 8. A Kuchi herding his flock in the uplands of Naran with his tent in the background. 146

Figure 9. Herders re-establishing their lowland settlement after return from high pastures. 146

Figure 10. Pastoralist children in Pakistan 149

CHAPTER 8

Figure 1. Map of Darma valley, India. 155

Figure 2. Bhotia woman.. 158

Figure 3. A shepherd in the process of transhumance. 169

CHAPTER 9

Figure 1. Modernising pastoralism: Gujjar pastoralists with GPS, Bakhtpura Village. 179

Figure 2. Pastoralist woman and her buffaloes, Lilunda village, Sariska Tiger Reserve. 183

Table 1. Considerations in *oran* institutional design. 184

Figure 3. Bhagwana Gujjar: a pastoralist with with herd of goats from Binak village. 185

Figure 4. A woman Gujjar pastoralist with her herd of goats from Vijaipura village. 186

Table 2. *Oran* significance to the local community. 191

Table 3. Trees found in local *orans*. 192

Table 4. Ethno-medical significance of the plants in the *oran*. 194

Figure 5. Pastoralism in Kraska (Sariska Tiger Reserve), where human and livestock use the same source of water 'rain water harvesting'. 195

Box 1. Changes to *orans*. 197

CHAPTER 10

Figure 1. The Hashemite Kingdom of Jordan. 202

Figure 2. The Tent from the back in Umm *eljammal*. 205

Figure 3. Tent in Umm *eljammal* with 'protected' *maharam* and 'open' *maqad*. 205

Figure 4. The Tent from the front in Aljaffer in south of Jordan. . 206

Figure 5. Overlapping structures between tent and house in Aljaffer. 210

Figure 6. The domain of the tent. 211

Figure 7. The stages of stone house development, taking a tent as a model in Aljaffer. 212

Figure 8. The development of the modern tent in Aljaffer 212

Chapter 1

INTRODUCTION

Ariell Ahearn and Allison Hahn

This volume presents the selected writing and reports of practitioners from pastoral nomadic communities across the Middle East, South Asia and Inner Asia to examine the interrelated themes of agency, risk and boundaries as they pertain to the wider fields of anthropology and human geography. The included scholars first met at the Localities and Livelihoods in Asian Drylands intensive workshop held at the School for Geography and the Environment at Oxford University in April 2015. Since then, they have worked together to examine the contemporary milieu of interdisciplinary research and international policy regarding pastoral nomadic communities.

    This unique group of scholars holds in common a body of literature concerning the contemporary relationships between pastoralist communities and the natural environment (Krätli 2001, 2009; Chatty 1996; Chatty and Colchester 2002). They are also informed by scholars who have focused on the ways that pastoral knowledge of animal husbandry and dryland environments are combined in dynamic socioeconomic systems that work with, rather than against, changing natural conditions (Dyer 2014, McGahey et al. 2014, Sternberg and Chatty 2013). Yet, when asked to speak of their own work, the 2015 workshop participants quickly identified the need for more scholarly attention to the long-term historical trends, government projects and political schemes that affect contemporary pastoralist communities. The problem, commonly highlighted by workshop participants, was that pastoralists are often faced with first combatting misconceptions about how pastoralist communities are formed and governed, and then addressing a specific question of policy or conservation. The resulting edited collection asks scholars and practitioners to address these broad questions of political administration, power dynamics and governance issues in communities ranging from Oman to Tibet and Mongolia.

Ariell Ahearn and Allison Hahn

This work owes a great debt to scholars of mobile pastoralism and activists who have fought to give voice to mobile peoples around the globe and it builds upon this effort. Indigenous peoples, professionals and scholars who met at the Wadi Dana Nature Preserve in 2002 established a framework to address the collective challenges faced by mobile peoples today, reaffirmed in 2012 at the Dana+10 Congress. At this meeting, the Dana Declaration was initiated in order to establish a common approach to include mobile peoples in environmental conservation efforts. The Dana Declaration states:

> Mobile peoples are discriminated against. Their rights, including rights of access to natural resources, are often denied and conventional conservation practices insufficiently address their concerns. These factors, together with the pace of global change, undermine their lifestyles, reduce their ability to live in balance with nature and threaten their existence as distinct peoples.
>
> Nonetheless, through their traditional resource use practices and culture-based respect for nature, many mobile peoples are still making a significant contribution to the maintenance of the earth's ecosystems, species and genetic diversity- even though this often goes unrecognized. Thus the interests of mobile peoples and conservation converge, especially as they face a number of common challenges. There is therefore an urgent need to create a mutually reinforcing partnership between mobile peoples and those involved in conservation. (Dana Declaration 2003, 195)

While the Dana Declaration directly engages with environmental conservation policies that wrongly perceive mobile pastoralism as the sole cause of degradation, it also addresses misconceptions around the organisation of pastoralist society and culture which continue to pose a risk to pastoralist livelihoods and cultures in Asia. International development discourse, which has entered into national policies through structural adjustment programmes, conservation projects and democracy-building initiatives, has been another source of misconceptions about mobile pastoralist livelihoods and land management systems. While some development planners believe that pastoralists are opposed to development, the studies collected in this text highlight the historical participation of pastoral nomadic communities in nation-state building projects, social institutions and economic processes. The collected studies also illustrate the varied ways that pastoralist households in Asian drylands have responded to a variety of development schemes that seek to reshape social organisation and land management. Utilising a diversity of methods from participant-observation and ethnographic interviews to surveys and archival research, the collected authors have worked to present pastoral-nomadic communities, which are often also their own communities, from an informed, first-hand perspective.

Introduction

The perspectives presented in this text are at times different from those found in development discourse and government documents. This difference is anticipated by scholars such as Riccardo Bocco, a scholar of sedentarisation programmes in the Middle East. He writes, 'Whether we look at Western or Arab experts, we can conclude that in general their writings are not based on knowledge gained from field studies' (Bocco 2006, 302). Indeed, much knowledge about pastoralist livelihoods is generated by officials and scholars who are based in settled communities with little lived or experiential understanding of mobile animal husbandry in arid environments.

Reading the reports of scholars who are fluent speakers of the language of their research area and who have spent long periods of time living with pastoralists produces a very different picture – that of resilient pastoralists, who are aware of and engaged in modernity and are making decisions about pastoralism and settlement from an informed and deliberative perspective. The material analysed throughout this book contains new perspectives on pastoral engagement in citizenship, land tenure, development projects, social networks and resource distribution. Reading these studies collectively so as to draw from the plethora of pastoralist experiences, this book aims to propose new research questions and help develop new theories for understanding social transformations.

Together, we, scholars from pastoralist communities and settled communities in Europe and the United States, aim both to better understand specific pastoralist communities and to encourage intercultural and cross-cultural dialogue. These studies emerge at a critical moment of contention for pastoralists, when their very livelihood is questioned and at times threatened by climate change, governmental policies, wars, unfavourable economic conditions and increasing urban–rural divides. Read as a holistic text, the following chapters address three commonly held misconceptions regarding pastoralists: that they live beyond state controls, lack formal governance structures and participate in unsustainable lifestyles. These perceptions also contain assumptions about the nature of the state as an entity separate from the realm of social relations.

In what follows, we introduce the region of Asian drylands and address each of these misconceptions, providing a summary of their emergence in contemporary discourse, the reasons that they are thought to be true and some of the problems that they produce for pastoralist communities. Then, we provide a brief overview of the collected texts with attention to the interplay of the themes of agency, risk, and boundaries.

Ariell Ahearn and Allison Hahn

Asian Drylands

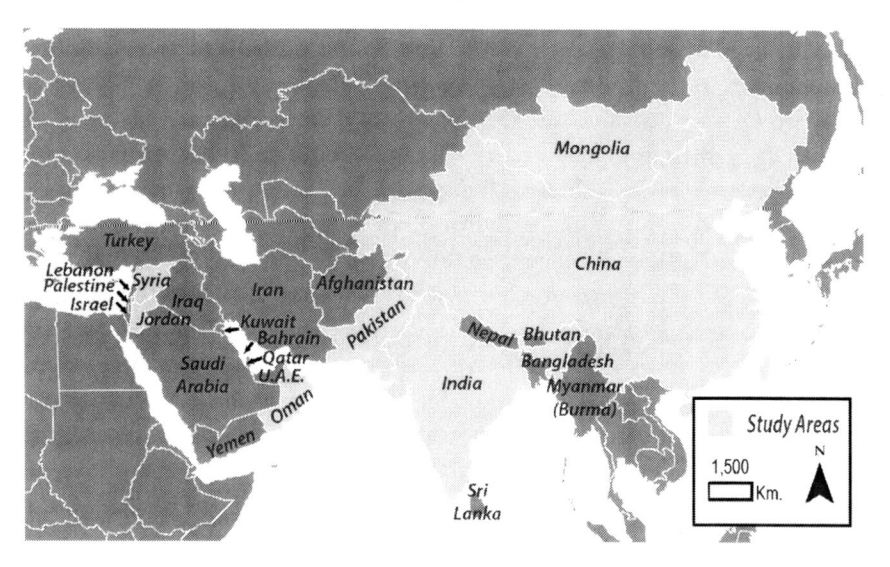

Figure 1. Map of study areas.

The regional focus of this book is Asian drylands. Drylands are defined by very low levels of precipitation and constitute around forty per cent of the earth's surface (Goudie 2012, 5). Dryland ecosystems, which include the vast grassland steppes of Central and Inner Asia, play an important role in regulating the earth's climate. Middleton (2016) has stated that, vegetation-wise, some drylands 'rival tropical rainforests for their species richness'. More than two billion people inhabit the earth's drylands, a number which is projected to increase into the future (Pravalie 2016, 262). Pastoralism is a central livelihood practice in dryland regions, characterised by mobile livestock that graze and browse wild grasses and brush. Pastoralist livestock are specially adapted to the different extremes of dryland regions and typically include breeds of yak and cows, goats, sheep, camels and horses. Approximately fifty per cent of domesticated livestock live on arid rangelands (Middleton 2016).

The dryland region of East Asia generally includes the contemporary states of Mongolia and the northwest region of China. This area is approximately 4.81 million square kilometres in size (Chen et al. 2014, 3) characterised by mountain grasslands, shrub lands, steppe and temperate forests. It also includes major deserts such as the Gobi, Taklamakan and Badain Jaran. The East Asia dryland region is a high altitude zone, with elevations up to 7,929 metres above sea level (Chen et al. 2014, 5). Climate change is having an impact on this

Introduction

region. The IPCC identified the Mongolian plateau as particularly sensitive to climate change (Chen et al. 2014, 8) in comparison to other world regions. In Asia, China has the largest dryland territory, while Saudi Arabia is unique for its hyper-aridity (Pravalie 2016). Beyond East Asia, the Asian drylands include the Arabian Desert, the Syrian Desert, Karakum, Kyzylkum and the Thar, located in the countries of Iraq, Iran, Jordan, Syria, Turkmenistan, Kazakhstan, Uzbekistan, India and Pakistan (Pravalie 2016).

These regions may also experience wide fluctuations in daily and seasonal temperatures. Mongolia, for example, sees temperatures more than forty degrees Celsius in the summer months and below minus forty in the winter months. Drylands are also the sites of particular climatic and environmental hazards, including 'drought, heat waves, extreme rainfall events, dust storms, wildfire and dzud' (Pravalie 2016, 262). Amongst these hazards, drought and pressure on indigenous water supplies such as shallow and deep aquifers are expected to present increasing challenges to dryland populations and states.

Land degradation and desertification remains an important concern in dryland regions and has sparked much debate amongst scientists, NGOs and policy makers. Desertification refers to the loss of vegetation in dryland regions, which may lead to the loss in top soils and increased erosion. While it has been acknowledged that both human and climatic factors contribute to land degradation, the extent of these factors is context-specific. The complexity of dryland environmental dynamics has been captured in the non-equilibrum model for understanding desert ecology. According to this model, vegetation in drylands is determined by precipitation, which is variable in time and place. This model is different from an equilibrium paradigm based on more predictable and consistent annual rainfall outcomes and vegetation production. Thus, identifying causes of land degradation using non-equilibrium models is complicated because vegetation cover is highly connected to climate conditions (Middleton 2016). Severe drought, flash floods and wind erosion are factors that contribute to land degradation and occur exclusive to human activity. The effects of livestock grazing on rangelands have been a focal point in debates around land degradation and land use policies. This view sees grazing as a primary cause of degradation and draws upon the more static equilibrium model's concepts of 'tragedy of the commons' and carrying capacity. Studies of degradation and pastoralism have revealed a far more complex and dynamic picture regarding dryland ecosystems and pastoralist production. A study of the legacy effects of livestock grazing on grasslands in Inner Mongolia (Han et al. 2014), for example, has shown that grazing increased the resilience of certain plant species and promoted carbon sequestration. The legacy effects of crop cultivation or fire on contemporary grazing areas, in combination with climatic conditions, have also been identified as a critical component in the study and analysis of desertification.

As Middleton (2016) points out, debates about desertification have been informed by different models for understanding desert ecosystems as well as widely different views of the place of pastoralism in these ecosystems. The chapters in this volume give further nuance to this debate and illustrate the effects of state policies on pastoralist land use and human relations to nature. The following sections address three misconceptions that appear in debates around dryland management and land use.

Misconception 1: Pastoralists Live Beyond State Control

Pastoralist communities, by definition, often live in remote regions, far from the permanent offices of government officials and international development organisations. This physical remoteness is often highlighted in international reports which suggest that pastoralists are unaware of or unaffected by state policies. Problematically, many reports focus exclusively on remoteness, rather than investigating the complex historic socio-economic relations which have resulted in the marginalisation of pastoralist communities (Aikman and Dyer 2012; Dyer 2001, 2006, 2013, 2014). As a result of this emphasis on remoteness, governments and international organisations commonly design interventions that bring pastoralist communities closer to the state. This oftentimes includes the temporary or complete sedentarisation of pastoralists so that services such as education can be provided.

The rhetoric of sedentarisation can be seen in modernisation, land privatisation and environmental conservation schemes (Anderson and Broch-Due 1999, Bocco 2006, Krätli 2001, Krätli and Dyer 2009). Statistically, these programmes may result in more children enrolling in a school, or more families within one hour of a hospital. However, such statistics overlook the ways that pastoralist communities are incorporated into these state services and their contradictory effects. Dyer's work on education amongst the Rabari pastoralists of Gujara, India illustrates how accessing formal schooling has become a way in which children are educated out of pastoralism (2014). Her work highlights the ways in which pastoralist knowledge and institutions are discriminated against by inflexible and narrow interpretations of the UN development goals and concepts of modernity. Krätli and Dyer (2009) have brought attention to

Introduction

Figure 2. Herder prepares for Naadam. Tov Aimag, Mongolia. Photo: Allison Hahn, June 2015.

these issues in their work on education amongst pastoralists, writing 'Typically, for children from nomadic households, there is an exceptionally unfavorable trade-off in curtailing informal learning and enduring forced separation from their family environment in order to seek the advantages of formal education within a school-based system' (p. 1). They advance alternative schooling formats which support both home-based education and mobile learning, calling on policy makers to value alternative livelihoods and develop innovative and inclusive social services.

In nations and communities with historic opposition to pastoral groups, the lack of access to educational institutions, markets and government offices may put additional pressure on communities to give up their traditions, languages and livelihoods. For example, the determination to settle herders is often bolstered by claims from state officials that herders are irresponsible and lazy or backward (Benwell 2013; Eriksen 2014; Williams 2002; Yeh 2007, 2013). The resulting policies include forced evictions from pasturelands, seizures of herds and forced settlement into public housing projects. As Yeh (2013) has pointed out in her work with Tibetan communities in China, the government portrays development as a 'gift' to the Tibetan people. Yet, the price of this gift is often exceptionally high and includes the loss of culture and livelihood. Agrawal (1999) also discusses the link between Indian development programmes and control of pastoralist mobility. The Pasture and Sheep Development Program, framed as a series of projects to improve pasture quality and livestock yields, attempted to re-organise pastoralist work to take place via collective groups on fixed plots of land. This project failed to improve pasture and livestock, but Agrawal argues that it was successful in exerting control over mobility by promoting a new form of state territoriality and spatial regulation.

Misconception 2: Pastoralists Lack Formal Governance

Scholars, mainstream media and travellers have often imagined nomads to be wandering across a vast, empty space, free of any constraints and acting however they choose. While contemporary policy makers and academics know that this perception cannot be true, the expectation that pastoralists are free agents and lack formal governance continues to permeate development discourse.

The results of this expectation were apparent in Mongolia during the early 1990s when development projects funded by the German Technical Cooperation, the Swiss Agency for Development and Cooperation, the World Bank and other aid agencies began pushing for the reorganisation of rural social and economic life under the concepts of 'collective' and 'community' action. These projects aim to foster environmental conservation, the reversal of grassland degradation and economic participation in markets for herder households by creating 'self-help groups' and 'pasture user groups' (see for example Fernandez-Gimenez et al. 2012, Schmidt 2006, Schmidt et al. 2002, Usukh et al. 2010). These projects essentialise pastoralist work by focusing on the revival of 'traditional' institutions that are imagined as a primary way to make pastoralism sustainable and viable into the future. These user groups were imagined to be a vehicle to manage rural pasture and adapt to changing economic conditions. For example, Klein et al. (2012) write, 'Many of the traditional strategies pastoralists have employed in the past are in flux and may not be readily available to them in the future. This will probably have profound effects on pastoralists' ability to adapt to their changing climatic, ecological and socio-economic situation and may impair their resilience in dealing with these ongoing-pressures.' (p. 8) This fatalistic account not only depoliticises pastoralist livelihoods and overlooks long political histories but also presents

Introduction

a very narrow interpretation of the diverse forms, identities and practices of pastoralism in Mongolia.

Bocco (2006) has given attention to the complex history of sedentarisation programmes launched in the Middle East from 1950–1990 by international organisations such as UNESCO, the FAO, the World Health Organization and other agencies. He illustrates the ways that environmentally deterministic frameworks are applied to pastoralist societies, where the decisions made by pastoralists are framed by environmental constraints rather than larger socio-economic processes or concerns. Bocco argues that development discourse focuses on managing pastoralist territories through participatory approaches that 'reinterpret or even mystify certain aspects of the recent past as well as use ideological re-adaptions to legitimize one or another of these policies' (p. 303). Similar to the community-based resource management 'pasture user groups' that have been organised in Mongolia, Bocco identifies the popularity of reviving the *hima* system in the Middle East. He writes, 'With its evocation of the principles of local participation and self-sustained development, the *hima* system cannot but appeal to the representatives of international agencies such as the World Bank or the IMF, who see in it the chance to apply their policies of economic liberalization and promote free enterprise through the "rediscovery" of a traditional system of resource management.' (p. 327) These accounts also overlook the many ways in which people who practice pastoralism also pursue other forms of work and maintain networks and relationships with people in distant regions.

Misconception 3: Pastoralist lifestyles are unsustainable

Garret Hardin's 1968 publication, 'The Tragedy of the Commons', has had a long-lasting impact on pastoralist communities. This metaphor, which is deduced from European sheep grazing by settled communities, presumes that pastoralists use land in unregulated ways resulting in pasture degradation and destruction of national environments. Using this metaphor, scholars and international organisations have justified land privatisation legislation. For example, when writing about the proposed Mongolian Pastureland law, Hannam, an international consultant and expert on rangeland legislation indicates, 'Mongolian rangeland is degraded because herders are unable to apply sustainable grazing practices. Mongolian grassland is not valued so its regulation and management have been avoided in the past. Herders continue to graze their livestock on public land unrestrained, where there is high competition for good pasture.'

(2012, 418) The drafting of this legislation and similar legislative documents from around the world reflects the dual expectation that herders exist outside of regulatory systems and are responsible for land degradation.

Government officials and development practitioners working in drylands throughout the world have presumed that pastoralism results in land degradation. Yet, scholars such as Chatty (2002) indicate, the contribution of state land tenure policies, such as the cultivation of crops on former pastureland, transportation infrastructure and mining projects, all also result in land degradation but are not attended to in development reports. Chatty's (2002) investigation of the Arabian oryx reintroduction project in Oman reveals the tension between pastoralists and state conservation projects. This project excluded the Harasiis from their traditional grazing lands and prevented them from receiving improvements in their water sources. The government prioritisation of preserving an oryx habitat to the detriment of local Harasiis livelihoods illustrates a process of dispossession which Chatty calls 'conservation without a human face'. (2002, 225) Similar state-led projects to remove pastoralists from rangelands have been implemented around the globe. Some projects are focused on economic outcomes while others are more oriented toward achieving an environmental result.

Organisations such as the International Union for Conservation of Nature and Natural Resources and the United Nations Environment Programme have made a strong effort to contest the misconception that pastoralist livelihoods are unsustainable. They advocate for increased investment in pastoralist systems and acknowledgment of pastoralism as a livelihood with 'green economy potential' (McGahey et al., viii). An IUCN report states, 'Pastoralism has been shown…to be between 2 and 10 times more productive per unit of land than the capital-intensive alternatives that have been put forward. Unfortunately many of these benefits go unmeasured and are therefore frequently squandered by policies and investments that seek to replace pastoralism with more capital intensive modes of production' (p. ix). The report highlights an issue that is common for many pastoralist societies – a lack of investment in services and infrastructure to enable mobility and more secure pastoralist systems. As the chapters in this book will illustrate, many of the root causes of the risks and insecurities that pastoralists face, which contribute to the sense that this lifestyle is unsustainable, emerge from specific histories, policies and programmes.

Introduction

Agency, Risk and Boundaries

The study of modern pastoralist communities requires attention to these misconceptions and to the ways that communities are moving beyond these misconceptions to continue their lifestyles. The essays collected here address those modern day adaptations through the articulation of agency, the definition and mitigation of risk and the conceptualisation and crossing of boundaries. Each chapter addresses all three concepts with careful attention to the ways that community members define and identify these concepts. Bumochir Dulam's chapter, 'The Afterlife of Nomadism', discusses identity politics and land use amongst the Deed Mongol pastoralists in Qinghai Province of northwest China. His ethnographic research reveals the prevalence of the discourse of 'unsustainable pastoralism' frequently used in reference to pastoralism in China by environmentalists. This framing posits that pastoralism contributes to land degradation, which can only be resolved with settled methods of fodder cultivation (agriculture). Bumochir illustrates how the Chinese state's concept of unsustainability clashes with Mongolian pastoralists' concepts of pastoralism in the independent state of Mongolia. He suggests that the Chinese government has framed pastoralism as environmentally harmful in an attempt to meet political goals and unify China's 56 nationalities. This fascinating account reveals the historical tensions over territorial control and land use between ethnic groups in China, which play out using environmentalist discourses. Bumochir's work raises questions about the political agency of people who identify as pastoralists within both China and independent Mongolia. He identifies the discourse of 'unsustainable pastoralism' as a barrier to achieving sustainable outcomes for pastoralist livelihoods, which are increasingly constrained and limited by economic opportunities and government policies.

Aman Singh also addresses the concept of agency through his investigation of community forests, called *orans*, in Rajasthan, India. His research examines the role of *orans* as locations of spiritual and cultural identity as well as providers of natural resources. Singh examines the ways pastoralist frame themselves as stewards of *orans*, and the counter-framing utilised by the Forest Department of India which depicts pastoralists as trespassers within the *orans*. Singh discusses the social and economic implications of this reframing for pastoralists in Rajasthan and examines the ongoing challenges faced by these communities. Singh's focus on Rajasthani pastoralists' relationship to common forest land highlights the agentive nature of relations with the land itself, which also is found in Mongolian attitudes towards nature. In the context of Mongolia, Empson (2011) and Humphrey (1995) discuss the ways that pastoralists believe landscapes to be alive and filled with human and non-human actors. Land spirits and non-human entities inhabit the landscape. And herders acknowledge and interact with these non-human actors through daily practices and ceremonial ritual events. Chatty (2012) has also discussed the mutually constitutive aspects of society and the natural environment in her work on the Harasiis pastoralists of Oman and their relationship with the Omani desert. The Mongolian concept of custodial land use (Sneath 2003), as opposed to exclusive or private land 'ownership', is informed by this value system and relational way of using natural resources. Aman's chapter also indicates the tension between tenure systems based on private use versus common use, which have opened up controversies over rights to land and formal tenure systems.

Haian Dukhan's chapter, 'From Reform to Revolt: Bashar al-Assad and the Arab Tribes in Syria', investigates the integration and social cohesion of tribal groups into the Syrian state. His research has revealed another facet in the study of agency – the role of patronage networks in economic distribution and political consolidation. Dukhan argues that the since the early 2000s, economic liberalisation programmes have ignored tribal constituencies and have contributed to Bashar al-Assad's failure to gain the support of the Arab Bedouin tribes. The resulting dispossession of rural Bedouin led to regional conflicts between tribal groups and partially fuelled uprisings against the state in tribal regions. Dukhan's chapter highlights the importance of Bedouin patronage networks in the formation of the state in Syria. His work also encourages us to think differently about how development organisations and programmes understand and attempt to impact on pastoralist agency. Dukhan discusses the creation of the General Commission for Badia Management in Syria by the Bashar al-Assad government in 2006. This agency failed to address the problems that emerged from Bedouin experiences of economic liberalisation, and focused its work instead largely on environmental conservation efforts that created protected areas for bird species while excluding Bedouin from their traditional grazing lands. The drought of 2008 further intensified the problems, and forced many to abandon the Badia for the suburbs of major cities. By focusing on certain outcomes without examining wider historical and political processes for the Bedouin in Syria, the programmes failed to address both humanitarian and environmental issues and led to the unraveling of state legitimacy in rural areas.

On the theme of risk, Gongbuzeren's chapter, 'Herder Participation in Modern Markets', examines the use of credit loans amongst Tibetans in Sichuan, China. His research shows that China's rangeland rental system, along with increasing expenses related to herding, has caused many herding households to

Introduction

turn to short-term lines of credit. Many development theories suggest that access to short-term credit will allow herders to quickly improve their livelihoods. However, Gongbuzeren argues that the lack of oversight amongst creditors, as well as herders' traditional distance from markets has resulted in cycles of debt amongst pastoralists. Gongbuzeren's analysis clearly articulates the increase in livelihood risks that herders face as a result of both China's rangeland household contract system and limited access to local markets. By requiring herding households to rent pasturelands, the rangeland household contract system has increased the cost of living and practising mobility as a pastoralist. The payment schedule for these contracts is timed to occur when herders have the least amount of cash-in-hand, and as such, herders have entered into cycles of debt from which, without better access to markets, they are unlikely to excape.

Nisthasri Awasthi focuses on changes in transhumance amongst the Rung pastoralists in the Darma valley of Uttarkhand, India. Here, the development and infrastructure for a 280 MN hydroelectric power project has brought Rung pastoralists into close contact with settled communities. Focusing on the effect of improved transportation infrastructure and access to formal education, Awashi finds that younger generations of Rung are less inclined to pursue pastoralist livelihoods. In this case, Nisthasri illustrates how the younger generation of Rung draw from negative popular discourse about pastoralism, resulting in their assessment of pastoralist livelihoods as risky or insecure. She predicts that due to these discourses, many Rung will settle and give up their pastoralist lifestyles.

On the topic of boundaries, in 'Environment as a Commodity and a Shield', Byambabaatar Ichinkhorloo investigates the Mongolian notion of *nutag* (homeland) as a foundation for rural identity, social networks and governance of pastures. Byambabaatar draws upon ethnographic field research to understand how traditional use of *nutag* to negotiate territorial rights clashes with neoliberal pastureland commodification. Then, he addresses the ways that individuals or groups outside of a local *nutag* are viewed as environmental deviants – often blamed for pasture degradation, illegal hunting or exploitation of land resources. This chapter investigates the ways that herders utilise network connections to negotiate territorial boundaries and determine who has a right to use the resources of a region. This study highlights the political nature of both formal and informal boundaries in rural Mongolia and critically responds to the expectation that pastoralists lack boundaries or borders.

Inam Rahim's work with the Kuchi pastoralists of Afghanistan and Pakistan further highlights the challenging boundary issues between states at the Durand line. The politically marginalised situation of the Kuchi in relation to the states of Pakistan and Afghanistan contrasts with places like Mongolia and Jordan, where nomadic pastoralism is regarded as a national tradition and legitmate livelihood. Rahim's discussion of Kuchi mobility illustrates the extensive range of their territory throughout Afghanistan and the North-South corridor of Pakistan. These historical migratory routes are changing due to the stricter international border controls as well as changing patterns of land use and land tenure among the migratory corridors. Rents from landlords pose significant obstacles to migration and access to pastureland, despite new opportunities that Kuchi have to provide meat supplies to the growing food industry of Pakistan.

Pastoralist material culture is examined in Wassef Al Sekhaneh's study of traditional and modern Bedouin housing in Jordan. His field report focuses on the tangible aspects of the Bedouin woven tent, its arrangement, and the gendered division of space. He shows how elements of traditional tents have been retained in more modern constructions and emphasises the intangible cultural values of honour, decency, dignity and respect. His concern is with the translation of cultural values and heritage of the Bedouin in contemporary architecture. This chapter emphasises the spatialisation of social organisation and reminds us of the significance of the home space as a social site in pastoralist societies.

Finally, Salah al Mazrui's chapter on conservation initiatives in Oman provides an ethnographic study of pastoralists living on the Jabal Akdhar mountain range. This study focuses on pastoralist's cosmology known as *hāwzat*, which locally means tribal space or enclosed area, and the effect of this cosmology on contemporary conservation projects. Salah's work traces the linguistic and cultural roots of *hāwzat* in an attempt to reframe debates regarding the role of indigenous knowledge in conservation decision-making. This chapter contributes to the theme of boundaries by bring attention to the tensions involved in different approaches to and perceptions of the 'proper' relationship between humans and nature.

Rather than attempt to align these definitions of pastoralism, the collected authors have played careful attention to the ways that community members articulate their own ways of life. In this way, the complexity of Asian pastoralist experiences is represented, leading to a broader understanding of community needs and histories. The collected texts have been divided into chapters, which provide an in-depth discussion of specific cultural contexts, and reports from the field which point to emergent trends and historic lineages that can inform our understanding of the diversity of pastoralist experiences.

Introduction

References

Agrawal, A. 1999. *Greener Pastures: Politics, Markets and Community Among a Migrant Pastoral People*. Durham NC: Duke University Press.

Bocco, Riccardo. 2006. 'The settlement of pastoral nomads in the Arab Middle East: International organizations and trends in development policies, 1950–1990'. In D. Chatty (ed.) *Nomadic Societies in the Middle East and North Africa: Entering the 21ˢᵗ Century*. Leiden: Brill, 2006. pp 302–330.

Chatty, D. 1972. 'Pastoralism: Adaptation and optimization'. *Folk* 14–15: 27–38.

Chatty, D. 1996. *Mobile Pastoralists: Development Planning and Social Change in Oman*. New York: Columbia University Press.

Chatty, D. 2006. 'Boarding schools for mobile people: The Harasiis in the Sultanate of Oman'. In C. Dyer (ed.) *The Education of Nomadic Peoples: Current Issues, Future Prospects*. New York and Oxford: Berghahn Books. pp. 212–230.

Chatty, D. 2007. 'Mobile peoples: Pastoralists and herders at the beginning of the 21st century'. *Reviews in Anthropology* 36 (1): 5–26.

Chatty, D. 2012. 'Authenticity in the desert landscapes of Oman: The Jiddat-Il-Harasiis, Oman'. In Lisa Mol and Troy Sternberg (eds) *Changing Deserts: Integrating People and their Environment*. Cambridge: The White Horse Press.

Chatty, D. 2013. *From Camel to Truck: The Bedouin in the Modern World*. 2nd ed., Cambridge: The White Horse Press.

Chatty, D. and M. Colchester (eds). 2002. *Conservation and Mobile Indigenous Peoples: Displacement, Forced Settlement, and Sustainable Development*. New York: Berghahn Books.

Chen, J. et al. 2014. 'State and change in dryland East Asia'. In J. Chen, S. Wan and G. Henebry, (eds) *Ecosystem Science and Applications : Dryland East Asia: Land Dynamics amid Social and Climate Change : Land Dynamics amid Social and Climate Change*. Berlin/Boston, DE: De Gruyter.

Dana Declaration 2003. 'Dana Declaration on mobile indigenous peoples and conservation'. *Nomadic Peoples* 7 (1): 159–164.

Empson, R. 2011. *Harnessing Fortune: Personhood, Memory and Place in Mongolia*. Oxford: Oxford University Press.

Goudie, Andrew. 2012. 'Introduction'. In Lisa Mol and Troy Sternberg (eds) *Changing Deserts: Integrating People and their Environment*. Cambridge: The White Horse Press.

Han, J. et al. 2014. 'Legacy effects from historical grazing enhanced carbon sequestration in a desert steppe'. *Journal of Arid Environments* 107: 1–9.

Klein, J.A., M.E. Fernandez-Gimenez, H. Wei, Y. Changqing, D. Dorligsuren and R.S. Reid. 2012. 'A participatory framework for building resilient socio-ecological pastoral systems'. In M. Fernandez-Gimenez, X. Wang, B. Batkhishig, J.A. Klein, and R.S. Reid (eds) *Restoring Community Connections to the Land*. Wallingford, UK: CABI.

Krätli, S. 2001. 'Education provision to nomadic pastoralists: A literature review'. *IDS Working Paper 126*. Available from: http://www.eldis.org/fulltext/saverio.pdf [accessed 7 October 2015].

Ariell Ahearn and Allison Hahn

Krätli, S. and C. Dyer. 2009. *Mobile Pastoralists and Education: Strategic Options.* Working Paper 1: London: International Institute for Environment and Development. Available from: http://pubs.iied.org/10021IIED.html [accessed 7 October 2015].

Humphrey, C. 1995. 'Chiefly and shamanist landscapes in Mongolia'. In E. Hirsch and M. O'Hanlon (eds). *The Anthropology of Landscape.* Oxford: Oxford University Press. pp. 135–162.

McGahey, D., J. Davies, N. Hagelberg and R. Ouedraogo. 2014. *Pastoralism and the Green Economy – a natural nexus?* Nairobi: IUCN and UNEP.

Middleton, N. 2016. 'Rangeland management and climate hazards in drylands: Dust storms, desertification and the overgrazing debate'. *Natural Hazards* doi:10.1007/s11069-016-2592-6

Pravalie, R. 2016. 'Drylands extent and environmental issues: A global approach'. *Earth-Science Reviews* **161**: 259–78.

Sneath, D. 2003. 'Land use, the environment and development in post-socialist Mongolia'. *Oxford Development Studies* **31**: 441–59.

Sternberg, T. and D. Chatty (eds). 2013. *Modern Pastoralism and Conservation: Old Problems, New Challenges.* Cambridge: The White Horse Press.

Chapter 2

THE AFTERLIFE OF NOMADISM: PASTORALISM, ENVIRONMENTALISM, CIVILISATION AND IDENTITY IN MONGOLIA AND CHINA[1]

D. Bumochir

Introduction

As a Mongolian whose grandparents were pastoralists, I had never seen herders growing grass and other forms of fodder to feed livestock until I first travelled to Qinghai Province in the north-west of China in the winter of 2002. From Xining, the capital of the province, it took more than seven hours to reach Qaidam Basin in a fully packed mini-bus with excess passengers sitting on small boxes in the aisle. Qaidam Basin starts from Lake Qinghai in the east and stretches to the west for about 700 kilometres, with a width of 300 kilometres (Kapp et al. 2011, 4). This is where the herds of the *Deed* ('High' or 'Upper Mongols') graze. These are an ethnic Mongol minority in a predominantly Tibetan area. For more than an hour the paved road followed the shore of Lake Qinghai. The pastures around the lake are considered greener and are occupied by Tibetan herders. Beside the lake, in addition to fenced *belcheer* (pasture in Mongolian),[2] there were ploughed fields. Later my Deed Mongol friends explained that the local government had reduced *belcheer* and livestock numbers around the lake and instructed herders to cultivate fodder for the remaining animals. Although

---

1. This research was supported by the European Research Council (project number 515115) in the Department of Anthropology, University College London.
2. To avoid connotations of 'pasture' as used in other parts of the world, I will use the Mongolian word *belcheer* for pasture with reference to all Mongol herders both in Mongolia and China.

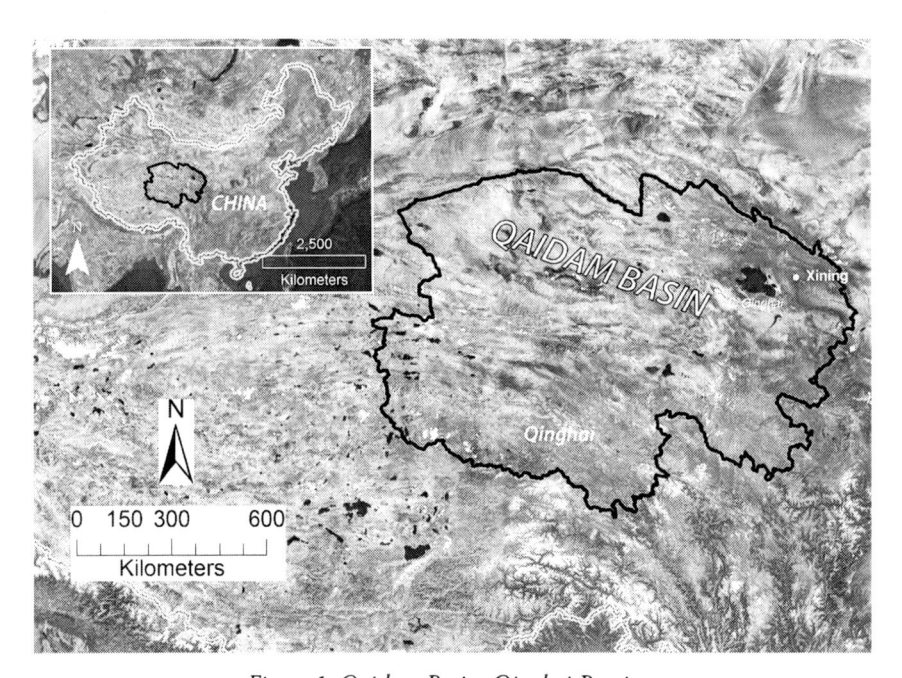

Figure 1. Qaidam Basin, Qinghai Province

I had known since I arrived in the area in early 2000 that such a development was expected, this was the first time I had seen it.

In the summer of 2007 I was on another fieldwork trip in the area and was due to meet up with Bat, the father of my Deed Mongol family in Qinghai. Herders from different villages of Züün *Xia*ng[3] (Mongolian *Hoshuu*) had gathered in the only street of the main village to attend an official talk delivered by the local party secretary. Bat was one of those attending and had arranged to give me a lift on his motorcycle to his summer *belcheer* afterwards. By the time I arrived the meeting was about to finish and herders were discussing amongst themselves how ridiculous it is to blame livestock and herders for destroying nature. On the ride to the summer camp, about an hour on a dirt road through the narrow corridors of fenced *belcheer*, Bat and I had a chance to chat about the meeting which had just occurred.

---

3. The Chinese administrative term *Xiang* is translated as 'township', but in rural areas denotes rather a group of villages.

The Afterlife of Nomadism

I asked, 'What does it mean that livestock and herders are destroying nature?' He laughed as he does all the time, and said, 'They are saying that our animals are eating bushes and grass, and we are hunting wild animals.' 'Who says that?' I asked. 'The State of the Chinese' (*kitadusyn tör*) he replied.

As a native of independent Mongolia, I thought that mobile pastoralism probably functioned this way ever since it first began, and I said, 'What else could your animals eat, except grass?' Bat replied immediately, 'They are telling us to plant grass to feed livestock.'

I thought that only people who do not know much about mobile pastoralism, such as non-Mongols and 'non-mobile pastoralists', could think of 'feeding livestock with planted grass', because most Mongol herders never planted anything and the main way of feeding livestock is to use natural resources. Then I wondered out loud, 'How many animals can you feed this way?' Bat said, 'Maybe 200.'

For me this sounded like a true 'end of nomadism' (Humphrey and Sneath 1999), if the state chooses 'green governmentality' (Williams 2000, Yeh 2005, Kolås 2014) and decides not to let herders occupy the mountain pasture which the local government contracted to them in the 1980s for fifty years. The majority of livestock of all the herding households, both Mongol and Tibetan, spend up to six months from June to December in the mountains, while young livestock stay with their mothers in fenced pasture in the Qaidam. Unlike the Qaidam Basin, the mountain *belcheer* is not fenced and is not owned privately but is still shared informally, with constant threats of Tibetans trying to invade the *belcheer* which has been traditionally occupied by the High Mongols. Since I have known Bat's family, they have always had 600 to 700 livestock, limited by the resources they have in the fenced *belcheer*. Certainly 200 fodder-raised animals will not provide enough income for Bat to support his family.

Unlike me, he seemed not to be taking the situation seriously and I discovered that he was right during my fieldtrip in 2014. Since the talk in 2007, not much had happened to the *belcheer* in Züün *Xiang* and Bat explained to me that the situation had eased for a while, possibly due to some Chinese scientists' argument that livestock and herders do not actually contribute to landscape degradation, a question to which I will return. However, the situation has been getting more and more serious in the last few years since 2014. The local government, following instructions from the state, introduced an argument to protect natural resources such as wild animals, plants and trees in the mountains. According to Bat, the official decree to stop herders occupying the *belcheer* in the mountain has not yet been passed but people expect it sooner or later. If this happens, then all the herders will have to use their available privately owned pastures in the Qaidam, usually used for only half of the year, for the entire year, and reduce their livestock numbers accordingly. Hence Bat would have to drop his numbers to 200.

The same situation is also alarming herders in neighbouring Baruun *Xiang*. In summer 2014 I visited Daichin, a herder in Baruun *Xiang* whom I have also known since the start of my fieldwork and who is related to Bat through marriage. There, I found that circumstances I had only known in the case of some Tibetan regions from my first fieldwork trips in the early and mid-2000s, were already developing among the Deed Mongol herders. Because Daichin is so worried about the mountain *belcheer* restrictions, he has started trying to cultivate some grass to feed his livestock in order to be prepared for the future, as advised by the local government.

The same changes have been affecting Mongol herders in Inner Mongolia. In the Chinese construction of pastoralism, Williams writes, Han Chinese scientists and government officials at national and regional levels explicitly express that 'Mongols never learned to look beyond their sheep to the soil, so today they have no regard for the land that farmers have cherished' (2000, 508). Despite numerous demonstrations by Mongol herders, which have occurred across Inner Mongolia since the year 2000, only a few Chinese have rejected the scientific establishment's negative discourse on pastoralism. The most famous counterreaction was that of Jiang Rong, who saw the construction as a history of misperception. In 2004, Jiang Rong (real name Lu Jiamin), a Chinese author, made an enormous contribution in promoting Mongol pastoralists' environmental stewardship in his bestselling semi-autobiographical novel *Lang Tuteng* [*The Wolf Totem*], based on his experience living with Inner Mongolian pastoralists during the cultural revolution. The novel has been translated into numerous languages including English (2008) and Mongolian (2010), and was made into a film called *The Wolf Totem* by the French director Jean-Jacques Annaud. Bulag writes about the author's intention 'Jiang mourns the demise of Mongol nomadic power under the relentless assault of Chinese agricultural civilization. Nomadic Mongols are, under his pen, invaluable to the Chinese, for they have injected much-needed virile blood (*shuxue*) into the Chinese, through repeated invasions and conquests throughout history.' (2010, 1) Besides conflict and cultural difference between Mongols and Chinese, an important point Jiang Rong repeatedly makes in his novel is about the current issue of 'unsustainable pastoralism'. His message is that the Chinese conventional construction of a backward, ignorant and 'unsustainable pastoralism' is in fact the opposite of the truth.

Building on Williams's work, I argue that scholars, policymakers and local and international NGOs have produced a new concept of pastoralism in the last two decades in Mongolia and China. Considerations of climate change and the need to conserve the environment have led scholars, politicians and development agencies to a search for causes of land degradation. Some have identified certain forms of pastoralism with different scales of mobility as one of the main human factors. Thus the environmentalist approach to pastoralism has constructed an image of a harmful 'unsustainable pastoralism' with negative effects on pasture and natural resources. I am not saying that environmentalists consider all pastoralists and their acts as always harmful. Instead I am referring to the specific ways in which pastoralist practices have been framed as harmful to nature in environmental discourses. Many scholars have critiqued this position, but it remains embedded in many government policies (Chatty and Colchester 2002, Dyer 2014). In contrast to the environmentalist view, Mongols both in Mongolia and China demonstrate that pastoralism involves complex reasoning, knowledge and techniques which prevent herders from overgrazing and causing damage to nature (Humphrey and Sneath 1999). Therefore, the environmentalist construction of pastoralism is different from the local understanding in Mongolia and Inner Asia and contradicts how herders actually perceive and interpret pasture degradation and their wellbeing in the natural environment.

This chapter does not aim to trace causes of land degradation, nor prove or disprove herders' impacts on natural resources. Since large numbers of livestock are suspected of being one of the causes of land degradation, another discussion focuses on what it means for herders to increase their livestock numbers. It is argued that large numbers of livestock can be a form of resilience (Murphy 2014, 106, 117) and risk management in the uncertain conditions of mobile pastoralism (Thrift and Ichinkhorloo 2015, 138) or alternatively that it is a way of showing prestige and social status (Borgerhoff Mulder et al. 2010, 38; Murphy 2014, 111–112). My concern is none of the above. I argue that the term 'pastoralism', which overtook the term 'nomadism', is now suffering the same fate. Many anthropologists stopped using the term 'nomadism' because of its implication of barbarism and backwardness. Only about two decades ago, Humphrey and Sneath carried out a research project, 'Environmental and Cultural Conservation in Inner Asia', from 1991 to 1995, and published their seminal work *The End of Nomadism?* in 1999. With the title they raise two ideas: one is the demise of the way of life while the other is the negative associations of the term 'nomad'. They 'prefer the term mobile pastoralism to nomadism because it does not bring with it the suppositions such as those' (Humphrey and Sneath 1999, p. 1) of 'low technology' (Khazanov 1984) and 'barbarian' (Sneath 2007, 39–41; Myadar 2011, 340; Bumochir and Chih-yu 2014, 417; Tsetsentsolmon 2014, 423). In the conclusion Humphrey and Sneath (1999) answer the question in the title:

> if what is imagined by 'the nomad' is the low-tech, rapacious, disorganised wanderer, then we think that this has been a rather rare character in Inner Asian history and only ever applied to a minority of the population. Maybe a few such individuals are around today. If we are talking about mobile pastoralism, on the other hand, this technique remains viable and useful in the modern age (Humphrey and Sneath 1999, 306).

They argue that pastoralism is sustainable when there is greater mobility, as in Mongolia and Tuva, while less mobility causes degradation in most of the cases in the regions of Buryatia and Inner Mongolia where mobility has been limited by state interventions (ibid., 54, 92, 293). They attempted to end the negative assumptions about the term 'nomad' by showing the sophisticated techniques of mobile pastoralists, with which I am in full agreement. If one considers the negative implication of 'nomadism' ending, then we can now talk about its afterlife.

The title of this chapter, 'Afterlife of Nomadism', engages with the second question in *The End of Nomadism?* I argue that the term 'unsustainable pastoralism' is the afterlife of the term 'nomadism'. Almost twenty years after Humphrey and Sneath's research, discussion of 'unsustainable pastoralism' has grown in the field of mobile pastoralism, even in Mongolia. Ahearn and Bumochir (2016, 89) pointed out:

> Government officials and herding communities themselves frequently devalue pastoral livelihoods and knowledge. Mongolian Prime Minister Enkhbayar expressed this view in 2001 when he called for the end of pastoralism and the movement of 90 percent of the population to urban areas within thirty years (Endicott 2012). Enkhbayar supported his policy by questioning the viability of pastoralism after severe drought and winter weather killed the livestock of 12,000 families from 1999 to 2001 (Sternberg 2010). His criticisms did not acknowledge the government's role in exacerbating this disaster (Sneath 2003; Sternberg 2010). Also, in Mongolia, some pastoralists evaluate their work as 'unskilled' and their own subjectivities as 'uncultured', despite the widespread celebration of 'nomadic' identities in nationalist discourse (Marzluf 2015).

The Afterlife of Nomadism

In addition to being perceived as 'unskilled' and 'uncultured', the afterlife of pastoralism has come to contain negative discourses which focus on damage to the environment. As a result of academic and political debates on whether or not pastoralists 'degrade pasture' and 'destroy natural resources', a suspicion and supposition of 'harmfulness' has already gained credence as an attribute of 'pastoralism'. This chapter shows a growing negative assumption about mobile pastoralism, which makes the use of the term pastoralism no longer preferable to nomadism. The preference of the word pastoralism to nomadism was one of the key reasons for Humphrey and Sneath to title their book *The End of Nomadism?* If the word pastoralism is now facing the same fate as nomadism, then I suppose the 'backwardness of nomadism' is not ending but has transferred its tragic fate to the term pastoralism, in the sense of carrying on a discourse on unsustainability and potential damage to environment.

Finally, I will look at how connotations of pastoralism as 'harmful' call into question the national pride and identity of Mongols, who consider 'mobile pastoralism' to have a defining role in the construction of their national identity as fundamentally different from sedentary agriculturalists and others. Mongols, both in Mongolia and China, are victimised by the same global approach but the two states, Mongolia and China, show different reactions to the same discourse. The importance of pastoralism to Mongolian national identity helps us understand why Inner Mongolia has recently seen increasing numbers of demonstrations resisting Chinese policy on pastoralism, which is actually ending pastoralism for many. Here, I follow Humphrey and Sneath's suggestion that in many places, the continued existence of mobile pastoralism as a viable economic practice is under threat (1999, 1). To be more precise, pastoralism is ending more rapidly in China, while Mongolia is struggling to preserve it. The last section of the chapter explains the different consequences in relationship to different constructions of the notion of 'civilisation' in Mongolia and China. Even though the view that pastoralism is unsustainable is growing in Mongolia, Mongolia cannot stop employing 'nomadic' pastoralism in the making of its national identity.

The Making of 'Unsustainable Pastoralism'

The Chinese State and Chinese scientists are not the first to condemn the destructive effects that humans have on nature. This is merely the Chinese version of the 'anthropocene' concept – human dominance of biological, chemical and geological processes on Earth. As Williams explains, Chinese government officials and scholars widely attribute land degradation to past and present anthropogenic forces, specifically those humans who practise mobile pastoralism. Though climatic and physical processes first formed China's deserts, they believe that humans have contributed immensely to their enlargement (2000, 508). The same also applies to Mongolia. Ian Hannam, an expert in international and national legal, policy and institutional systems for natural resource management, advised the governments of Mongolia and many other Central Asian countries on environmental law and land management policy and has contributed to new legislative and institutional structures. According to his advice,

> Mongolian rangeland is degraded because herders are unable to apply sustainable grazing practices. Mongolian grassland is not valued so its regulation and management have been avoided in the past. Herders continue to graze their livestock on public land unrestrained, where there is high competition for good pasture. They use public pasture and water free of charge and without initiative to protect and properly use it (Hannam 2012, 418).

For many living in pastoral regions with little industry, 'harmful pastoralism' is a replica of the 'anthropocene' notion, which was originally targeted at the growth of industrialism. The idea and term 'anthropocene' were first developed in the early 1980s by Stoermer and Crutzen (Crutzen and Stoermer 2000, 17; cf. Chakrabarty 2009, 204). In 1995 Crutzen and his colleagues Molina and Rowland were awarded the Nobel Prize in Chemistry for their discovery of growing depletion in the ozone layer:

> For the past three centuries, the effects of humans on the global environment have escalated. Because of these anthropogenic emissions of carbon dioxide, global climate may depart significantly from natural behaviour for many millennia to come. It seems appropriate to assign the term 'Anthropocene' to the present ... human-dominated, geological epoch, supplementing the Holocene – the warm period of the past 10–12 millennia. The Anthropocene could be said to have started in the latter part of the eighteenth century, when analyses of air trapped in polar ice showed the beginning of growing global concentrations of carbon dioxide and methane (Crutzen 2002, 23).

The alarming rise in global concentrations of carbon dioxide and methane is one aspect of the negative effects of human activity. Although the connection of the anthropocene with industrial carbon dioxide and methane is far removed from pastoralism, its overall concept which addresses the escalated 'effects of humans on the global environment' also alarms non-industrial others to reflect on their mode of production. Chakrabarty (2009) presents the idea of humanity as a 'geological agent' with the capacity to transform, and even to destroy, its own conditions of existence. This idea has been widely adopted in novels and the film industry. As Weik von Mossner puts it 'it is indeed quite interesting to see how often texts and films that attempt to imagine the risks of the Anthropocene mix and fuse fictional and non-fictional modes of narration' (2016, 85). In other words, this concept of 'anthropocene' operates as a global slogan and call to save the world. Not only novels and films but also scholarly disciplines are now forced 'to radically rethink the scope of human agency' (ibid., 87). In the field of pastoralism, one might reflect on Hardin's concept of the 'tragedy of the commons' (Hardin 1968), which discusses a different form of human effect on nature. Hardin contended that where many actors graze their livestock on communal land, it is in each individual's interest to keep adding to the number of his or her animals, even if the land is facing overgrazing and degradation. Although Hardin did not use the term 'anthropocene', this over-use and eventual destruction of resources can be seen as another form of anthropogenic forces. Hardin suggested that the way out of this destructive cycle was to introduce private ownership of land. Individuals who owned both land and livestock would have an interest in maintaining the potential of the land and preventing overgrazing (Sneath 2003, 444). In response to Hardin, Ostrom proposed a solution to protect natural environments, which gained her a Nobel Prize in 2009: to organise 'community based natural resource management' (1990) whereby community groups collectively use and protect common land. The solution was widely accepted by national and international NGOs and policy makers as a way to engage with or sometimes against mobile pastoralists, as I will illustrate in the following.

Hardin coined the concept 'unsustainable pastoralism' and argued that pastoralism is harmful. He proposes privatisation as a solution. On the other hand, Ostrom claims that pastoralism does not have to be harmful, especially when there is some sort of community-based pasture management. Ostrom's claim neither follows Hardin, nor suggests the opposite. She implies that, if there is no community-based pasture management, for example in Mongolia and North China, then pastoralism can be harmful. In this way Ostrom, in my reading of her implication that pastoralists have the potential to harm the environment in the absence of management, shares Hardin's basic attitude towards pastoralism. This is the angle adopted by International NGOs and development practitioners in Mongolia and China. Besides the actual content of Hardin and Ostrom's work, what matters is the way in which it is read and the argument applied in policies and related programmes. Here, I must also admit that I am not arguing whether or not pastoralism harmful to the environment; instead my main concern is to show how different agencies, policy makers, activists, development practitioners and scholars can read it differently and popularise their reading of this literature.

Not long after Ostrom's winning of the Nobel Prize, I first heard of her solution in Inner Mongolia and China, when my colleagues asked me if people in Mongolia believe in the theory of the commons. Many of them were concerned that the Chinese State was taking advantage of the prestige of the Nobel Prize to use Ostrom's argument against the Mongol herders. Even though 'grassland' is privatised in China,[4] the argument became a justification for the Chinese authorities to continue taking 'grassland' away from Mongol herders, by eliminating pasture and forcing urbanisation. People talked about the 'ghost town' in Ordos as an example, where all the herders were encouraged to move to the new town, flats were sold to them at a discount and compensation was given for loss of livelihood, which might be enough to live on for up to three years. The question was what would the future livelihoods of the herders be after they finished the money provided as compensation? A student of mine from Ordos told me that many people had started opening souvenir shops since the reinvention of the region as a tourist area centred on Chinggis Khan's mausoleum (cf. Bulag 2010, 60).

A few years after my experience in Qinghai, starting from spring 2012, I was involved in a similar discussion, but this time in Mongolia to do research for the Green Gold Project (2004–2016) funded by the Swiss Agency for Development and Corporation (SDC). The Green Gold Project, 'partnering with the Mongolian State',[5] acknowledges and builds on Hardin's 'tragedy of the commons' theory and Ostrom's work on 'governing the commons' (Ostrom 1990). Green Gold argues that, since 1990, pasture has been left to public ownership without state regulation and control (cf. Sankey et al. 2012, 153; Himmelsbach 2012, 165–166), while the number of herding households and livestock numbers have dramatically increased, leading them to take advantage of publicly owned common rangeland. According to Green Gold, this is a factor in rangeland degradation in combination with climate change. In order to create an 'owner' for the public rangeland (*belcheeriig ezentei bolgoh*) who can control and regulate the pasture, Green Gold established community groups

---

4. According to the 50 year contracts mentioned above, which is often termed privatisation although pasture is still ultimately state-owned.
5. Quoted from Green Gold Website (http://www.greengold.mn/index.php/en).

they call *Belcheer ashiglah heseg*, meaning 'Pasture User Groups'.[6] Other projects, namely the German Technological Corporation's 'Nature Conservation and Buffer Zone Development Project' (1995–2002) and its successor 'Conversion and Sustainable Management of Resources: Gobi Component' (2002–2006), the World Bank's Sustainable Livelihoods Program (SLP) (2002–2012) and the UNDP's Sustainable Grassland Management Project (SGMP) (2002–2007) (cf. Upton 2012, 225–226; Kamimura 2013, 188) adopted the same approach and formed over 2,000 local herders' groups across the country. Following Ostrom's proposed solution to the 'tragedy of the commons', all the foreign projects initiated various 'community based natural resource management' interventions and instructed local people to collectively own and protect common pasture. All this was done as a result of the belief that Mongolian pastoralism does not have a satisfactory sustainable management system, and did not acknowledge the formal and informal forms of land management that already exist (see, for example, Sneath 2003). Therefore the discourse states, 'since 1999, Mongolia has become a de facto testing-ground for community-based rangeland management, with the establishment of over 2000 'herder groups' or 'pasture user groups' facilitated by over twelve different donor and NGO-sponsored programs' (Fernandez-Gimenez et al. 2008, 3, cited in Kamimura 2013, 188). The debate has neither proven nor disproven whether degradation exists and what causes it; instead, the discussions have created more suspicion of pastoralism and have left many simply in doubt.

Thus, within the last two decades, both in Mongolia and China, a new approach has been used to target pastoralism as being harmful to natural resources. Williams calls this approach 'scientific knowledge construction' (2000). Following Williams, I call this the 'environmentalist construction of pastoralism' and argue that it is a different concept of pastoralism from the traditional one. In the environmentalist construction of pastoralism, livestock and mobile herders are blamed for the destruction of the natural environment, and this blame is the focal point in the new conceptualisation of pastoralism. Studies by scholars, local and international NGOs, stakeholders and policymakers engage with topics such as climate change, rangeland degradation, desertification, the *zud* winter disaster, loss of herds, risk management and poverty to produce a range of publications contributing to the construction of a discourse of pastoralism through the lens of environmental determinism. Many of these works explore and explain causes of land degradation by addressing the issue of the

---

6. By 2013, Green Gold had set up over 700 pasture user groups across seven *aimags* (provinces) (http://www.greengold.mn/index.php/en).

increase in livestock numbers in Mongolia (e.g. United Nations Development Program 2007, Bayanmonkh 2009, Index Based Livestock Insurance Project Implementation Unit 2009, Sheehy and Damiran 2009, Whitten 2009, Sternberg 2010, Reeves 2011, Leisher et al. 2012) and search for solutions and alternative approaches in pastoralism without digging deeper into the root political causes of the problems identified.

However, many scholars also argue against Hardin and criticise him for oversimplifying the diversity and complexity of pastoralists' land use and regulations (McCay and Acheson 1987, Feemy et al. 1990), while many works claim that mobile pastoral forms of land utilisation do not necessarily cause degradation (e.g. Goldstein et al. 1990, McCabe 1990, Buzdar 1992, Wesche and Retzer 2005, Klein et al. 2007, Wesche et al. 2010, Cheng et al. 2011). Also an increasing number of scholars have expressed their concerns about the under-recognition of spatial and temporal dimensions (Addison et al. 2012, 135) and ignorance of indigenous practice and herders' extensive knowledge of ecology (Humphrey and Sneath 1999, Williams 2000, Fernandez-Gimenez 2000) that safeguards natural resources. For instance, Sneath finds that indigenous Mongolian notions of 'land ownership' can be described as 'custodial' (2001, 43). It is striking to find some studies which prove that privatisation and enclosure do not help (Little and Bronkensha 1987), but instead actually abolish existing practices and in the long run tend to lead to more ecosystem problems (Williams 1996, 307) and degradation than traditional mobile pastoralism (Hoshino et al. 2009, Suruga et al. 2014). The same contradiction is also evident in the diverse results produced by different community based rangeland management schemes (CBRM). Some show improved livelihoods and better resource conditions (Usukh et al. 2010, Fernández-Giménez et al. 2012, Leisher et al. 2012), while others appear ineffective (Upton 2008, Murphy 2011, Addison et al. 2013).

As a result of the discourse on environment and pastoralism in the last decade, we now find a different understanding of pastoralism in China, as Williams (2000) describes, based on scientific knowledge construction, while Sneath finds similar problems in Mongolia as environmentalists' agendas 'reflect a familiar western interest in promoting western conservationist ideology and establishing and expanding protected areas to harbour wildlife and biodiversity' (Sneath 2003, 441). Following this discussion, I argue that recent discourses on pastoralism have created a new understanding – an environmentalist construction of unsustainable pastoralism – directly or indirectly associated with the prestige of several Nobel Prize winning arguments. The idea of 'unsustainable pastoralism' conflicts with the existing so-called traditional, local, indigenous understandings of pastoralism as sustainable and helping to preserve nature. But these are, in fact, also another construction, a product of the history and culture of the Mongols both in Mongolia and China.

Pastoralism in the Making of National Identity and Civilisation

Mr. President,
>Distinguished Members of the European Parliament,
>Excellencies, Ladies and Gentlemen,
>I would like to begin with something simple: thank you.
>…
>I am the youngest of eight sons. For generations, my family lived as 'nomadic' herdsmen in the western highlands of my country, in the ranges of the Altai Mountains. My mother and father never dreamt that, one day, their youngest son would speak from this respected podium to the most caring hearts of democracy: the European Parliament. But this is not about me. I am here to speak for my people and about my country.[7]

On the 9 June 2015, the President of Mongolia, Ts. Elbegdorj made a speech to the European Parliament, in Strasbourg, France. He started his speech about Mongolia's transition to democracy and the European Union's support and cooperation, by explaining that he was born and grew up in the 'nomadic' pastoralist way of life. 'Nomadic' pastoralism is an essential element for many Mongolians to identify 'Mongolness.' Unlike the environmentalist approach explored in the previous section, such employment of 'nomadic' pastoralism does not imply anything negative and harmful. Just the opposite – it implies pride in the successful achievement of modernity, democracy and a market economy from the basis of so-called 'barbarian nomadic' pastoralism. This is not only a pride in democracy but also a pride in the 'nomadic' and pastoral cultural background in promoting and enabling a vibrant democracy. Many believe there is an actual connection between 'nomadism' and democracy. For example, Sabloff argues that Mongolia's democracy predates the 1989 democratic revolution by 800 years, being rooted in the political culture of Chinggis Khan (2002, 26). This also explains why the President was so enthusiastic in proudly announcing his 'nomadic' and pastoralist background.

The following year a similar statement was made by the Prime Minister of Mongolia, Ch. Saikhanbileg, at the Credit Suisse 19th Annual Asian Invest-

---

7. http://www.president.mn/eng/newsCenter/viewNews.php?newsId=1568

ment Conference in April 2016 in Hong Kong. His mission was to attract and welcome investors with his portrayal of Mongolia's glorious democracy and global free market environment, providing different business opportunities and investment confidence. To answer a question regarding agriculture and economic diversity, the Prime Minister mentioned Mongolia's 'rainbow policy' (*solongoruulah*) to diversify the national economy with seven different colours, one of which is mining, while agriculture is another, largely potential, colour in the diversification. Moreover, he also said,

> We have the most democratic livestock in the world. Why do we say democratic? Because they are free to choose where to go and what to eat. This is really unique. 300,000 people are still having a 'nomadic' style of life. Because of this uniqueness, our lamb and beef is the tastiest food in the world. Very organic![8]

According to his point 'very organic', the purpose of his statement was not only promote mining investment and advertise democracy in Mongolia, but also to advertise 'nomadic' pastoralism as a potential sector in the diversification of the nation's economy.

At the national level, pastoralism does not have the negative connotations it has for the environmentalists and conservationists cited above. A positive attitude to pastoralism is common not only in the government but also among scholars, herders and the general public. In 2002, the Council for Sustainable Development of Mongolia (led by the Prime Minister), published a collection of articles, *Tulkhtai khögjil – Mongolyn ireedüi* [*Sustainable Development – Mongolian Future*] by Mongolian economist Dagvadorj, who states,

> For Mongolians nomadic pastoralism is about how herders tend livestock and use its products to meet their economic consumptions, animals adopt to the environment and increase its number, nature with the help of nomadic civilization remains preserved with its original characteristics, which is a resource for future herders and animals. This way of life provides sustainable development conditions for nomadic civilization and pastoralism (Dagvadorj 2002, 19).

Similarly, other Mongolian scholars writing on 'nomadic' civilisation and pastoralism also reveal the same stance. For instance, Dulam (2013) writes that Mongols inherited 'nomadic' civilisation not because they are savage and barbarian, but because of the environmental conditions of their homeland. Most importantly, he states that Mongols realise nature cannot be produced again in the same way that it originally was and that 'nomadic' pastoralism can

---

8. https://www.credit-suisse.com/microsites/conferences/aic/en/media-hub/virtual-aic/investment-mongolia.html

play a role environmental conservation (Dulam 2013, 29). According to these authors, pastoralism is a fundamental element in the construction of 'nomadic' civilisation. In fact, the construction of 'nomadic' civilisation is a reaction to depictions of the Mongols by their sedentary neighbours and other foreigners, which claimed that nomads were backward and uncultured barbarians (Khan 1996, 127–31; Humphrey and Sneath 1999, 1; Sneath 2007, 39–41; Bumochir and Chih-yu 2014, 417; Tsetsentsolmon 2014, 423; Bayar 2014a, 440–43). Insiders' construction of Mongolian national identity in the twentieth and early twenty-first centuries often tried to oppose foreign definitions (Bumochir and Chih-yu 2014, 417–420). According to Tsetsentsolmon, the notion of '"nomadic civilisation" emerged in opposition to the negative presentations of the "uncivilised" Mongolians' (2014, 435). She further elaborates in detail the history of the reconstruction of 'nomadic' culture and 'civilisation' in the Soviet and post-Soviet era, mainly by leading Mongol scholars. Subsequently, the Mongolian version of the concept 'nomadism' and 'pastoralism' has had very positive connotations, even playing a crucial role in national pride and an honoured place in building a national identity. Its level of importance is confirmed even in the National Security Concept of Mongolia. In the version passed in 2007, article 47.1 was entirely dedicated to the preservation and enhancement of 'nomadic' civilisation.[9]

On the other side of border, in China, the situation of pastoralism is completely different. Here, mobile pastoralists have been historically conceived of by the Chinese as a 'barbaric other' (Khan 1996, 129) or as *yin* (versus *yang*), where the 'negative' force, the land of the northern groups, is dark and cold (Bayar 2014a, 441), therefore often rejected. Khan (1996) and Bayar (2014a) argue that this understanding is a by-product of Chinese imagination of pastoral Mongols in the history of China. Starting from the Zhou dynasty (1046–771 BC), Bayar shows the Chinese construction of the people in the north as *yeman* (barbarian), *cuye* (rough) and *culu* (rude) who need to be tamed with *wenming* civilisation. *Wenming* refers to a high style of writing used to express a kind of thought that one only achieves after cultivating one's imagination. Despite historical and political negative attitudes, the Chinese Communist Party (CCP) had to accept, reconstruct and employ pastoralism in the Chinese construction of nationalism and civilisation in order to unite the 56 nationalities (for education, cf. Borchigud 1995, 278). The non-Han minority nationalities were embraced (Bulag 2010) and after some hundred

---

9. http://www.openforum.mn/index.php?sel=resource&f=resone&obj_id=750&menu_id=3&resmenu_id=3 Last accessed 27 April 2015.

years nomadic culture was finally politically accepted, with use of the term *youmu wenming*, literally 'nomadic civilisation' in Chinese (*negüdel-ün bolbasun* in Mongolian in Inner Mongolia) (Dulam 2013, 15). The term was eventually replaced by a different term, *cao yuan wen hua* in Chinese and *tal-a nutag-un soyol* in Mongolian, meaning 'grassland culture'. This modification occurred in parallel with the recognition of 56 'nationalities' or 'ethnic groups', in order to make one homogeneous nation *zhonghua minzu* (Chinese Nation) and civilisation *zhong guo wenming* (Chinese civilisation). In the words of Bulag, the concept of 'grassland culture' now forms part of the communist Chinese narrative of national harmony (Bulag 2010, 108). Bayar writes that,

> There have been shifts in the official and semi-official discourses of national unity and ethnopolitics, moving towards the aim of stronger national integration and solidarity in China. The affirmative action policies towards minority nationalities have come under increasing criticism. The so-called 'second generation nationality (ethnic) policy' (*dier- dai minzu zhengce*), proposed by two academics (Hu Angang and Hu Lianhe), deliberately aims to weaken the ethnic identity of minorities and to strengthen identification with the Chinese nation (*zhonghua minzu*) among ethnic groups (Bayar 2014b, 378).

In this way, in the 2000s, the CCP's unification project employed pastoralism and 'nomadic' culture not in the form of 'nomadic civilisation' but under the concept of 'grassland culture', a term apparently absent in Mongolia. Moreover, Bayar describes Chinese government-sponsored research projects designed to promote the concept of 'grassland culture' as one of the three great components of Chinese civilisation (Bayar 2014a, 450). Whereas in Mongolia 'nomadic' culture is regarded as the product of an independent civilisation of the steppes, in Inner Mongolia, 'grassland culture' is one component of a larger, inclusive category – *Huaxia* 'Chinese civilisation' (Bumochir and Chih-yu 2014, 418). For historical and political reasons, the concept of 'nomadic' civilisation found in Mongolia is therefore absent in China. Instead, according to Harrell, Chinese civilisation puts the minority nationalities under communist 'civilising projects' (Harrell 1995, 12–14).

  China is more keen to construct a different civilisation of industrialism and urbanisation. More precisely, the consequences in Mongolia and China are different, mainly because of the different missions of the two states. In China, the state is encouraging herders to reduce livestock numbers, minimise pasture and give up pastoralism, inciting demonstrations by herders in different parts of Inner Mongolia and other regions in China with Mongol pastoralists. When I visited Inner Mongolia in 2013, many of my colleagues told me

The Afterlife of Nomadism

that the Chinese Government openly stated, 'China does not need peasants and pastoralists because they are burdens in the development of the country. Therefore, Chinese future policy will be to eliminate peasants and pastoralists.' This is based on remarks made by the Chinese Prime Minister Li Keqiang. Since the beginning of 2012, Li Keqiang repeatedly stressed the importance of urbanisation in the future development of the country, versus the agricultural sector. He often mentioned the unnecessary difference between urban and rural livelihoods, which should be equalised by eliminating poverty in rural areas.[10] At the same time, social media in Mongolia started to feature various cases of Inner Mongolian ex-herders whose *belcheer* and livestock had been taken over by the local governments. The herders were demonstrating against the government, some saying they failed to obtain compensation, some stating that the compensation was inadequate, others questioning how they are supposed to live once they finish the compensation.[11] The elimination of pastoralism very much stimulates the existing crisis of 'Chinese identity' (*Zhonghua minzu* and *Zhongguo ren*) conflicting with local, regional, cultural, ethnic and national identities. Borchigud writes that, historically for non-Han minorities, there is dissonance between their ethnic identities and their national identity (1995, 162). The main problem lies in the fact of 'ending pastoralism' for those people and making them not only 'ex-pastoralist' but also 'ex-Mongols' who are no longer able to possess the 'nomadic' and 'pastoralist' (*nüüdelchin* and *malchin*) identity. For example, Deed Mongols in Qinghai always consider Mongolness to be deeply connected to mobility and pastoralism, in opposition to Chinese agriculture, sedentary way of life and urbanisation. For them, there is not much chance to pursue a Mongolian way of urbanisation as is being done in Mongolia (for urban education cf. Borchigud 1995). Therefore, to be a pastoralist is the only and ultimate way to remain an authentic Mongol. I was surprised when the father of my family in Qinghai, Bat, told me that the enclosures are actually a good thing for them. Only by way of making a contract with the Chinese State to use the *belcheer* for fifty years and fencing it have they been able to preserve Mongolness within the gated space. Otherwise, as Bat explains, their *belcheer* and *nutag* homeland would have been invaded by the neighbouring Chinese, Tibetans, Hui and Salar Muslims a long time

---

10. Li Keqiang made a speech at a conference in Lanzhou, the capital of Gansu, neighbouring Qinghai, in August 2013. The title of the conference was 'Development and Poverty Alleviation in the North West of China' http://news.xinhuanet.com/politics/2013–08/19/c_117004247.htm Last accessed 25 April 2014.
11. I hesitate to reveal details about Mongol herders' demonstrations in rural China for the safety of the local people.

ago. Evidently many Deed Mongols are grateful to pastoralism for enabling them to maintain a unique identity. Many more scholars from Mongolia, Inner Mongolia and elsewhere also address the importance of 'nomadism' and pastoralism in the construction of Mongol national identity (e.g. Khan 1996, 143; Tsetsentsolmon 2014, 423). Khan poses a question of 'Why the pastoral?' and responds that the symbolisation and universalisation of pastoral identity for the whole Mongol population of Inner Mongolia is a form of resisting subordination, assimilation and Sinification.

> [T]he imagery of pastoralism has inevitably become the most salient rallying point and identity marker because, as a mode of economy and way of life, pastoralism is not only the most effective distinguishing marker of opposition to Han Chinese, it is also intimately connected to the Mongols' proud past as a powerful nation that once ruled over the Middle Kingdom and beyond (Khan 1996, 143).

Pastoralism, therefore, cannot be limited to producers and herders, and reduced to an economic activity; it is in fact an indispensable part of national identity. Being a mobile pastoralist is upheld as a unique feature of the Mongols in contrast to their two gigantic neighbours, Russia and China. In such a manner, mobile pastoralism is unreservedly engaged in the construction of national identity and nation-building.

The same also applies to the Mongols in Mongolia. Therefore, repeated attempts to privatise (*ezemshüüleh*) *belcheer* since the early 1990s have failed. The State would certainly be condemned by the public for jeopardising the most important feature of national identity, by restricting the mobility of mobile pastoralism. In the last attempt made in Spring 2014, the government of Mongolia introduced a draft law of land use (*Gazryn tuhai bagts huuli*) including the privatisation of winter and spring *belcheer* to community-based groups. The attempt resulted yet again in tremendous disagreement in parliament, which later involved wider public discussion, with some people collecting votes to resist the *belcheer* privatisation. The Mongolian public was devastated by the news of the draft law, and social media were immediately packed with discussions, angry reactions and counterattacking comments. A Facebook group 'Not supporting the land law' (*Gazryn huuliig demjihgui*) opened and reached 19,723 members (as at 27 April 2014). Many argued that it is in the national interest for land not to be privately owned but to belong to the state. People widely cited the former MP Dashbalbar's statement that privatisation of the land could end in 'civil war' (Sneath 2001, 42–43 and 2003, 444–45). For the Mongols, *belcheer* does means not only an economic resource; instead it is an open, free, wild, wide, organic and natural landscape which is their homeland. As such, it is the treasure and pride of the nation that can never be owned by anyone except the state and the public. In this sense the land plays an important role in the construction of the Mongol Nation State, so that it is no surprise that many people actually mentioned 'war'. Everyone who initiated and supported the *belcheer* privatisation was regarded as an enemy of the country. In this way, Mongolia intends to remain a homeland for mobile pastoralists by supporting mobility of pastoralism, while China does the opposite.

Conclusion

It is fashionable in the history of humanity for states to construct their own narrative of national civilisation. The nation state of Mongolia may be the only state built by a single nation whose history is entirely 'nomadic' and pastoral until the twentieth century. Therefore, compared to many states with agricultural, sedentary and urban histories, it is not a surprise that this state and its rulers are constructing its unique civilisation (cf. Bumochir and Chih-yu 2014) based on 'nomadic' and 'pastoral' identity. Myadar deconstructs Mongolia's imaginary nomadic identity and argues that it is not only a western construction but also a Mongolian self-representation endorsed by the state.

> While Mongolian nomadic identity was appropriated and perpetuated in Western Orientalist discourse, the myth is also a Mongolian-produced self-fiction: a fiction that both glorifies and blasphemes nomadic identity. Mongolians have channelled Western curiosity into a telescoped version of Mongolia with staged authenticity and primitivity. The state's fiction of 'true' nomadic identity manipulates enchanted tourists, foreign donors and visitors alike, while reifying and fossilising 'nomadic characteristics' in order to construct signifiers and symbols that are different from other cultures. These symbols, in turn, serve to articulate an imagined cultural identity and social bond for those who identify with them (Myadar 2011, 338).

Because 'nomadism', 'pastoralism' and the concept of mobility play an essential role in defining not only national identity but also national civilisation, unlike in China, the leaders of the Mongolian State are always hesitant to issue any policy which jeopardises mobile pastoralism. For example, the above-mentioned failed attempts to pass land privatisation law over the last two decades. The politics of pastoralism in Mongolia and in China are entirely different. Chinese rulers and scientists undervalue pastoralism while Mongol leaders and scientists hesitate to express any approaches against pastoralism, including the employment of the environmentalist construction of 'unsustainable pastoralism'.

Beyond Mongolia and China, there is a clear contrast and even contradiction between the value of pastoralism as seen by the Mongols and the environmentalists. This sits in further contradiction with the discourses of international agencies and NGOs which operate in Mongolia and fund interventions based on the concept of an 'unsustainable' pastoralism. Unfortunately, to be grateful for and proud of pastoralism is now globally questioned. Moving into the future, to what extent is the Mongolian State able to utilise 'mobile pastoralism' in the building of the nation state? Maybe the answer lies in the National Security Concept (Ündesnii ayulgüi baidlyn üzel barimtlal)[12] article emphasising the importance of 'nomadic civilisation'. In the version passed in 2007, article 47.1 was entirely dedicated to the preservation and enhancement of 'nomadic civilisation'[13] and it was eliminated in the new version passed in 2010. In this way, is Mongolia gradually attempting to abandon mobile pastoralism because of global environmentalist pressure?

References

Addison, J., M. Friedel, C. Brown, J. Davies and S. Waldron. 2012. 'A critical review of degradation assumptions applied to Mongolia's Gobi Desert'. *The Rangeland Journal* 34: 125. doi:10.1071/RJ11013

Addison, J., J. Davies, M. Friedel and C. Brown. 2013. 'Do pasture user groups lead to improved rangeland condition in the Mongolian Gobi desert?' *Journal of Arid Environments* 94: 37–46.

Ahearn, A. and D. Bumochir. 2016. 'Contradictions in schooling children among Mongolian pastoralists'. *Human Organization* 75: 87–96.

Bassett, W.W. 1986. 'The myth of the nomad in property law'. *Journal of Law and Religion* 4: 133–52.

Bayanmonkh, P. 2009. 'State policy to increase living standard of herders and to adjust extensive livestock farming to climate changes'. In *International Conference on Climate Change and Adaptive Capacity Development: Combatting Desertification and Sustainable Grassland Management in Govi Region, Mongolia.* October 2009, Ulaanbaatar, Mongolia.

---

12. The official government website for the National Security Concept (Ündesnii ayulgüi baidlyn üzel barimtlal) announces that it is the second most important state document after the constitution. Available at http://www.nsc.gov.mn/?q=ns-concept

13. http://www.openforum.mn/index.php?sel=resource&f=resone&obj_id=750&menu_id=3&resmenu_id=3 Last accessed 27 April 2015.

Bayar, N. 2014a. 'A discourse of civilization/culture and nation/ethnicity from the perspective of Inner Mongolia, China'. *Asian Ethnicity* 15: 439–57, doi:10.1080/14631369.2014.939329

Bayar, N. 2014b. 'Nation-building, ethnicity and natural resources: The perspective of an Inner Mongolian coal truck driver across the China–Mongolia border'. *Inner Asia* 16: 377–91

Borchigud, W. 1995. 'Impact of urban ethnic education in modern Mongolian ethnicity'. In Stevan Harrell (ed.), *Cultural Encounters on China's Ethnic Frontiers*. Seattle: University of Washington Press.

Borgerhoff Mulder, M., I. Fazzio, W. Irons, R.L. McElreath, S. Bowles, A. Bell, T. Hertz and L. Hazzah. 2010. 'Pastoralism and wealth inequality'. *Current Anthropology* 51: 35–48. doi:10.1086/64856

Bulag, U.E. 2010. *Collaborative Nationalism: The Politics of Friendship on China's Mongolian Frontier*. Lanham, MD: Rowman and Littlefield Publishers

Bumochir, D. and S. Chih-yu. 2014. 'Introduction'. *Asian Ethnicity* 15: 417–21, doi: 10.1080/14631369.2014.942055

Buzdar, N. 1992. 'The role of institutions in the management of commonly-owned rangelands in Baluchistan'. In Michael Dove and Carol Carpenter (eds), *Sociology of Natural Resources*. Karachi, Pakistan: Vanguard Press.

Chakrabarty, D. 2009. 'The climate of history: Four theses'. *Critical Inquiry* 35: 197–222.

Cheng, Y., M. Tsubo, T. Ito, E. Nishihara, E. and M. Shinoda. 2011. 'Impact of rainfall variability and grazing pressure on plant diversity in Mongolian grasslands'. *Journal of Arid Environments* 75: 471–76.

Crutzen, P. 2002. 'Geology of Mankind', *Nature* 415: 23.

Crutzen, P.J. and E.F. Stoermer. 2000. 'The Anthropocene'. *IGBP [International Geosphere–Biosphere Programme] Newsletter* 41: 17.

Dagvadorj, D. 2002. *Tulkhtai khögjil – Mongolyn ireedüi* (*Sustainable Development – Mongolian Future*). Ulaanbaatar.

Dulam, S. 2013. *Mongol Soyol Irgenshiliin Utga Tailal*. Mongol soyolyn chuulgan tsuvral, vol. XII. Ulaanbaatar: Bit Press.

Dyer, C. 2014. *Livelihoods and Learning: Education for All and the Marginalization of Mobile Pastoralists*. New York: Routledge.

Endicott, E. 2012. *A History of Land Use in Mongolia: The Thirteenth Century to the Present*. New York: Palgrave Macmillan.

Feemy, D., B. Fikret, B. McCay and J. Acheson. 1990. 'Tragedy of the commons 22 years later'. *Human Ecology* 18: 1–19.

Fernandez-Gimenez, M.E. 2000. 'The role of Mongolian 'nomadic' pastoralists' ecological knowledge in rangeland management'. *Ecological Applications* 10: 1318–26.

Fernandez-Gimenez, M.E., A. Kamimura and B. Batbuyan. 2008. *Implementing Mongolia's Land Law: Progress and Issues: Final Report, a Research Project of the Central for Asian Legal Exchange (CALE)*. Nagoya, Japan: Nagoya University.

D. Bumochir

Fernández-Giménez, M.E., B. Batkhishig and B. Batbuyan. 2012. 'Cross-boundary and cross-level dynamics increase vulnerability to severe winter disasters (dzud) in Mongolia'. *Global Environmental Change* 22: 836–51.

Goldstein, M., C. Beall and R.P. Cincotta. 1990. 'Traditional conservation on Tibet's northern plateau'. *National Geographic Research* 6: 139–56.

Green Gold Website. http://www.greengold.mn/info.php?t=intro. Accessed 28 January 2017.

Hannam, I. 2007. *Report to United Nations Development Program Mongolia on Review of Draft Pastureland Law of Mongolia.* UNDP: Sustainable Grassland Management Project.

Hannam, I. 2012. 'International perspectives on legislative and administrative reforms as an aid to better land stewardship'. In Victor Squires (ed.), *Rangeland Stewardship in Central Asia.* Dordrecht: Springer. pp. 407–29.

Hardin, G. 1968. 'The tragedy of the commons'. *Science* 162: 1243–8.

Harrell, S. 1995. 'Introduction: civilization projects and the reaction to them'. In Stevan Harrell (ed.), *Cultural Encounters on China's Ethnic Frontiers.* Seattle: University of Washington Press. pp. 3–36.

Himmelsbach, R. 2012. 'Collaborative pasture management: A solution for grassland degradation in Mongolia'. In Julian Dierkes (ed.), *Changes in Democratic Mongolia: Social Relations, Health, Mobile Pastoralism, and Mining.* London: Brill. pp. 165–94.

Hoshino B., M. Kaneko, T. Matsunaka, S. Ishii, Y. Shimada and C. Ono. 2009. 'A comparative study of pasture degradation of Inner Mongolian fenced and unfenced land based on remotely sensed data'. *Journal of Rakuno Gakuen University* 34: 15–22.

Humphrey, C., and D. Sneath. 1999. *The End of Nomadism?: Society, State and the Environment in Inner Asia.* Durham: Duke University Press.

Index Based Livestock Insurance Project Implementation Unit. 2009. 'Index Based Livestock Insurance Project Summary Report on Implementation 2005–2008.' Ministry of Finance: Ulaanbaatar, Mongolia.

Kamimura, A. 2013. 'Pastoral Mobility and Pastureland Possession in Mongolia'. In N. Yamamura, N. Fujita and A. Maekawa (eds), *The Mongolian Ecosystem Network: Environmental Issues Under Climate and Social Changes.* Japan: Springer. pp 187–203.

Kapp, P., J.D. Pelletier, A. Rohrmann, R. Heermance, J. Russell and L. Ding. 2011. 'Wind erosion in the Qaidam basin, central Asia: Implications for tectonics, paleoclimate, and the source of the Loess Plateau'. *GSA Today* 21: 4–10, doi: 10.1130/GSATG99A.

Khan, A. 1996. 'Who are the Mongols? State, ethnicity and the politics of representation in the PRC'. In Melissa J. Brawn (ed.), *Negotiating Ethnicities in China and Taiwan.* Berkeley: Institute of East Asian Studies, University of California, Berkeley. pp. 12S-159.

Khazanov, M.A. 1984. *Nomads and the Outside World.* Trans. Julia Crookenden. Cambridge: Cambridge University Press.

Klein, J., J. Harte and X.-Q. and Zhao. 2007. 'Experimental warming, not grazing, decreases rangeland quality on the Tibetan Plateau'. *Ecological Applications: A Publication of the Ecological Society of America* 17: 541–57.

Kolås, Å. 2014. 'Degradation discourse and green governmentality in the Xilinguole grasslands of Inner Mongolia'. *Development and Change* 45: 308–28.

Leisher, C., S. Hess, T.M. Boucher, P. van Beukering and M. Sanjayan. 2012. 'Measuring the impacts of community-based grasslands management in Mongolia's Gobi'. *PLoS ONE* 7: e30991.

Little, P. and D. Brokensha. 1987.'Local institutions, tenure, and resource management in East Africa'. In David Anderson and Richard Groves (eds) *Conservation in Africa: People, Policies and Practice*. New York: Cambridge University Press. pp. 193–209.

Marzluf, Phillip P. 2015. 'The pastoral home school: Rural, vernacular, and grassroots literacies in early Soviet Mongolia'. *Central Asian Survey* 34: 204–18.

McCay, B.J. and J.M. Acheson (eds). 1987. *The Question of the Commons: The Culture and Ecology of Communal Resources*. Tucson: University of Arizona Press.

McCabe, T. 1990. 'Turkana pastoralism: a case against the tragedy of the commons', *Human Ecology* 18: 81–103.

Murphy, D.J. 2011. *Going on Otor: Disaster, Mobility, and the Political Ecology of Vulnerability in Uguumur, Mongolia*. Ph.D thesis, University of Kentucky. Retrieved from http://uknowledge.uky.edu/cgi/viewcontent.cgi?article=1168andcontext=gradschool_diss (168)

Murphy, D.J. 2014. 'Booms and busts : Asset dynamics, disaster, and the politics of wealth in rural Mongolia'. *Economic Anthropology* 1: 104–123. doi:10.1111/sea2.12007

Myadar, O. 2011. 'Imaginary nomads: Deconstructing the representation of Mongolia as a land of nomads', *Inner Asia* 13: 335–62

Newman, R.P. 1992. *Owen Lattimore and the 'Loss' of China*. Berkeley: University of California Press.

Ostrom, Elinor 1990. *Governing the Commons: the Evolution of Institutions for Collective Action*. Cambridge: Cambridge University Press.

Reeves, J. 2011. 'Mongolia's environmental security, Chinese unconscious power and Ulaanbaatar's state weakness'. *Asian Survey* 51: 453–71. doi:10.1525/as.2011.51.3.453

Rong, J. 2008. *Wolf Totem*. Hamish Hamilton: London.

Sabloff, Paula L.W. 2002. 'Why Mongolia? The political culture of an emerging democracy', *Central Asian Survey* 21:19–36. doi: 10.1080/02634930220127928

Sankey, T.T., J. Sankey, K. Weber and C. Montagne. 2012. 'Changes in the pastoral land use and their effects on rangeland vegetation indices'. In Julian Dierkes (ed.), *Changes in Democratic Mongolia: Social Relations, Health, Mobile Pastoralism, and Mining*. London: Brill. pp.151–164.

Sheehy, D., and D. Damiran. 2009. 'Temporal study of Mongolian pastureland ecological condition (1997–2008): Draft'. *Consultancy Report to the World Bank*, NEM02.

Sneath, D. 2001. 'Notions of rights over land and the history of Mongolian pastoralism'. *Inner Asia* 3: 41–58.

Sneath, D. 2003. 'Land use, the environment and development in post-socialist Mongolia'. *Oxford Development Studies* 31: 441–59.

Sneath, D. 2007. *The Headless State: Aristocratic Orders, Kinship Society and Misinterpretations of Nomadic Inner Asia*. New York: Columbia University Press.

Sternberg, Troy. 2010. 'Unraveling Mongolia's Extreme Winter Disaster of 2010'. *Nomadic Peoples* 14: 72–86.

Stuart, K. 1997. *Mongols in Western/American Consciousness*. Lampeter: Edwin Mellen Press.

Suriga, M. Hashimoto, B. Hushino, S. Ganzorig, Saixialt, Y. Hai, K. Manayeva, and Ts. Purevsuren. 2014. 'Grazing behavior of livestock in settled and 'nomadic' herders households in Mongolian plateau'. *Journal of Arid Land Studies* 24(1): 187–189

Thrift, E.D. and B. Ichinkhorloo. 2015. 'Management of dzud risk in Mongolia: Mutual aid and institutional interventions'. In Trans-disciplinary Research Conference: Building Resilience of Mongolian Rangelands, pp. 136–141.

Tsetsentsolmon, B. 2014. 'The 'gong beat' against the 'uncultured': contested notions of culture and civilization in Mongolia', *Asian Ethnicity* 15: 422–38, doi: 10.1080/14631369.2014.947060

Upton, C. 2008. 'Social capital, collective action and group formation: Developmental trajectories in post-socialist Mongolia'. *Human Ecology* 36: 175–188.

Upton, C. 2012. 'Mining, resistance, and pastoral livelihoods in contemporary Mongolia'. In Julian Dierkes (ed.) *Changes in Democratic Mongolia: Social Relations, Health, Mobile Pastoralism, and Mining*. London: Brill. p. 223.

Usukh, B., H.P. Binswanger-Mkhize, R. Himmelsbach and K. Schuler. 2010. *Fostering the Sustainable Livelihoods of Herders in Mongolia via Collective Action*. Ulaanbaatar, Mongolia: Swiss Agency for Development and Cooperation (SDC), Mongolian Society for Rangeland Management.

Yeh, E.T. 2005. 'Green governmentality and pastoralism in Western China: "Converting Pastures to Grasslands"'. *Nomadic Peoples* 9: 9–30.

Weik von Mossner, Alexa. 2016. 'Imagining geological agency: Storytelling in the Anthropocene'. In Robert Emmett and Thomas Lekan (eds) 'Whose Anthropocene? Revisiting Dipesh Chakrabarty's "Four Theses"', *RCC Perspectives: Transformations in Environment and Society* 2: 83– 88.

Wesche, K., and V. Retzer. 2005. 'Is degradation a major problem in semi-desert environments of the Gobi region in southern Mongolia?', *Enforchung biodiversity Ressourcen der Mongolei (Halle Saale)* 9: 133–46.

Wesche, K., K. Ronnenberg and I. Hense. 2010. 'Effects of a large herbivore exclusion on Southern Mongolian desert steppes'. *Acta Oecologica* 36: 234–41, doi:10.1016/j.actao.2010.01.003

Whitten, T. 2009. *The Destructive Side of Goats*. The World Bank Blogs. http://blogs.worldbank.org/eastasiapacific/the-destructive-side-of-goats. Accessed 28 January 2017.

Williams, D.M. 1996. 'Grassland enclosures: Catalyst of land degradation in Inner Mongolia'. *Human Organization* 55: 307–13.

Williams, D.M. 2000. 'Representation of nature on the Mongolian steppe: An investigation of scientific knowledge construction'. *American Anthropologist* 102: 503–19.

Chapter 3

ENVIRONMENT AS COMMODITY AND SHIELD: RESHAPING HERDERS' COLLECTIVE IDENTITY IN MONGOLIA

Byambabaatar Ichinkhorloo

Introduction[1]

With the 'transition' from state socialism to a 'market economy' in Mongolia since 1990, competition for better access to and control over natural resources has been increasing among local herders, mining companies, conservation agencies, central and local governments and other actors such as wildlife hunters and legal or illegal loggers. Local herders, members of socialist collectives (*negdel*), received livestock[2] when these were privatised in 1991–1994 and became the dominant users of local environmental resources including wildlife, pasture, water and forests. Due to economic crisis and the state's weakened control over environmental resources, until the mid-2000s many people, including but not limited to herders, used their social network contacts in urban areas to commodify environmental resources, mainly wildlife and forest resources, to maintain their livelihoods. Meanwhile, the Mongolian government joined fourteen multilateral and/or UN-led environmental conventions in 1993–2003 and went on to develop 27 national environmental policies and programmes between 1996–2006. These conventions and national programmes led to a boom

---

1. This chapter is based on my Ph.D. research at the National University of Mongolia in 2013–2015 and some of its funding was provided by the Green Gold Pasture Ecosystem Management Project in Mongolia. I am very grateful to Bumochir Dulam, Caitlin McElroy and Galen Murton for their helpful comments and to the organisers and participants of the Third Oxford Interdisciplinary Desert Conference where I presented a first draft.

2. Livestock covers five types of animals: sheep, goats, cattle, horses and Bactrian camels.

in conservation projects. At the same time, the government made ambitious efforts to attract foreign investment in natural resource extraction in the new millennium. This brought mining companies as new competitors to herders, especially with regard to use of pasture, water and hunting.

As many different actors now claim a legal or informal right to environmental resources, competition has increased and accusations of environmental damage are often used as a justification for resource control. A particularly urgent question is, who is a legitimate and capable agent for environmental protection: the government of Mongolia, conservation agencies or local people? In order to legitimise their right to protect the environment, these agencies often accuse each other of being 'inefficient and slow on protection', or 'responsible for environmental damage' (Addison et al. 2012, Brown 2010, Laurie et al. 2010, MNET and Tourism 2008, Schmidt 2006, Wingard and Zahler 2006). Environmental movements and civil society organisations in Mongolia further fuel this debate, targeting the government and mining companies in particular.

This chapter focuses on why herders think they are the only legitimate users of rural resources and how these perceptions are derived. Moreover, research findings show how local people use and protect their resources and what the hidden realities behind these social relations are. A discourse analysis of self and other (Bunzl 2004, Castells 2009, Fuary 2000, Humphrey and Ujeed 2012, Rasmussen 2011) is used to examine herders' assumption of legitimacy made on the basis of their collective identity, or '*nutag*.' The term *nutag* in Mongolian usually refers to territory and land, and it is later used as a term to describe the territory of administrative units along with its natural resources (Gongor 1978). Herders develop their *nutag* identities based on their shared belief system, traditional customs, access to resources and local space inhabited by all living and non-living beings, including spiritual beings (Baival 2012, Fernandez-Gimenez 1999, Murphy 2011, Sneath 1993, 2010). According to common belief among many senior herders, all beings form a whole in every specific place, which has a structure and internal hierarchy. Humans, who sit in the middle of this hierarchy, receive a mandate or blessing from higher-ranked spirits and *nutag* beings to use environmental resources, together with a duty to protect lower beings such as wildlife, grass and other resources. The revival of this spiritual belief system and traditional customs has played an influential role in changing herders' perceptions of property ownership and sense of belonging to place.

This chapter demonstrates that notions of self and other are central to debates and contestations about land use and degradation in Mongolia. First,

Environment as Commodity and Shield

I argue that the rapid changes in the national property regime and donor-led conservation efforts are misleading people, especially herders, into commodifying their environmental resources and pasture. Secondly, any local environmental problems derived from commodification-related negative consequences are blamed mainly on non-local people, using a discourse of otherness. Thirdly, collective identity (*nutag*) is reshaped as a resistance to the advancing capitalist economy and emerging inequality in Mongolia. Finally, government conservation efforts are producing an anti-mining, resource-based and environmentally 'defensive' collective identity in Mongolia. Herders' perception is that belonging to the world of 'self' or the *nutag* 'community' gives them legitimacy to use the resources in a specific locality for community members and to exclude other, non-*nutag* people. In return, this encourages people to rely more on the connections between urban and rural communities to leverage claims of belonging to a particular *nutag* to better access and utilise resources. For this reason, people often develop and strengthen their social networks and connections to other places.

After reviewing research methods used and the conceptual framework, the chapter explains the socio-economic background of rural Mongolia, situating herders in the environmental and natural resource debates. I then make use of the discourse of legitimacy of resource use to examine herder practice with regards to environmental resources such forest wood, wildlife and pasture. In the last two sections, I examine how herders in Mongolia construct their *nutag* identity through a discourse of otherness, how this identity governs herders' actions on resource use and protection of the environment, and the consequences which this has.

Methods

This research was conducted across a variety of physical and social landscapes in three different *sums* (districts) in three different *aimags* (provinces) of Mongolia. Bayanjargalan *sum* in Dundgovi *aimag* is the main research site and represents the semi-arid Gobi region. Tes *sum* in Uvs *aimag* represents the steppe ecosystem in the far west of Mongolia. The third site, Tariat *sum* in Arkhangai *aimag*, represents the forested *khangai* region (see Figure 1). Research across these three *sums* was conducted over the course of two years, including seven months in total of on-site fieldwork. Methodologically, data was produced through participant observation together with semi-structured interviews with 83 informants (31 people in Tes, 35 in Bayanjargalan and seventeen in Tariat).

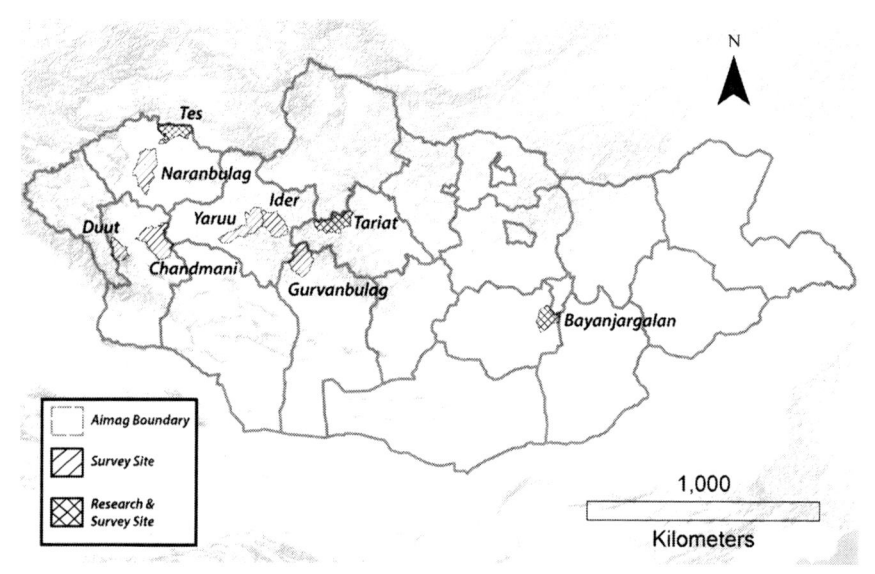

Figure 1. Research sites: Tes in Western Mongolia, Tariat in Central Mongolia and Bayanjargalan in Southern Mongolia; Survey sites: Uvs, Khovd, Zavkhan, Dornogovi and Bayankhongor aimags.

This qualitative data was augmented by wide-ranging survey data conducted under the National University of Mongolia's research project 'Socio-cultural dimensions of pastoral economy' (where I worked as a researcher for two years). This survey interviewed 288 respondents in nine *sums* in five *aimags*, including 23 questions focusing on herders' perceptions about environmental degradation and protection, and another ten questions about environmental discourse.

In addition, I reviewed a range of administrative level and other secondary source materials collected in the target *sums*. In order to understand the socio-economic conditions of the *sums*, data was collected primarily from the citizen *khural*,[3] the *sum* governor's office about official decisions and surveys including environment protection, resource use permissions and mining. I also visited three mines in Bayanjargalan and interviewed three officials and two mining company workers in order to find out how mining workers interact with local communities over environmental resources and wildlife hunting.

---

3. The citizen *khural* (council) in a *bag* (brigade; subdivision of a *sum*) is a meeting of all the citizens; at the *sum* and *aimag* level it consists of representatives.

Environment as Commodity and Shield

Conceptual framework

Themes and theories of political ecology serve as a guiding framework for this study. As summarised by McCarthy (2002), four key principles include: a) access to and control over rural lands and resources; b) informal and common property rights, relations and regimes; c) changing land use patterns under national and international conservation agendas; and d) transformations of property and production relations as a result of capitalist market integrations (pp. 1284–1290). Further drawing on Sikor and Lund's (2009) distinction between property and access, this study considers property as 'claims which are considered legitimate' and access as 'the ability to benefit' (p. 6). Herders in Mongolia have access to a wide range of state-owned or 'common' environmental resources through social networks, but legitimate authority over private property including livestock, shelters and mobile and immobile assets remains predicated on purchase and privatisation. Moreover, herders belong to 'residence-based groups', or spatially-bounded organisations which are used in elaborating a territorially-based co-management concept (Fernandez-Gimenez 2002). Mearns (1993) further demonstrated herders' view of entitlement to resources: 'newcomers frequently justify their entitlement to use common pasture on the grounds that they have family ties in the area' (p. 97). However, it is not necessary that people or households that form residence-based groups or informal institutions are all related by blood.

This study is also informed by debates over entitlements and endowments framed by Sen (1981). In explaining local people's access to resources and their control, the 'entitlement framework' is used by Leach et al. (1999) to argue that people rely on many different formal and informal institutions that are involved in natural resource management through their environmental endowment and entitlement (p. 240). The term 'entitlement' is defined as 'alternative sets of utilities derived from environmental goods and services over which social actors have legitimate effective command and which are instrumental in achieving well-being', whereas endowment is 'the rights and resources that social actors have' (Leach et al. 1999, 233).

In his early research on rural Mongolians' social relations, Sneath (1993) argued that a 'network of social relations of obligation' was formed in parallel with the official structure of collectives and farms during the socialist period in Mongolia. These networks controlled access to a whole range of resources, including services and produce. Private ownership of assets was restricted and access to state-owned resources was strictly controlled by officials or authorities who acted as 'patrons' in the social networks. Since the socialist regime in Mongolia collapsed, the social network has continued to serve as the basis of access to resources (Ichinkhorloo and Yeh 2016), especially environmental resources, for rural and even urban Mongolians. Privatisation of the livestock and assets of former collectives gave herders the opportunity to own property along with access to environmental resources such as pasture (Ahearn 2016) and wildlife.

According to Sneath, the former approach to management of livestock husbandry as a 'socio-technical system' has been transformed into an 'atomized pastoral sector of subsistence-oriented pastoral producer households' (Sneath 2004, 179). In Mongolia, a 'neo-classical economic and conservationist discourse' has become the government's main policy on land use and rural development (Sneath, 2003, 453). Accordingly, herders in post-socialist Mongolia are in the process of adapting to a new property regime while creating their own new form of a 'socio-technical system'. In this process, herders are drawn into a project of nation-building through 'asserting collective identity, reconstruction of tradition and deploying of sense of belonging' as argued by Sneath (2010, 261). In the context of collective identity (*nutag*), Sneath's argument can be advanced to suggest that 'networks continue to be of vital importance for accessing resources and opportunities, and the claims of regional and local collective identities are often seen as highly influential' (2010, 257). Following these lines of argument, this research examines tensions between an ongoing process of 'atomized households' joining forces around public property and environmental resources in response to intervention by other competing agencies, and the emergence of formal and informal institutions through which people get access to and control over resources through mechanisms of 'environmental entitlements'.

Socio-economic changes and inequality

The collapse of the planned economy in 1990 and de-collectivisation in 1991–1994 led to a return to rural life for large numbers of Mongolians. Livestock husbandry was a natural alternative livelihood after the collapse of planned industry, and contributed over 35 per cent of GDP in 1993–2000 (see Figure 2). This created employment opportunities and self-sufficiency for 270,000 households or almost one million people. By 1999, two thirds of the population (1.6 million out of 2.38 million) were living in 21 provincial centres and 323 *sums* (NSO 2014b). Livestock numbers had increased by 23 per cent compared to 1990. However, the number of herding households fell significantly after 2000 (see Figures 3 and 4).

Environment as Commodity and Shield

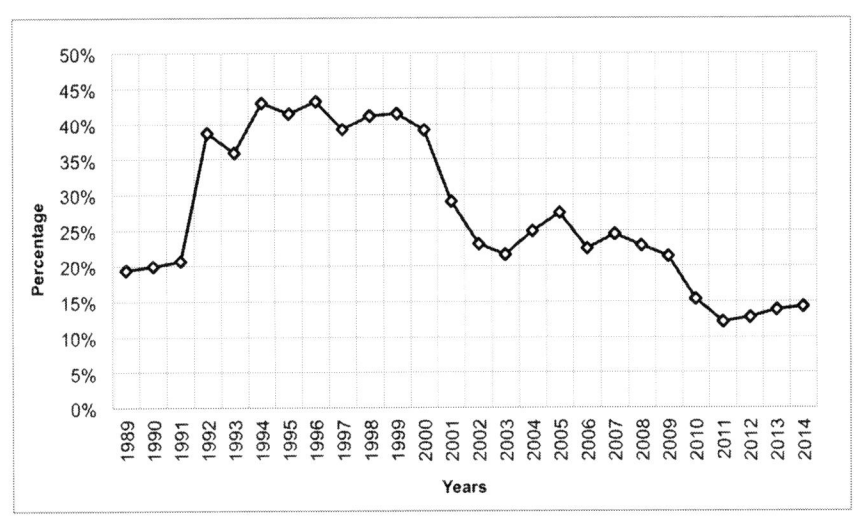

Figure 2. Comparison of livestock sector production to Gross Domestic Product of Mongolia (at current prices; NSO, 2014b).

After thirty years of socialist collectives, Mongolia's policies changed to neoliberalism, a system which has led to privatisation of national resources and new free market orientations towards resource management (Harvey 2005, 2). Complicating this neoliberal agenda in Mongolia (and elsewhere), however, is that local knowledge of the free market system and private property management was inadequate and assets were often privatised in ways leading to perverse outcomes. A common local experience with neoliberal schemes in Mongolia is illustrated by the privatisation of wells. When wells were privatised, the mechanical components were often divided into three distinct parts – the motor, shelter and well cement structure – and then distributed to three different people, thus rendering the well effectively useless.

Beginning in the 1990s, animal husbandry became increasingly associated with poverty in Mongolia. Following widespread efforts at privatisation and a subsequent period of economic decline in the 1990s, people fell back on livestock herding as the main source of survival and self-sufficiency. Mongolian husbandry is mainly subsistence-oriented, such that, with the exception of a few households, it lacks the financial or management capacity to develop husbandry commercially (Chuluundorj 2012, Janzen 2011). As a result, pastoralists generally receive government incentives rather than paying taxes. The government reduced taxes on livestock and pasture several times, eventually exempting herders from all taxes[4] in 2008 and providing them with subsidies (premiums) for cashmere in 2008 and wool and skins since 2011 and 2014 respectively. According to large scale household socio-economic surveys (NSO et al. 2004s NSO and World Bank 2009s NSO 2011, 2012, 2015), poverty persisted among herders throughout the 1990s and 2000s, reaching 56.1 per cent in 2010 after the 2009–2010 *zud*.[5] As numbers of sheep, goats, cattle, horses and camels grew significantly from 32.7 million to 51.9 million between 2010 and 2014, poverty declined sharply from 56.1 per cent to 27.9 per cent. At the same time, as a direct outcome of neoliberal reforms, livestock became increasingly concentrated in the hands of a few while overall herd sizes decreased, as illustrated in Figures 3 and 4 showing the trajectory for 1994–2013.

Along with significant state subsidies, incentives and increases to herd sizes, poverty and income inequality have grown across Mongolia's herding communities in the past two decades. In 1998, for example, herders who owned up to 200 livestock constituted 87 per cent of total households and owned 63 per cent of total livestock. By 2013, this level of ownership fell to 64 per cent of households and 23 per cent of total livestock. Conversely, the percentage of herders with more than 500 livestock increased from 1.4 per cent in 1998, when they owned 5.5 per cent of total livestock, to ten per cent of herders and forty per cent of total livestock in 2011 (See Figures 3 and 4). Moreover, even though livestock husbandry is mainly subsistence oriented, about 36 per cent or 75,000 households own almost 77 per cent of total livestock.

Government policies to support a majority of relatively poor herders have been exploited by wealthier livestock owners, whose herds have increased dramatically. These policies include the elimination of rangeland taxes (user fees), which had been calculated per head of livestock, in 2008; the introduction of cashmere subsidies of 5,000 tugriks (US$ 3.5) per goat in 2009; and

---

4. Livestock taxes were calculated in sheep unit. A horse or a cow equals 5 sheep. A goat equals 5 sheep and a camel 2 sheep. It is 100 tugriks per sheep in central region near Ulaanbaatar, Erdenet and Darkhan, 75 tugriks in the northern and southern regions and 50 tugriks in far western and eastern regions. Also herders do not pay livestock product sale taxes. The only taxes imposed on herders are gun, pet and garbage taxes. In 2008, government provided herders with 5,000 tugriks per kilogram of cashmere due to cashmere price decline in the international market and 2,000 tugriks per every kilogram of wool sold to national wool factories. In addition, 15,000 tugriks per horse or cattle skin and 3,000 tugriks per sheep or goat skin have been provided to herders since 2014.

5. Extreme winter weather causing heavy livestock mortality.

Environment as Commodity and Shield

the introduction of price premiums of 2,000 tugriks (US$ 1.5) per kilogram of sheep and camel wool in 2012. These statistics represent how state liberalisation led to increasing wealth differentiation and dispossession in Mongolia.

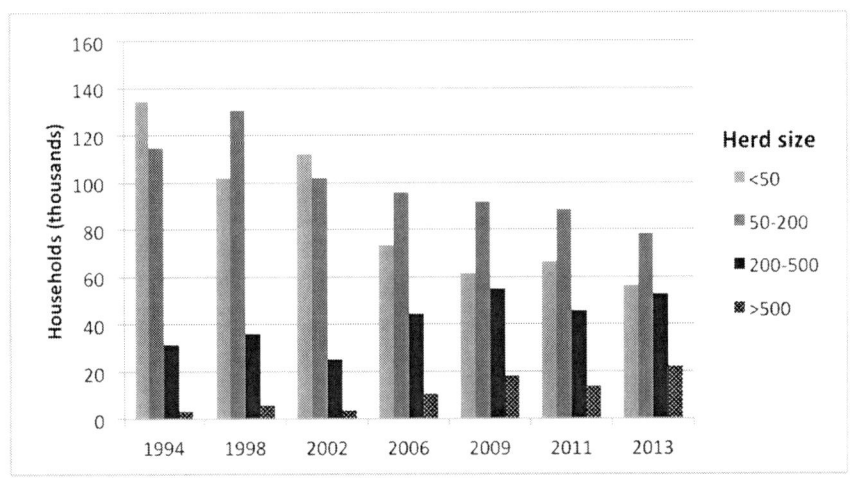

Figure 3. Number of herder households in Mongolia by herd size. Source: Livestock Censuses 1994–2013 (NSO, 2014a).

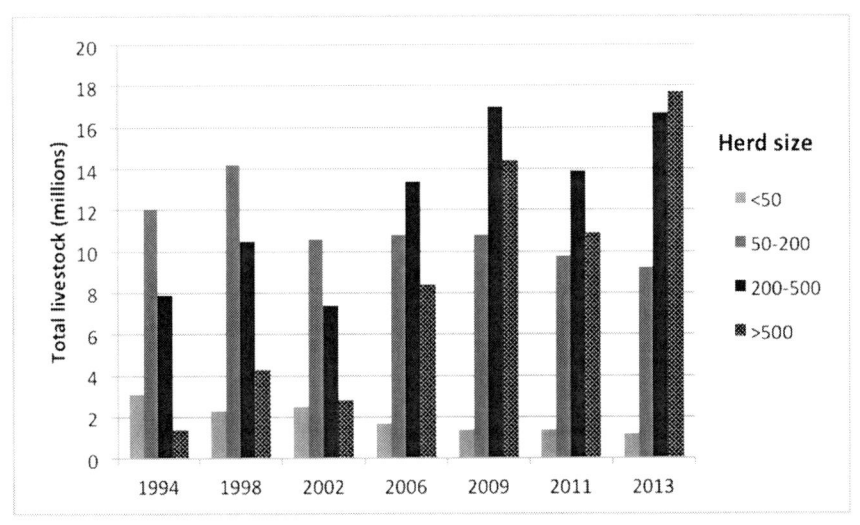

Figure 4. Total livestock in Mongolia by household herd size. Source: Livestock Censuses, 1994–2013 (NSO, 2014a).

Byambabaatar Ichinkhorloo

Herders' role in environmental degradation and competition for resources

The fact that inequality is deepening amongst already-marginal herders coincides with intervention by government and development agencies in environmental resource management. The herders' efforts to secure their subsistence and maintain basic livelihoods by accessing environmental resources (pasture, water etc.) have been met by accusations of environmental damage from both local and international organisations. Environmental degradation was first raised publicly by environmental and conservation programmes, including the Mongolia Action Plan for Sustainable Development for the 21st Century. These programmes were initiated following Mongolia's ratification of the Convention on Biological Diversity in 1993 and the UN Framework Convention on Climate Change in 1994, the Convention on International Trade in Endangered Species of Wild Fauna and Flora in 1995 and the UN Convention to Combat Desertification in 1996 (MNEM 1998). In the mid-1990s, Mongolia's pastures were considered to be in a healthy condition compared to those of China and Russia, and were characterised by year-round livestock mobility and the delivery of efficient services to mobile herders (Humphrey and Sneath 1999). However, according to the Government of Mongolia, by 1997, almost 34 per cent of the total territory of Mongolia had been degraded compared to its condition in the 1950s (MNEM 1997). The new government established in 1998 after parliamentary elections re-asserted that pastoral herding was one of the drivers of pasture degradation and increasing desertification, as a result of competitive self-interests of herders (MNET 2008). In 2010, the proportion of degraded land across Mongolia was estimated at 77.8 per cent (MEGDT 2015). That is, within one decade 33 per cent of Mongolia's land was classified as degraded and overall livestock numbers doubled.

According to a 2015 report by the Green Gold Ecosystems project implemented by the Swiss Agency for Development and Cooperation (SRC), the principal cause of land degradation was livestock overgrazing. The report's key recommendation was to control livestock numbers and revive pasture fees. Furthermore, development practitioners argued that, 'as a result of overgrazing, poor herd rotation practices, mining vehicle tracks – and compounded by climate change – biodiversity is declining, weeds are encroaching, soils are eroding and deserts are advancing' (Brown 2010, 11). However, commodification of all services and privatisation subsequently led herders to new competitive practices and pursuit of individual interests. In sum, pasture overgrazing and land degradation became the dominant concern among development decision

Environment as Commodity and Shield

makers and projects, especially after the *zud* disasters of the 2009–2010 winter and two consecutive winters in 1999–2001 (Viguier et al. 2010).

International organisations increasingly advise methods to reverse negative trends of overgrazing through pasture fragmentation. This includes the establishment of residence-based herder groups with exclusive rights to use environmental resources. Furthermore, many government and donor agencies report that uncontrolled opportunistic hunting by local herders has led to the total extinction of wildlife locally, while wildlife habitats are increasingly destroyed by livestock and mining operations (Addison et al. 2012, Laurie et al. 2010, Sneath 2003). These assessments and advocacy, especially the promotion of exclusive rights, have influenced herders to change their view towards more individualistic behaviour and to adopt an attitude of not sharing resources with others. These assessments are documented by much grey literature produced and funded by development agencies such as the United Nations Development Programme (Laurie et al. 2010), the World Bank (Wingard and Zahler 2006), the Swiss Agency for Development and Cooperation (SDC) (MFA et al. 2015, Usukh et al. 2010) and the German Agency for International Cooperation (GIZ) (Schmidt 2006). In parallel, these agencies have advised the Government of Mongolia to improve its legal framework, establish more environmental or pasture management institutions, increase the size of protected areas at the national level (Addison et al. 2012, Batkhishig et al. 2012, Dorligsuren et al. 2012, Ericksen 2014, Marin 2008, Upton 2012) and even to privatise pastureland to herders, a recommendation that is strongly opposed by herders (Sneath 2003). The government and Mongolian parliament have followed these recommendations through adoption of the National Mongolian Livestock Programme in 2010. This programme has enabled the institutionalisation of livestock husbandry and established a new state agency in every *sum*, while promoting herders' 'communities' to take over pastoral management and decisions.

Government measures and interventions to stop degradation have been heavily influenced by development agencies and donors. However, these parties are mainly concerned with overgrazing and have targeted herders, further complicating land management problems. Many donor organisations promoted conservationist (environmentalist) ideas through their public awareness and capacity building projects (Sneath 2003, 453). These interventions are also justified by discourses based on an imagination of ecologically-benign and homogenous groups of herders or ideal 'communities', rather than evidence-based research. These discourses argue that herders manage resources more effectively based on their close relationship to nature. These more effective practices include

Figure 5. Herder family in seasonal movement to autumn encampment in Tes, Uvs aimag. Some herders, often senior, instruct youths to practice cultural traditions threatened by modernity while keeping camels in use. Photo: Byambabaatar Ichinkhorloo.

Figure 6. Senior herder at the one of local horse races at Ovoonii naadam, where people extend their social networks and gain prestige. The herder is being interviewed by Byambabaatar Ichinkhorloo in Bayanjargalan, Dundgovi aimag. Photo: Byambabaatar Ichinkhorloo.

management of pastureland under pre-collective traditional 'socio-economic' or 'territorial units' called *neg nutgiinkhan* (Bazargur et al. 1993, 7, 11).

However, previous research in the field has failed to consider how development advice and misunderstandings connected with the transformation from the socialist to the neoliberal model have changed public perceptions about protection of the environment and concepts of individual responsibility. After the *zud* winter disasters of 1999–2001 and 2009–2010, public opinion was divided over the herders' responsibility for these events. As Ericksen (2014) observed, the herders who lost livestock during the *zud* were called 'lazy' and irresponsible, and blamed for their individualistic actions which were said to have contributed to rangeland degradation. However, she argued that there is a conflict between the socialist legacy that encouraged government and community to support individual herders, and current neoliberal approaches (p. 47). Before the start of open market systems in 1991, all herders were members of collectives (*negdel*), and the state through the *negdel* organisation was the owner of all livestock, excluding 50–75 privately-owned livestock per household, as well as all other facilities and resources. As the owner, the state was responsible for managing livestock and resources during the socialist period. As a result of this model, herders formerly sought and received support from the state for everything from transportation for seasonal movements to overcoming harsh winters. The change to a market system in 1990 gave individuals total responsibility for their own private property, namely livestock. In response to this change, urban populations that did not benefit from neoliberal privatisations frequently criticise herders for seeking support from the state against harsh winter conditions.

Blamed by donor countries and development agencies involved in environmental programmes on one hand, and threatened by the advance of mining over their pasture and water sources on the other, in the early 2000s herders started to vigorously assert their right to use resources, especially pasture, water and wildlife. As McCarthy (2002) identifies, herders use their collective identity to establish the legitimacy of their claim. 'Effective property claims and rights in this broader sense can arise and derive their power and legitimacy from a wide array of sources beyond the legal, including customary usage, community sanction, economic power, regulatory practices, moral authority, and more' (McCarthy 2002, 1289). According to interviews with herders, many believe that they are the legitimate users of natural resources, especially pastures, wildlife, woodlands, minerals and medicinal plants. On the basis of *nutag* identity, these herders often claim rights of resource use and accuse mining companies (Chuluun and Byambaragchaa 2014) or others of stealing their resources, damaging the environment and threatening their livelihoods.

Nutag collective identity and otherness

Nutag is both a traditional and dynamic concept. A traditional term, *nutag* was socially constructed and promoted by the state during the socialist period (Sneath 2010). In subsequent post-socialist decades, however, herder conceptualisations of *nutag* identity have changed to include the power to exclude others from resources.

Recent scholarship provides a preliminary understanding of the relationships between terminology and collective identity for rural Mongolians. Depending on the season, the term '*nutag*' is used by herders interchangeably with *neg goliikhon*, people of one river basin, or *neg usniikhan*, people of the same water source, and *neg nutgiinkhan*, people from one *nutag* place (Fernandez-Gimenez 1999; Mearns 1996, 314; Sneath 1993, 201). These terms indicate that members of one *nutag* share their pasture land, especially during winter and spring time (Fernandez-Gimenez 2002, 62). Others refer to how *nutag* members imagine the community or informal pastoral institution (Bazargur et al. 1993) and how the concept is used in nation state building (Sneath 2010, 2014).

According to Tsevel's Mongolian dictionary (1966), *nutag* more broadly represents territory on three levels: an administrative unit of settlement, different seasonal or temporary grazing areas and an encampment area. However, the term also encompasses a broad meaning of community, belonging, territory, inhabitants and social attributes of inhabitants such as family, locality, clan, region, ethnicity and nationality (Murphy 2011, 264). Baival (2012) argues that herders making up a single *nutag* identity can be treated as a 'community' and furthermore suggests using the '*nutag* framework' as a basis for building community resilience. However, previous research on *nutag* has been limited to studying its socio-economic implications: how this identity is related to conservation and capitalist market integration in rural Mongolia and its internal structure and regulatory power over natural resources.

Following the informal commodification of pastureland under the name of seasonal campsites, herders have started to make great use of *nutag* identity for purposes of both land access and social identity. On the one hand, herders claim rights to resources based on *nutag*. On the other hand, however, herders are motivated to strengthen their social or *nutag* identity networks in order to secure their resource access. Twelve years have passed since the revision of

Environment as Commodity and Shield

*Figure 7. Private pasture enclosure for livestock emergency grazing during dust and snow blizzard in Bayanjargalan, Dundgovi aimag. The fencing supported by Development and environmental agencies encourages informal ownership of pasture and resource competition.
Photo: Byambabaatar Ichinkhorloo.*

Mongolia's land law in 2002, which opened the gate for issuing certificates for winter and spring campsite land for herders. This certificate provides possession rights over just 0.07 hectares of land for building or previously built winter or spring livestock shelter for herder households. However, herders also utilise informal mechanisms to leverage this certificate to cover surrounding pastures. Furthermore, livestock numbers have reached over 51 million head and the campsite certificates have brought pasture commodification. For example, in Bayanjargalan, herders have started to rent out their winter shelters for over one million tugriks[6] and they sell and buy shelters for the purpose of expanding their pasture area, despite the fact that no one is allowed to possess pastureland legally.

Herders establish *nutag* identity across multiple scales of landscape and kinship. According to herders, the *neg amniikhan* or the *one valley people* are identified by residence in the same winter camp area, and the *neg goliikhon* or the *one river basin people* by summer camp area. However, summer camp area households outnumber the households residing in nearby winter camps, because

---

6. Approximately US$ 500 or 330 GBP.

herder households from different winter camp sites move to and are crowded into one summer camp area as a result of dense and rich summer vegetation cover. Therefore, the lowest level of *nutag* identity refers to the households and people who occupy winter camps around the same mountain or valley. This *nutag* identity is the strongest. As the scale of territory gets larger, the *nutag* collective identity becomes looser. At the *aimag* or provincial level, different *sums* form their own *nutag* identity around the *sum* administrative unit. At the national level, herders prefer *sum nutag* identity rather than *aimag* identity. The *sum* is further divided into three to twelve *bags* that are headed by the *bag* governor and head of the citizen *khural*. As such, a *nutag* identity is stronger at the *bag* level than at the *sum* level.

Nutag collective identity can be explained by the 'self' versus 'other' model, where the 'self' is a member of the *nutag* and the 'other' is everyone else. For the purposes of this study, I use the 'self' as a member of *nutag* people and 'other' as non-member people. From the herder's perspective, people who do not belong or are not included in *nutag* identity are 'others'. As a result, the *sum* or *aimag* administrative units are divided into many different smaller *nutag* identity groups. These 'self' or *nutag* identified people share the same territory or proximate residence, history, norms, memory, resources and most importantly, spiritual or social belief system. They can be of different ethnic descent or ancestry but they are united under this identity. This collective identity is dynamic and its members can change over time. But people who left this *nutag* group and live in urban areas are still considered 'virtual' or distant members of it. In addition, *nutag* people always exclude 'others' or outside people from their area, mainly at the *bag* and *sum* levels. For example, a herder who is related to one of the illegal hunters coming from Ulaanbaatar explained,

> My brother is in-and-out between Bayanjargalan and Ulaanbaatar. We grew up together in this place but police, together with local people in the neighbouring *sum*, caught him while he was hunting. If he were here (where he grew up), we would tell them 'get off'.

This case shows that the brother is still an active member of his *nutag* but powerless in other places. If a herder from this *nutag* group is active in another place, people who live in the other *nutag* place often exclude the herder. Quite simply, this *nutag* identity is everywhere.

Herders are quickly adapting to an emerging resource management system that is locally regulated by *nutag* identity and ongoing commoditisation of resources. As many local people often legitimise access to local resources to their own *nutag* people, outside people find a way to use resources that belong

Environment as Commodity and Shield

to other *nutag* people by expanding their social networks. *Nutag* groups have hierarchical systems and the exclusionary power of these groups varies depending on distance and social networks. As such, *nutag* identity provides social identity and land access as well as livestock security.

Nutag groups are also highly political and carry on feuds just as they maintain networks. During the *otor*[7] movement, herders often experience the following types of difficulties:

> During the 2004–2009 droughts, I had gone for *otor* almost five years. I collected the *nutag* people's horses and went for *otor* with my elder son and other *nutag* herders. I was so brave at that time I had collected almost 1,000 horses. It was easy to negotiate with people in the neighbouring *sums* because I know them. But it was difficult to graze 1,000 horses in one place for a month. So I moved to other places. This way I passed almost Dornogivi and reached Khentii. I always relied on my acquaintances or relatives who have ties with our *nutag*. Of course I gave them one or two horses for their food and always helped them. For example I first water livestock of that *nutag* people and then I water my horses. But in Darkhan *sum* of Khentii *aimag* I had no acquaintance. So I met with local *nutag* people and asked who is indirectly who is a senior and prestigious person among them. Then I met that senior person and explained my difficulties and even offered two horses. He sat listening and then finally allowed us to stay for two months. But I stayed a little longer, almost four months there. Their pasture was good because it is a khangai type of eco-region which includes dense grasses that grow in the Khangai mountains. These people did not like us and when two months passed, they sent their *bag* governor. He came and demanded we should move within a week. I explained and asked to extend a month. Then later on the *bag* governor came and asked us to transfer our registration to that *sum*. But later on, drunken youths of that *nutag* divided our horses into three and chased our horses about fifty kilometres off.

The above narrative illustrates that even a small tie with one *nutag* person provides power and access rights. The informant also explains the interrelation between *nutag* access rights by social networks and legal legitimacy. Even though different *nutag* 'communities' come under the same administrative units, for example *sum* or *aimag*, and pasturelands are public and free to everyone by law, every *nutag* community has special exclusionary power over its own (residence-based) places by traditional informal laws. Therefore, it is no surprise that *bag*

---

7. Herders' movement in search of fresh grazing in addition to regular seasonal movements. This *otor* movement often occurs during autumn for fattening animals. If there are climatic difficulties, herders move to other places that are not affected or less affected by droughts or *zud*.

and *sum* governors cannot mediate or handle pasture conflicts among herders from different *nutag*s especially in the event of *zud*. Likewise, with regard to illegal hunting mentioned in the next section, the *sum* environmental inspector together with her rangers and policeman cannot protect wildlife effectively.

Claims to *nutag* are also widely used in disputes over land use and environmental degradation. Across Mongolia, environmental damage and conservation failures are often blamed on non-local agents such as outside people, mining companies, the government and development agencies. For example, most illegal hunting and logging is attributed to temporary visitors, outside company workers or neighbouring *sum* or *aimag* people, and reduction of water supply in wells is supposed to be the direct impact of any mining in the *sum* or *aimag*.

While apportioning blame is not the purpose of this paper, it bears noting that a revitalisation of *nutag* identity is widely used to claim rights to resource use and refute the accusations of environmental agencies and conservation programmes. In the research survey, 79 per cent of respondents answered that herders can protect their environment and natural resources by themselves. In many other non-western societies, resource and habitat taboos and informal institutions like *nutag* identity are widely used in resource management and conservation (Colding and Folke 2001, Upton 2010). Thus, it is essential to recognize that herders in Mongolia use their own *nutag* collective identity and their spiritual and social belief system and customs in the management of natural resources.

Legitimacy of resource use among herders

According to Suchman, 'Legitimacy is a generalised perception or assumption that the actions of an entity are desirable, proper, or appropriate within some socially constructed system of norms, values, beliefs, and definitions' (Suchman 1995, 574). The entity can be an individual or a group of people such as herders who have shared and socially constructed beliefs and values. As Sikor and Lund (2009) argue: 'the exercise of authority is intimately linked to claims of legitimacy of the particular institution. This often involves a general, historically-based claim as well as a specific claim to legitimacy' (p. 7). In taking this conceptualisation further, the claim to legitimacy is linked to authority that is exercised by institutions (Fortmann 1995; Rocheleau and Ross 1995, cited in Sikor and Lund 2009, 7) and is continuously re-established through conflict and negotiation.

Environment as Commodity and Shield

According to Mongolian herders' perception, they are the 'legitimate users' of both biotic and abiotic natural resources because they were born in that locality. Detailed interviews with herders reveal that many individuals consider these resources as 'ours' or 'our *nutag* people's' and the government as just the manager. To consider how herders distinguish 'us' from 'others', the section below asks: why do herders think they are the legitimate users of natural resources, specifically wildlife, trees, rangelands, pasture, water sources such as rivers and lakes, even minerals exploited by mining companies? Under the notion of legitimacy discussed above, it seems that herders actually have a socially or historically accepted claim over resources and the following empirical data shows that herders are challenging governments and other agents for their legitimacy of authority over their local resources. Survey results show that 74 per cent (n=288) agree that the environment where they live is seriously degraded and 65 per cent oppose sharing of environmental resources with outside people, even with relatives who do not live in that *sum* or *bag* but come from outside (NUM 2015).

Using conceptualisations of legitimacy and practices of *nutag* as an informal institution, the following interviews demonstrate how herders perceive themselves as legitimate users of environmental resources and how they exclude people who do not belong to their *nutag*. Self-identification is a matter of similarity and solidarity, of belonging and community, of 'us' and 'we' (Jenkins 2008). Local people, especially herders, often distinguish locals from outsiders when it comes to hunting and use of natural resources (Scharf et al. 2010, 325). In Bayanjargalan *sum*, the environment inspector and rangers make great efforts to protect marmots and gazelle that used to be hunted without licenses. The reason for protection is clear: numbers of these species have fallen significantly and they are about to be included in the list of threatened species. As a result, the Ministry of Environment has prohibited hunting them.

Preliminary interviews with environmental inspectors about illegal hunting in this *sum* indicated that there were no serious issues and that all official decisions prohibiting hunting issued by central government had been introduced. However two weeks later, I encountered local people hunting gazelle using motorcycles. When I met the inspector again and asked about this incident, such was the reply:

> Just four staff is not enough to control all this illegal hunting in this *sum*. When rangers chase illegal hunters by motorcycle those illegal hunters just run away in their four-wheel drive car or jeep. Sometimes I go on patrol with our policeman but this is rare. Instead we focus more on illegal hunting of marmot and wild

sheep in the protected area. For marmots, illegal hunting occurs a lot especially by outside people from neighbouring *sums* or *aimags* because our *sum* is the only place with marmots. So we usually cooperate with and rely on our local *nutag* herders. If these local people were doing such acts, that is a crime.

These two meetings indicate that the inspector connects illegal hunting with people from outside and hesitates to admit local people's hunting activity (or does not want to accept it). According to the inspector, local people have similarities in belonging to the *sum* administrative unit and solidarity of not hunting illegally, whereas outside people are different from the locals in belonging and solidarity. This is the simple form of *nutag* identity at the *sum* level.

In contrast to the above narrative, interview and survey data show that herders effectively use conservation advocacy and the environmental agenda to put environmental blame on outside people or other institutions. Hedging or defence of one's own *nutag* community is common among local people and they often defend the exclusionary (resource-based) customary practice of their *nutag*. When conservationists or government environmental agencies raise issues of illegal activities or local environmental damage, herders often put the blame for environmental despoliation on non-local people and organisations, or link it to mining companies:

> We believe spiritual beings who master water and mountains own local resources. Local *nutag* people only receive fortunes (*khishig hurteh*) blessed by the water and mountain owners. They have power to bless and punish local people on resource uses. In most cases they act like our father and mother and protect us and help us. If we do wrong actions they punish us. If outside people come and dig our land or kill these wild animals that belong to those masters, we have to stop them. Otherwise our share will be reduced and there will be less rain or no water ... or punishment on us.

This herder underscores the ways in which spiritual beliefs shape management of natural resources and conservation activities at the individual and *nutag* level. During the socialist period, this practice or spiritual belief system was weakened by socialist ideology and it is being revived these days as a means of resistance to the 'market' economy and emergent resource competitors at local levels.

Another herder, whose winter campsite is very close to the gazelles' grazing area, was asked whether she noticed any hunting around this area and if so, who was doing it.

> Well, local *nutag* young men happen to hunt gazelle and marmots. These days, we have no rights to hunt and some people do it in a secret way. Anyway, these *nutag* people are nothing, but those travelling people from mining companies

just kill and they use gazelle meat for their food in order to save money from purchasing meat from herders. People who are in and out from those mining companies and who are passing through our *sum* and *nutag* often hunt these animals. We do not know how many people are going through our *sum* and their number is countless. But we herders are here and it is clear who is who and we will not escape from our *nutag*.

This perception that herders have lived for centuries using local resources and are the legitimate people to do so is widespread among herders. Instead of pursuing them, they believe the state or government should control those outside people and their 'illegal' use of local resources.

In response to the survey question 'who would best organise environmental conservation activities', most herders (79.2 per cent, n=288) supported individual herders as the most effective agents of environmental protection, though 77.1 per cent thought that there should be strong state regulation (NUM 2015). In sum, the conflict over access to environmental resources has started the long process of re-establishing perceived legitimacy in Mongolia.

In Tes *sum*, herders gave similar accounts of their practices over resource use. The Tes river basin includes forested areas, mainly willow, and open pastureland, and suffers cold wind from Lake Uvs in winter. The administration of the *aimag* protects this river basin and the lower reaches of the river that feed into the lake are included in the national Strictly Protected Area. According to the administration of the protected area, the most critical problem in Tes *sum* is illegal logging of forests for fuel and commercial logging for making *ger*, the traditional Mongolian dwelling. This forest is not only a winter encampment for herders but also a habitat for endangered wildlife such as wetland hogs, rare amphibians, and various migratory birds. In the early 2000s, people commonly burned areas of forest in order to prevent cross-border livestock theft between Mongolia and the Republic of Tuva.

To better understand this situation, I interviewed a herder who was preparing wooden poles from willow forests, and another family that was logging wood for their winter fuel. For the first woodman there was no problem because he was preparing these poles in his *bag* territory, his homeland or *nutag*. But the other family collecting fuelwood came from the centre of the *sum*. This family used their social network in that area to avoid repercussions and they stopped by two families on the way to appease them with vodka. Also this family left the *sum* centre early and came back with fuelwood at night to hide from officials.

Figure 8. Abandoned vegetable field enclosed with support from donor project to motivate collective action of herders who are busy with livestock all year round in Tariat sum. *Photo: Byambabaatar Ichinkhorloo.*

Figure 9. Winter fuel wood collection in the Tes river basin in autumn that is often practiced through formal permission from local government or informal nutag *identity access. Photo: Byambabaatar Ichinkhorloo.*

Environment as Commodity and Shield

From the cases above, it appears that *nutag* herders often exercise their right to log woods in their locality and do not seek official permission from the *bag* or *sum* administration. Herders who do not belong to a specific *nutag* have no access to natural resources in that area. The above interviews further suggest that herders distinguish local herders from others or outside people. Within the logic of legitimacy-perception, these local herders believe that they have a right to the natural resources if they belong to the *nutag*. However, there is also a strong sense of custodianship of the natural resources for all locals, rather than ownership among herders (Sneath 2001, 2004). This custodial relationship is often connected to the spiritual and social belief system.

Numerous studies document socially accepted norms and spiritual beliefs among local herders regarding natural resources (Chimedsengee et al. 2009, Humphrey et al. 1993, Humphrey and Sneath 1996, Sneath 2001, Upton 2010). Herders often claim that wildlife and natural resources belong to people of the given *nutag* only, and they justify their access rights and perceived legitimacy assumption by reference to their religious belief. While this belief is often practised among local people, they do not often impose it on outside people. In response to the survey question (NUM 2015) 'can local spirits and deities punish outside people who desecrate the environment', 49.3 per cent of respondents answered 'no' and 22.9 per cent of herders answered 'do not know.' In contrast, 53.5 per cent of herders agreed that local spirits and deities punish local herders for their transgressions against the environment. According to social norms and corresponding to Humphrey et al. (1993), if a *nutag* herder hunted more wild animals than he was allocated (blessed with) from these *nutag* masters, there would be punishment or revenge (social discrimination).

Data analysis shows that herders strongly exclude 'others', or people outside of their *nutag* community and the resources that belong to it. These social norms are not written down and are perceived differently by different people. A main criterion is not to damage or degrade natural processes of growth or sustainability. If the *nutag* master allowed the resource, the *nutag* individual can take it. As suggested by one informant, the idea is to 'take it if you are given or if you encounter wild animals or resources but do not search for them for commercial purposes'. In both cases, an individual member of the *nutag* is responsible for his actions and for damage done by others. The notion of responsibility for protection of the *nutag* in turn unites *nutag* people.

Consequences of herders' legitimacy assumption

Herders' livelihoods are dependent on their rights to access and control natural resources. *Nutagarkhakh,* or the preference for relying on people from one's *nutag* while discriminating against others, is increasing among herders. This is one type of adaptation strategy for local people and a social response to conservation efforts, commodification of resources and economic neoliberalism. In order to get around exclusionary limitations, rural people regularly expand their social networks to areas where they usually go on *otor* movements and otherwise have access to resources.

However, the rights of individual access and control conflict with the collective approach. Although *nutag* collective identity is influenced by the nation-building project, it helps herders to connect with each other and to reduce impacts of ongoing commodification projects that encourage commercialisation and exclusion, such as herders' possession rights to campsites as well as the granting of mining licenses by the government.

Problematically, the new collective forms of *nutag* identity have constructed an assumption of legitimacy that is leading to more social and spatial fragmentation in Mongolia. On the one hand, local people argue that they benefit from the assumption of legitimacy over resources because they earn cash by leasing shelters and commercialising environmental resources to outside people. On the other hand, however, mobility for these same local people becomes restricted and pasture areas shrink as mechanisms of commodification deepen social and economic inequalities.

Nutag collective identity is also exploited politically in elections for parliament and for the local citizen *khural* (Sneath 2010). For example many citizen *khural* members have double or triple *nutag* identities acquired on the basis of where one's parents were born as well as one's natal and/or adolescent home. These multiple belongings to several places – or what Sneath identifies as 'context-specific groupings, dependent on a particular discourse or point of reference' (2010, 262) – allow politicians and business people to generate political support and garner votes that in turn lend access to natural resources. Ultimately, the global trend of supporting community participation in the use of resources and decisions of redistribution, as well as the decentralisation of resource rights to local people (Arellano-Yanguas 2011, Ballard and Banks 2003, Bridge 2004), have helped the development of *nutag* identity in Mongolia.

Environment as Commodity and Shield

Conclusion

In the past two decades, Mongolian herders have adapted to a new socio-economic or socio-technical system that brings many new institutions and users of resources. Most recently, conservation organisations, development agency driven projects and government environmental programmes have intervened in the management of resources that were primarily the purview of herders in past centuries. In addition, private mining companies, and urban people passing through or spending vacation time in the countryside, have competed with herders for pasture, water, wildlife and other natural resources. As a result, new competition for resources has challenged herders in multiple ways with respect to various institutional agendas and programmes. While some actors blame herders for environmental degradation, others encourage herders to organise artificial 'communities' and commercialise the environment. Across these relationships, herders are cast either as environmentally destructive and opportunistic or as environmentally benign and the only people capable of protecting the local environment and natural resources.

The ongoing changes to social and economic conditions across Mongolia have generated new identities for rural people, especially herders. Resource competition and commodification have led rural people to construct and reshape collective *nutag* identities in order to enable local people to exclude external or outside people from their local resources. This *nutag* identity has roots in herders' traditional spiritual and social belief systems and is based on herders' resource use interests and sense of belonging to places of home. Traditional beliefs remain powerful for rural Mongolian herders, as shown in ceremonies such as *ovoo* worship, morning libation of tea and praying to spirits to cure diseases. Spiritual beliefs and the socially accepted norms discussed above also reveal that *nutag* people's sense of legitimacy over resources is getting stronger. This legitimacy is even accepted by outside people and increasingly used by politicians for opportunistic purposes.

With respect to resource management and environmental conservation, the modern form and practices of *nutag* present distinct tensions between individual agency and collective interest. The global trend of supporting community participation in decision-making or resource management, as introduced by conservation agencies, has influenced herders to revitalise this collective identity in order to claim ownership over environmental resources. This demonstrates that herders have started to see their environment as a commodity and have in turn commodified pasture, wildlife and other natural resources. At the same time, however, herders have reshaped their former *nutag* identity toward individualistic and neoliberal subjectivity, and it is used as a shield to defend them from environmental accusations. Moreover, *nutag* identity and what goes with it further creates social problems such as social and spatial fragmentation and increasing cost of access to environmental resources for outsiders, as well as inequality among *nutag* people. Other social problems include future conflicts over resources between herders and formal legitimate agencies, since herders' *nutag* identity has more legitimacy power in daily life than those legal legitimate powers. Ultimately, this modern form of *nutag* identity is fuelled by the decentralisation efforts of the government and development agencies. If these institutional and structural changes are not managed well by the multiple actors and stakeholders – including herders, the Mongolian government and international agencies alike – we can expect to see increased local internal and external conflicts, particularly over environmental resources.

References

Addison, J., M. Friedel, C. Brown, J. Davies and S. Waldron. 2012. 'A critical review of degradation assumptions applied to Mongolia's Gobi Desert'. *The Rangeland Journal* **34**: 125. doi:10.1071/RJ11013

Ahearn, A. 2016. 'The role of kinship in negotiating territorial rights: Exploring claims for winter pasture ownership in Mongolia'. *Inner Asia* **18**: 245–64.

Arellano-Yanguas, J. 2011. 'Aggravating the resource curse: Decentralisation, mining and conflict in Peru'. *Journal of Development Studies* **47**: 617–38. doi:10.1080/00220381003706478

Baival, B. 2012. *Community-based Rangeland and Social Ecological Resilience of Rural Mongolian Communities*. Ph.D. thesis, Colorado State University.

Ballard, C. and G. Banks. 2003. 'Resource wars: The anthropology of mining'. *Annual Review of Anthropology* **32**: 287–313. doi:10.1146/annurev.anthro.32.061002.093116

Batkhishig, B., B. Oyuntulkhuur, T. Altanzul and M.E. Fernandez-Gimenez. 2012. 'A case study of community-based rangeland managment in Jinst Soum, Mongolia'. In M.E. Fernandez-Gimenez, X. Wang, B. Batkhishig, J.A. Klein and R.S. Reid (eds), *Restoring Community Connections to the Land*. Wallingford: CAB Inetrnational. pp. 113–136.

Bazargur, D., C. Shiirevadja and B. Chinbat. 1993. *Territorial Organization of Mongolian Pastoral Livestock Husbandry in the Transition to a Market Economy, Research Report to Policy Alternatives for Livestock Development in Mongolia Project*. Institute of Development Studies, University of Sussex.

Bridge, G. 2004. 'Contested terrain: Mining and the environment'. *Annual Review of Environment and Resources* **29**: 205–59. doi:10.1146/annurev.energy.28.011503.163434

Brown, N. 2010. *Final Report: Change the Mentality not the Culture*. FAO OSRO/MON/001AUS, OSRO/MON/002/CHA. TCP/MON3301. Ulaanbaatar.

Bunzl, M. 2004. 'Boas, Foucault, and the 'native anthropologist': Notes toward a neo-Boasian anthropology'. *American Anthropologist* **106**: 435–42. doi:10.1525/aa.2004.106.3.435

Castells, M. 2009. *The Power of Identity*. Oxford: Wiley-Blackwell. doi:10.1002/9781444318234

Chimedsengee, U., A. Cripps, V. Finlay, G. Verboom, V.M. Batchuluun and V.D.L.B. Khunkhur. 2009. *Mongolian Buddhists Protecting Nature*. Bath: Alliance of Religions and Conservation.

Chuluun, S. and G. Byambaragchaa. 2014. 'Satellite nomads: Pastoralists' tactics in the mining region of Mongolia'. *Inner Asia* **16**: 409–26. doi:10.1163/22105018-12340026

Chuluundorj, K. 2012. 'Mongolia's economic and social development and future trends'. In B.M. Knauft, R. Taupier and L. Purevjav (eds), *Mongolians after Socialism: Politics, Economy, Religion*. Ulaanbaatar: Admon Press. pp. 43–52.

Colding, J. and C. Folke. 2001. 'Social taboos: "invisible" systems of local resource management and biological conservation'. *Ecological Applications* **11**: 584–600. doi:10.1890/1051-0761(2001)011[0584:stisol]2.0.co;2

Dorligsuren, D., B. Batbuyan, B. Densambu and S.R. Fassnacht. 2012. 'Lessons from a territory-based community development approach in Mongolia: Ikhtamir pasture user groups'. In M.E. Fernandez-Gimenez, X. Wang, B. Batkhishig, J.A. Klein and R.S. Reid (eds), *Restoring Community Connections to the Land*. Wallingford: CAB International. pp. 166–89.

Ericksen, A. 2014. 'Depend on each other and don't just sit: The socialist legacy, responsibility, and winter risk among Mongolian herders'. *Human Organization* **73**: 38–49.

Fernandez-Gimenez, M.E. 1999. 'Sustaining the steppes: a geographic history of pastoral land use in Mongolia'. *The Geographical Review* **89**: 315–42.

Fernandez-Gimenez, M.E. 2002. 'Spatial and social boundaries and the paradox of pastoral land tenure: A case study from postsocialist Mongolia'. *Human Ecology* **30**: 49–78.

Fortmann, L. 1995. 'Talking claims: Discursive strategies in contesting property'. *World Development* **23**: 1053–63.

Gongor, D. 1978. *Khalkha Tovchoon: Socio-economic Structure of Khalkha Mongolians (XI-XVII Centuries), vol II*. (1st ed.). Ulaanbaatar: Institute of History, Academy of Science, People's Republic of Mongolia.

Harvey, D. 2005. *A Brief History of Neoliberalism*. New York: Oxford University Press.

Humphrey, C., M. Mongush and B. Telengid. 1993. 'Attitudes to nature in Mongolia and Tuva: a reliminary report'. *Nomadic Peoples* **33**: 51–61.

Humphrey, C. and D. Sneath (eds). 1996. *Culture and Environment in Inner Asia: Volume 1. The Pastoral Economy and the Environment*. Cambridge: The White Horse Press.

Humphrey, C. and D. Sneath. 1999. *The End of Nomadism?: Society, State and the Environment in Inner Asia (Central Asia S.)*. Durham: Duke University Press.

Humphrey, C. and H. Ujeed. 2012. 'Fortune in the wind: An impersonal subjectivity'. *Social Analysis* **56**: 152–67. doi:10.3167/sa.2012.560211

Ichinkhorloo, B. and E.T. Yeh. 2016. 'Ephemeral "communities": Spatiality and politics in rangeland intervention in Mongolia'. *Journal of Peasant Studies* **43**: 1010–34.

Janzen, J. 2011. 'Mongolian pastoral economy and its integration into the world market under socialist and post-socialist conditions'. In J. Gertel and R. Le Heron (eds), *Economic Spaces of Pastoral Production and Commodity Systems*. Farnham and Burlington: Ashgate Publishing Limited. pp. 195–210.

Jenkins, R. 2008. *Social Identity*. New York: Routledge.

Laurie, A., J. Jamsranjav,O. van den Heuvel and N. Erdenesaikhan. 2010. 'Biodiversity conservation and the ecological limits to development options in the Mongolian Altai: formulation of a strategy and discussion of priorities'. *Central Asian Survey* 29: 321–43. doi:10.1080/02634937.2010.528188

Leach, M., R. Mearns and I. Scoones. 1999. 'Environmental entitlements : Dynamics and institutions in community-based natural resource management'. *World Development* 27: 225–47.

Marin, A. 2008. 'Between cash cows and golden calves: Adaptations of Mongolian pastoralism in the "Age of the Market."' *Nomadic Peoples* 12: 75–101. doi:10.3167/np.2008.120206

Maureen, F. 2000. 'Torres Strait and Dawdhay: Dimensions of self and otherness on Yam Island I Mauree n Fuary'. *Oceania* 70: 219–30.

McCarthy, J. 2002. 'First world political ecology: Lessons from the Wise Use movement'. *Environment and Planning A* 34: 1281–1302. doi:10.1068/a3526

Mearns, R. 1993. 'Territoriality and land tenure among Mongolian pastoralists: variation, continuty and change'. *Nomadic Peoples* 33: 73–103.

Mearns, R. 1996. 'Community , collective action and common grazing: The case of post-socialist Mongolia'. *The Journal of Development Studies* 32: 297–337.

MEGDT, Ministry of Environment, Green Development and Tourism. 2015. *Report on the State of the Environment of Mongolia 2013–2014 submitted to State Great Khural*. http://www.parliament.mn/monitoring/info/categories/131/pages/19829

MFA, (Ministry of Food and Agriculture), SDC, (Swiss Agency for Development and Cooperation), ALAGC, (Administration of Land Affairs Geodesy and Cartography), GG, (Green Gold Project) and IRIMH, (Information and Research Institute of Metreology and Hydrology). 2015. *National Report on the Rangeland Health of Mongolia*. Ulaanbaatar.

MNEM. 1997. *National Plan of Action to Combat Desertification in Mongolia*. Retrieved from http://www.unccd.int/ActionProgrammes/mongolia-eng2000.pdf. Accessed 31 January 2017

MNEM, (Ministry of Nature and Environment of Mongolia). 1998. *International Conventions (Olon ulsiin konventsi)*. Ulaanbaatar.

MNET (Ministry of Nature, Environment and Tourism). 2008. *Report on the State of the Environment of Mongolia 2006–2007 by Ministry of Nature, Environment and Tourism*. Ulaanbaatar

Murphy, D. J. 2011. *Going on Otor: Disaster, Mobility, and the Political Ecology of Vulnerability in Uguumur, Mongolia*. Ph.D. Dissertation, University of Kentucky.

NSO (National Statistical Office of Mongolia). 2011. *Urkhiin Niigem Ediin Zasgiin Sudalgaa (Household Socio-Economic Survey)*. http://www.1212.mn/files/HSES_2010_mn.pdf

NSO (National Statistical Office of Mongolia). 2012. *Urkhiin Niigem Ediin Zasgiin Sudalgaa (Household Socio-Economic Survey)*. http://www.1212.mn/files/HSES_2011_mn.pdf

NSO (National Statistical Office of Mongolia). 2014a. *Mal toollogiin dun (Livestoc Census 1990–2014)*. http://www.1212.mn (under folder 'census')

NSO (National Statistical Office of Mongolia). (2014b). *Mongolian Statistical Yearbook (1989–2014)*. http://www.1212.mn (under folder 'yearbook')

NSO (National Statistical Office of Mongolia). 2015. Statistikiin Medeelliin Negdsen San (Statistics Database). Retrieved from http://www.1212.mn. Accessed 6 October 2015.

NSO (National Statistical Office of Mongolia) and World Bank. 2009. *Urkhiin Niigem Ediin Zasgiin Sudalgaanii 2007–2008 onii ur dun (Household Socio-Economic Survey)*. http://www.1212.mn/files/HSES_2007–2008_mn.pdf

NSO (National Statistical Office of Mongolia), World Bank and UNDP. 2004. *Household Income Expenditure and Livelihoods Standards Survey*. Ulaanbaatar

NUM (Department of Anthropology and Archaeology National University of Mongolia). 2015. *Collective Action in the Pastoral Economy of Mongolia: Cooperation, Herd and Pasture Management, Economic Decisions, and Livestock Health*. http://www.slideshare.net/GreengoldMongolia/report-on-collective-action-in-the-pastoral-economy-of-mongolia

Rasmussen, S. 2011. 'Encountering being, identity, and otherness: Reconsidering Guimaraes's "Amerindian anthropology and cultural psychology" and Amerindian perspectivism, with insights from anthropology of religion, African humanities, and collaborative ethnography'. *Culture and Psychology* 17: 159–76. doi:10.1177/1354067X11400953

Rocheleau, D. and L. Ross. 1995. 'Trees as tools, trees as text: struggles over resources in Zambrana-Chacuey, Dominican Republic'. *Antipode* 27: 407–28.

Scharf, K.M., M.E. Fernandez-Gimenez, B. Batbuyan and S. Enkhbold. 2010. 'Herders and hunters in a transitional economy: The challenge of wildlife and rangeland management in post-socialist Mongolia'. In I.T. Du Toit, R. Kock and C. Deutsch (eds), *Wild Rangelands Conserving Wildlife While Maintaining Livestock in Semi-Arid Ecosystems*. West Sussex, UK: Blackwell Publishing. p. 400

Schmidt, S.M. 2006. 'Pastoral community organization, livelihoods and biodiversity conservation in Mongolia's southern Gobi region'. *USDA Forest Service Proceedings RMRS-P*, **39**: 18–29. Retrieved from http://nzni.org/wp-content/uploads/2011/06/SCHMIDT-Pastoral-Community-Organization.pdf Accessed 31 January 2017.

Sen, A. 1981. *Poverty and Famines: An Essay on Entitlement and Deprivation*. Oxford: Clarendon Press.

Sikor, T. and C. Lund. 2009. 'Access and property: A question of power and authority'. *Development and Change* **40**: 1–22. doi:10.1111/j.1467–7660.2009.01503.x

Sneath, D. 1993. 'Social relations, networks and social organziation in post-socialist rural Mongolia'. *Nomadic Peoples* (old series) **33**: 193–207.

Sneath, D. 2001. 'Notions of rights over land and the history of Mongolian pastoralism'. *Inner Asia* **3**: 41–58.

Sneath, D. 2003. 'Land use, the environment and development in post-socialist Mongolia'. *Oxford Development Studies* **31**: 441–59. doi:10.1080/1360081032000146627

Sneath, D. 2004. 'Property regimes and sociotechnical systems: Rights over land in Mongolia's "Age of the Market".' In K. Verdery and C. Humphrey (eds), *Property in Question: Value Transformation in the Global Economy*. Oxford: Berg. p. 324.

Sneath, D. 2010. 'Political mobilization and the construction of collective identity in Mongolia'. *Central Asian Survey* 29: 251–67. doi:10.1080/02634937.2010.518009

Sneath, D. 2014. 'Nationalising civilisational resources: sacred mountains and cosmopolitical ritual in Mongolia'. *Asian Ethnicity* 15: 458–72. doi:10.1080/14631369.2014.939330

Suchman, M.C. 1995. 'Managing Legitimacy: strategic and institutional approaches'. *Academy of Management Review* 20: 571–610.

Upton, C. 2010. 'Living off the land: Nature and nomadism in Mongolia'. *Geoforum* 41: 865–74. doi:10.1016/j.geoforum.2010.05.006

Upton, C. 2012. 'Managing Mongolia's commons: Land reforms, social contexts, and institutional change'. *Society and Natural Resources* 25: 156–75. doi:10.1080/08941920.2011.597494

Usukh, B., H.P. Binswanger-Mkhize, R. Himmelsbach and K. Schuler. 2010. *Fostering the Sustainable Livelihoods of Herders in Mongolia via Collective Action*. Ulaanbaatar: Selengepress Co. Ltd.

Viguier, L., B. Ichinkhorloo and T. Tsend-Ayush. 2010. *Dzud National Report 2009–2010: Report of the Study, Project 00074253*. UNDP/NEMA.

Wingard, J.R. and P. Zahler. 2006. *Silent Steppe: The Illegal Wildlife Trade Crisis in Mongolia*. Washington D.C.: Mongolia Discussion Papers, East Asia and Pacific Environment and Social Development Department, World Bank.

Chapter 4

FROM REFORM TO REVOLT: BASHAR AL-ASSAD AND THE ARAB TRIBES IN SYRIA

Haian Dukhan

Introduction

The death of Hafez al-Assad and the succession of his son, Bashar, brought an end to the system of government that Hafez had built up over decades. Hafez al-Assad built an authoritarian state based on patronage networks that connected his regime to the society. These networks allowed the state to become the major source of employment for the tribes and to clientise their Sheikhs through distributive social policies, thus securing the regime's survival. In contrast to his father's rule, under Bashar these patronage relationships have been affected by the policies of privatisation and liberalisation. Privatisation and liberalisation of the economy have created new economic and social players that have transformed the nature of the authoritarian regime from a populist one into a regime that is connected mainly with the bourgeoisie and the upper class, neglecting the rural tribal constituency that was a vital part of Hafez al-Assad's authoritarian state. Drawing on different data gathered through interviews as well as written literature, this chapter will explore the policies that Bashar al-Assad carried out towards the Arab tribes in the period from 2000 until 2010. The chapter starts by outlining how Bashar al-Assad narrowed the coalition supporting his rule to depend mainly on his family and the urban entrepreneurial class, excluding the lower and middle strata in the periphery. It will then trace the disintegration of the social contract between the regime and the Arab tribes as a result of the regime's failure to deliver adequate development services in their regions. Losing the support of the tribes undermined the stability of the regime, resulting in different clashes between the tribes themselves, the tribes and the Kurds, and

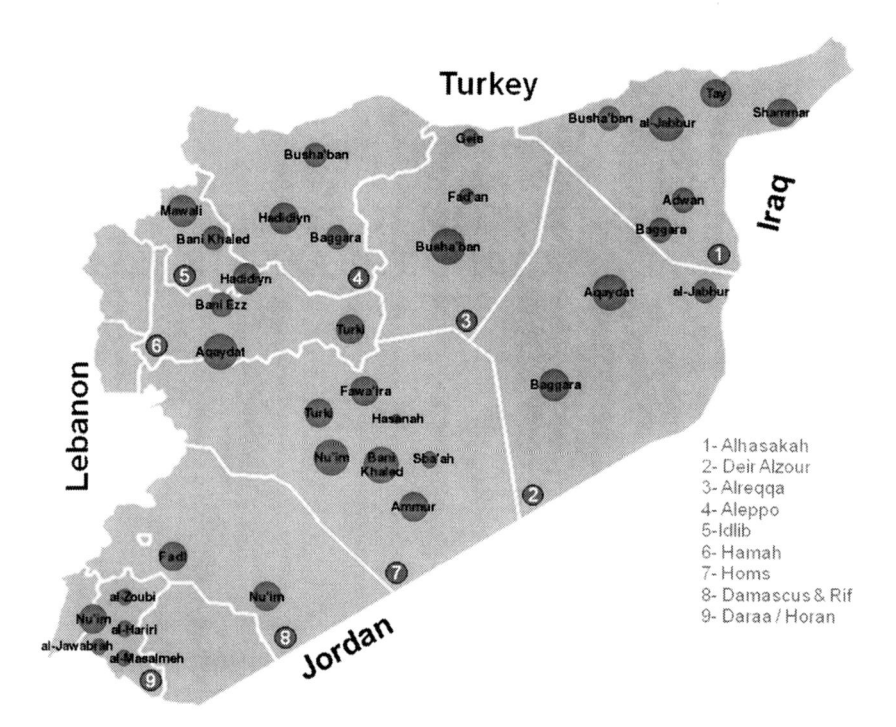

Figure 1. Tribes' Presence in Syria.

the tribes and the Druze, which will be investigated in detail in this chapter. This chapter will argue that Bashar al-Assad's policies towards the Arab tribes chipped away the regime's ideological pillars and threatened the longer-term cohesion of its social base, which paved the way for the uprising to start in the tribal regions.

Methodology

Research and fieldwork for this chapter represent part of the author's Ph.D. research on the relationship between the state and the Arab tribes in Syria from the late Ottoman Empire until the present time. The review of some of the literature (academic literature and reports by government, donors and international organisations) and historical information, as well as contact with the community concerned in this research, started during a work experience placement. This experience combined working with international organisations such as the International Union for the Conservation of Nature (IUCN), Food and Agriculture Organization of the United Nations (FAO), government bodies such as the Ministry of Agriculture and the General Commission for Badia Management and Development.[1]

Because I lived in the Syrian Badia and worked on issues related to the tribes, I am looking at the topic from a different perspective to someone who only knows about the situation from the literature. I am actually privileged to have had close and lengthy contact with the community and therefore could provide an alternative view to those of scholars who may have fallen into an unintentional or unconscious 'othering' of or orientalist outlook on the Bedouins and their way of life. I could present a more representative account of the tribes given my facility of communication and understanding of their customs, which is important in qualitative research and is not within the reach of non-Bedouin or western scholars. However, subjectivity can be dangerous because emotional, cognitive and physical experiences seem to contradict so much of the rational-actor worldview on which social science is premised (Ellis and Flaherty 1992). While being conscious of the influence of the author's subjectivity on data collection and data analysis processes, I also had to function as a researcher conducting research using objective methods and procedures (Rajendran 2001).

In general, my methodology involved the creation of and a review of a database derived from the literature written on the tribes including academic texts, media outlets and material published on the internet. I have also used direct interviews, which occurred during my visit to Turkey in July 2014, and Skype interviews with tribesmen and influential tribal leaders.

Bashar al-Assad: Narrowing the base of alliances

During Hafez al-Assad's time, the state comprised three institutions: the Ba'ath Party, the military apparatus and popular organisations. These pillars played a major role in connecting the top of the regime to its base, but were gradually eroding after 2000. With high population growth, the state institutions were no longer able to provide the same level of jobs as before. By the beginning of the uprising in 2011, the youth unemployment rate was 48 per cent (IFAD 2011). Bashar al-Assad considered the party apparatus and the worker

---

1. The Syrian Badia is an area of semi-arid steppe covering 10 million hectares of the central and north-eastern part of the country.

and peasant unions to be obstacles to economic reform and thus he ceased to fund them, which disabled their powers of patronage (Hinnebusch 2012, 99). Under Hafez, the Ba'ath Party and the popular organisations had become a vast patronage network (Hinnebusch 1989, 26). Many people joined the party as a strategy for protecting and 'diversifying the interests' of their tribe (Hinnebusch 1990, 188). Bashar al-Assad was not well aware of the role that these organisations played in connecting the top of the regime to its rural base so he considered them useless and decided to cut their funding, not realising that by doing this, he was changing the patron–client relationship that had preserved the regime for decades.

Under Hafez, the government also made credit available to the tribes wishing to invest in their herds. Emergency fodder stocks were created and fodder exports were stopped in order to have enough during droughts. Artesian wells were dug and enclosures were constructed in flood paths to retain rainwater in different parts of the Syrian steppe to provide water for herds. Hospitals, schools and veterinary units were established in most of the tribal regions. After witnessing a drastic decline in the economic support previously received from the government under Hafez, the tribes started to become a less stable base for the regime. This can be seen in different clashes between the tribes and the Kurds, the tribes and the Druze and the tribes amongst themselves from 2003 until 2010, which indicate that the regime started to lose hold of its major constituency as a result of the retreat of its economic benefits. In contrast to the previous era, during which the countryside benefited from Hafez al-Assad's policies, only certain cities, such as Damascus, Aleppo, Tartus and Latakia, were reaping the benefits of the economic opening-up, and poverty ratios were significantly higher in tribal areas (Khatib 2011, 206).

When many tribesmen were asked why they opposed Bashar al-Assad's regime, their answer was that they no longer benefited from the oil and gas fields that existed in their lands. 'Where are the Syrian oil revenues?' (Macleod 2011). Deir Ezzor has huge oil and gas resources which were estimated by the International Monetary Fund in March 2010 to earn the state about $3 billion per year – money, the tribes say, they see precious little of (ibid.). 'We see foreign and national companies working in the oil fields but our sons have no jobs in these oil companies', Abu Khalaf, of the Aaqidat tribe said; 'We get the bad smoke, the pollution and diseases, but no money'. Nizzar al-Assad, a Syrian businessman from the coast, came to Deir Ezzor and established a huge oil company that collaborated with Petro Canada to invest in oil and gas fields located mainly in the eastern part of the country that is inhabited by the tribes.

From Reform to Revolt

Ninety per cent of those who were employed by Nizzar's company were people from the Syrian coast, i.e. Alawites, said Nawaf al-Bashir, Sheikh of Baggara.[2] 'Very few of our tribesmen were given basic jobs in this company like dustmen, truck drivers or cleaners.' 'We were deprived of the oil wealth although the Syrian constitution states that when a natural resource is discovered somewhere, people who live close to it, have the priority to get the jobs and the benefits', he added. In another interview, Mohammad Assaf from the Tay tribe stated: 'It was not only the oil jobs that we were deprived of. Even teaching vacancies with the Ministry of Education in al-Hassakeh were taken by the Alawites, who came all the way from Latakia and Tartous to teach our children. We had many unemployed people who had university degrees; sitting at home and doing nothing while people who had high school certificates were given the priority to teach in our schools.'[3] This change prompted Leverett (2005, 36) to note that 'the balance of urban versus rural Sunnis has shifted in favour of the former', changing the nature of the relationship that existed between the regime and its people.

The regime of Bashar al-Assad embarked on a set of liberalisation policies that have mainly benefited the upper middle class, the Syrian bourgeoisie and certain tribal leaders. In the tribal regions, 'the dismantling of state farms and the renting out of undeveloped land confiscated during the land reforms put an end to 43 years of collectivist experiments in the field of land reform, including 38 years under the rule of the Ba'ath party' (Ababsa 2013, 34). The majority of those who benefited from these reforms were tribal leaders who were linked to the regime leadership. For example, in the Amur tribe Mohammad Said Bukhaytan's family members[4] were allowed to rent and herd their cattle over a large area of state-owned land near Palmyra, while other members of the same tribe were banned from doing so. Despite continuous complaints from other tribesmen to the peasant union and Ba'ath Party branch about these concessions granted to Bukhaytan's family, noone seemed to pay attention. The economic liberalisation meant that the regime started to restructure its social base away from the lower-middle classes (Hinnebusch and Zintl 2015, 286) of which tribes constitute a large part. The regime started to move from a populist

---

2. Skype interview with Sheik Nawaf Bashir of the Baggara tribe.
3. Skype interview with Mohammad Assaf, a teacher from the Tay tribe.
4. Mohammed Bukhaytan built his career in the security service, eventually attaining the rank of Assistant Secretary of the Syrian Regional Command of the Ba'ath Party, the second highest position in the political party after the Syrian president. He then tended to adopt policies that supported his tribe, particularly his family living in Palmyra.

authoritarian phase to a phase in which public sector assets are appropriated to the president's clan and those who support them (ibid.).

During Bashar's decade of power, a private business class started to become prominent. A major part of this Syrian business community 'grew under government patronage and care' (Seifan, 2010, 9). Another part was established by the children of government officials (ibid.) and tribal leaders who enjoyed special privileges and influence. For example, the sons of Sheikh Mohammad Nazzal el-Sheikh of Fwaira in Homs were granted big trading concessions in Homs.[5] The growth of this group of *'awlad al-sulta'* (children of authority) in the tribal community alienated them from the rest of the tribe and created vivid class divisions within the tribe itself. The children of the tribal leaders were able to own luxurious palaces by the Syrian coast while their fellow tribesmen were living in shanty slums in the suburbs of the cities.

The regime gave a free hand to the Assad-Makhlouf family clan (Hafez al-Assad's own family and his in-laws), which led to the over-concentration of opportunities and patronage in the hands of the regime elite at the expense of the traditional regime clients in the rural areas (Heydemann 2007). For example, this family was given the exclusive concession for mobile phones in Syria in 2001 and continued to hold it until the upsurge of the Syrian uprising. On the other hand, as part of Bashar's campaign to fight against corruption, a few Sunni figures were ousted from the regime's close circle after 2000. The campaign reached its highest point when the Syrian media started accusing the previous Prime Minister Mahmoud al-Zoubi, who belongs to the al-Zoubi clan in Dar'a, of corruption (Gambill 2000). The Syrian media announced that al-Zoubi's assets were confiscated and that he was no longer part of the Ba'ath Party regional command (Ghadbian 2001). Earlier, in 1998, a highly-placed Sunni officer, Hikmat Shihabi, had been accused of embezzlement and corruption and been dismissed from his position as a result (Moubayed 2001). This was seen as a response by Hafez al-Assad to Shihabi's opposition to the prospect of Bashar succeeding his father.

The second tier of the regime after the Alawites continued to be people from the rural areas of Houran and Deir Ezzor. Although prominent figures from the tribes continued to rise in the state apparatus, such as Bukhaytan, mentioned above, from the Amur tribe and Ryad Hijab from the Sukhni tribe, who became Prime Minister, these figures were notorious for their corruption and their interest in their closely-knit families rather than their whole tribe. Moreover, these people belonged to very small tribes that did not have

---

5. Interview with Sheikh Mohammad Mzeid.

From Reform to Revolt

demographic or political weight on the ground. Bashar al-Assad's dependence on small tribes to support his rule is noteworthy. Both the Amur and Sukhni tribes mentioned above are looked down upon by other tribes like the Baggara and Aaqidat. By contrast, Hafez al-Assad relied on these and other larger tribes to support his regime.

By 2005, Syrian opposition figures, including some religious and tribal leaders like Sheikh Nawaf al-Bashir of the Baggara tribe and Mohammad Mzeid Terkawi of Aneza, signed the Damascus Declaration which was a statement that called for 'peaceful, gradual', reform 'founded on accord, and based on dialogue and recognition of the other' (Wright 2008, 232). Sheikh Nawaf said that the National Council of the Damascus Declaration was very active in the tribal regions and many youth from different tribes joined the council and supported its calls for reform in the country.[6] The regime responded with repression, arresting 22 members of the National Council of Damascus Declaration (Syrian Human Rights Committee 2007). Sheikh Nawaf and Sheikh Mohammad were interrogated for many hours for signing the declaration, according to interviews with both of them.

All these developments showed the regime narrowing its coalition from party, state institutions and major Sunni figures to revolve around the Alawites and in particular the Assad clan, which was considered by many as a dangerous move (Wieland 2013, 12). Members of the regime were no longer the sons of the rural middle class that Battatu (1999) has neatly described (Perthes 2004, 109). Rather, the new rulers came mainly from the Alawite sect and urban middle classes located on the Syrian coast and the two main cities (Damascus and Aleppo) (ibid.).

Development and 'modernisation' policies in the tribal regions

After coming to power in 2000, Bashar's first speech stressed the 'need for a strategy of development that is comprehensive and has clear steps and measures to achieve it' (Seifan 2010, 7). Although Bashar al-Assad tried to follow in his father's steps by investing in development projects in the rural areas, he failed to create a broad co-optation of the tribes like his father. This section will argue that the Syrian government's efforts during Bashar's rule concentrated on the development of 'useful Syria', which comprises Damascus, Aleppo and the coast. As a result, the tribal regions were neglected, weakening patronage links between the regime and its people. In combination with the govern-

---

6. Interview with Sheikh Nawaf Bashir.

ment and non-governmental bodies' neglect, the situation was worsened by a prolonged drought in the tribal areas. The ecological and economic situation contributed to a sharp increase in internal migration, especially to Damascus, Homs and Aleppo, and external migration alike (Danish Immigration Service 2010, 13). This migration was described as 'the largest internal displacement in the Middle East in recent years' with 65,000 families being displaced to the cities of Damascus, Homs and Aleppo (Ababsa 2015, 209). This has led to the transfer of complete tribes from the countryside to city suburbs, creating belts of poverty surrounding the cities.

The problem of poverty was acute in the tribal regions of the country, particularly in the northeast, which led to the loss of livelihood for thousands (Abboud 2015, 51). Poverty was generally more prevalent in the rural than in urban areas of Syria (62 per cent in rural areas) with the North-Eastern region (Raqqa, Deir Ezzor and Hassakeh) having the greatest incidence and severity of poverty (UNDP 2005, 33). Official data published in 2005 indicated that unemployment reached twenty per cent in the whole country, with a particular rise in the Jazirah region to the east and in the southern region where it reached 51 per cent (Zisser 2006, pp. 117). Stephen Starr (2012, 124) describes the situation in the Syrian Badiya during his visit to Palmyra in 2009, where he noticed visibly malnourished children sitting in rags on street pavements and jobless young men driving motorbikes around the town for hours without any prospect of education, healthcare or any other positive element. To tackle all these issues, Bashar al-Assad issued a presidential decree in 2006 to establish the General Commission for Badia Management and Development. Having its headquarters in Palmyra, the commission's mission was to develop the Badia by improving human and natural resources and developing infrastructure in the tribal regions for economic and social development programmes that include increasing fodder production, establishing pastoral and environmental reserves, digging wells and stabilising sand dunes (Louhaichi and Tastad 2010, 5).

The commission failed to tackle poverty and unemployment issues in the tribal regions for many reasons. First, the majority of its directors were from Damascus, Homs and Aleppo and had no knowledge or experience of how to deal with the local problems. They were employed to lead the commission in Palmyra without giving people from the tribes themselves the opportunity to deal with their issues. Second, the commission was riddled with corruption, spending most of its resources on staff rather than on serious daily challenges like drought or poverty. Third, the commission focused to a large extent on wildlife and environment conservation, ignoring the tribes' main problems. For

From Reform to Revolt

example, Dukhan (2014, 71) describes how the commission set up a protected area around Palmyra in 2009 in a joint project with the International Union for Conservation of Nature to protect endangered species of birds which stay in the project area for six months of the year only. By excluding them from the protected area and thus limiting their grazing area, this project led to the impoverishment of the Amur tribe (Dukhan 2014). Conservation efforts and funds were directed to protect six bird species, ignoring the needs of the tribe that has inhabited the project area for centuries. Fourth, the commission had connections to certain tribal leaders who benefited as a result. All the relatives of Nawaf al-Fares, one of the Aaqidat tribal sheikhs and the Syrian ambassador to Iraq, were given the right to access the grazing reserves in Deir Ezzor because of his connections to the regime. All other people from the same tribe of Aaqidat, the second largest in Deir Ezzor, were not allowed to access the same areas.[7] Fifth, the commission was unable to solve many critical issues that emerged in the tribal regions. For example, in 2007,[8] Mawali tribesmen attacked the headquarters of Petro Canada Company that had gas concessions in the tribe's traditional grazing land. The commission was asked to mediate between the company and the tribe and find a satisfactory solution for both sides. Its only attempt to solve the problem was to arrange a meeting with the Sheikh of Mawali tribe and threaten him with asking the Syrian army to interfere militarily against his tribe. Instead of finding a solution based on giving some job opportunities for tribesmen on their traditional grazing land, the commission was playing the role of security apparatus and not a development agency.

When it comes to the non-governmental bodies' development efforts, the First Lady Asmaa al-Assad set up 'the Syria Trust for Development' which aimed to emerge as the pioneer of the development sector in Syria by trying to control and manipulate the sector to be compatible with Bashar's overall approach to social reform (Ruiz de Elvira 2012, 22). In this category, the Fund for Rural Development of Syria (FIRDOS) focuses on conducting development initiatives in the rural areas of the country. FIRDOS is active in six governorates (Aleppo, Idlib, Latakia, Homs, Hama, Quneitra) (Donati 2014, 45) none of which are in the Eastern part of the country which was badly stricken by poverty and unemployment. According to Mohammad Assaf of Tay Tribe in Hassaka, the First Lady visited many rural areas of Syria where FIRDOS had development projects but she never paid a visit to the drought-stricken Eastern part of the

---

7. Interview with Sheikh Nawaf al-Bashir of the Baggara tribe.
8. From my personal experience of working with the General Commission for Badia Development

country. In fact, the only project that FIRDOS was involved in when it comes to tribes' development, was the Bald Ibis protected area described above, which aimed *hypothetically* at developing the living conditions of the Amur tribe in the protected area. Asmaa al-Assad did visit the protected area to observe the endangered species of birds and appear in the international media as a protector of nature, but she never met with anyone from the Amur tribe who were suffering from the drought, and were gradually evicted from their traditional grazing land to set up the protected area.[9]

The drought that hit the entire Middle East in 2008 was terrible for Syria, forcing the country to seek international aid and food supplies for one million tribesmen living in the north-eastern governorates of Al-Raqqa, Hassaka, and Deir Ezzor, the poorest region in Syria (OCHA 2010). Although the drought was a natural phenomenon that was outside the regime's control, many other factors contributed to this situation or aggravated it. First, the overuse of underground water resources by allowing people to dig wells irresponsibly led to the depletion of rivers like Balikh and Khabour (Ababsa 2015, 205). Second, despite the fact that the Tigris River crosses Syria, the government did not invest any money in bringing the water to al-Hassaka governorate. Only on 7 March, one week before the uprising, did Bashar al-Assad lay the first stone of a $2.1 billion irrigation project on the Tigris River (Ibrahim and Razzouk 2011). Third, overgrazing as a result of the increase in herd numbers caused rapid desertification. These herds were not mainly owned by the tribes. After 2000, many businessmen from the cities established commercial livestock enterprises by renting pastures in the tribal regions and organising the delivery of stock, meat and dairy products to the markets, damaging the local range resource (Dukhan 2014, 72). Fourth, the removal of subsidies on agricultural inputs like fuel and fodder and fertilisers (Hinnebusch 2012, 102) left the tribes hit by the drought without any hope of surviving in the regions.

Between 2006 and 2009, around 1.3 million tribesmen were affected by this situation and an estimated 800,000 people lost their livelihoods and basic food supports (Solh 2010). During this period, yields of wheat and barley dropped 47 per cent and 67 per cent, respectively, and livestock populations plummeted (ACSAD 2011). In 2009, 42 per cent of tribespeople were suffering from anaemia due to a shortage of dairy products, vegetables and fruits (Ababsa 2014, 207). Hundreds of villages were abandoned in the eastern part of the country because people could no longer afford to pay for water to be

---

9. From my personal experience of working with the General Commission for Badia Development

From Reform to Revolt

brought to their villages after the sharp increase in fuel prices.[10] This disaster accelerated the migration of whole tribes from the countryside to the suburbs of major cities in Damascus, Aleppo, Homs and Palmyra, leading to the creation of impoverished tribal belts in the suburbs of the cities. As Kilcullen and Rosenblatt (2014, 36) explain, the tribe 'had come to the city, planting itself outside and growing in. Tribesmen brought their customs to the city. They turned their slums into compact versions of their mud houses and tents. It was not poverty, but tradition, that had put a whole family in one room.' Thus, 'tribe' not only describes people who live in their tribal land but those poor migrants living in the slums surrounding Syria's cities.

Three examples of these tribal belts around Damascus, Homs and Palmyra will be described briefly. The first example is Hajr Aswad Suburb in Damascus, situated about six kilometres from the capital. After the arrival of the drought, Hajr Aswad became a hub for migrants from Hassakeh, particularly the Jabbour and Tay tribes. The influx was huge and upon their arrival, tribesmen looked for houses to rent. One of the most challenging issues was the chronic housing shortage, which has led to a dramatic rise in housing prices and increase in the construction of informal housing units. According to Mekhlef Said, a Tay tribesman who moved to live there, people looked down upon them. 'They called us gypsies when we belong to the noblest tribes. It was such a catastrophe for us.'[11] Under such conditions, school dropout rates were high and enrolment significantly declined (UN 2010). Crime rates were on the rise in Hajr Aswad because of poverty (Irinnews 2009). The new residents of this impoverished district were unable to find permanent employment and so were excluded from health and welfare systems (Zisser 2006, 116). A sense of solidarity continued to exist between the tribesmen who moved to Hajr Aswad. People who managed to get a job were helping their families and those who were closely knit to them.

The second example is Baba Amr suburb in Homs. It is one of the poorest suburbs in Homs. After the wave of drought, the suburb attracted a large number of migrants from Fwaira and Nu'im tribes. Many young tribesmen were commuting daily to Lebanon to work in the construction sector. Feelings of sectarianism were on the rise among those tribes who saw the Alawites in the city living in better conditions and having better jobs.[12]

The third example is Brykat suburb in Palmyra where Amur and Bani Khaled tribespeople were forced to settle, under the pretext of projects to combat

---

10. Interview with Sheikh Ahmad Melhem of the Jabbour tribe.
11. Interview with Mekhlef Said, a Tay tribesman.
12. Interview with Sheikh Muhammad Mzeid Terkawi.

desertification. The tribes live in Brykat in conditions of extreme poverty, surviving on the products of a few sheep, goats and chickens (Dukhan 2014, 71). Their houses were built randomly without construction licenses and there are no organised streets or proper services of sanitation, water or electricity (ibid.). Family sizes are large and the birth rate is very high. The dense population in such a small area has negative consequences for public hygiene, especially where living spaces are shared with livestock (ibid.). In all these cases, Bashar al-Assad's regime appears to have produced impoverishment for the tribes, who were left to face their deteriorating natural environment without any real support from the government.

Under Bashar al-Assad's rule, the policies of economic liberalisation affected the agriculture sector too. The new policies included the privatisation of all Syrian state lands according to Decision 83 on 16 December 2000 (Ababsa 2014, 213). This led to the 'renewal of large latifundia, which exceed all property ceilings fixed by the successive land reform laws' (Ababsa 2011, 106). This was in clear contradiction to the Ba'ath Party ideology that aimed to limit private ownership of land. Eighty per cent of those who received land from the government did not use their land but sold it, and the main purchasers were sheikhs of the Hleissat tribe who used the land for their big business of sheep herding (Ababsa 2004, 19). Some of the Hleissat Sheikhs confirmed this to Ababsa by saying: 'the Hleissat are the ones who buy this land because it is our land! We, the former owner, received only 30 hectares out of thousands of hectares we had long time ago. We do everything to get back our land confiscated by the Nasserites and the Ba'athists. Why did not the government simply give us our land back?' (ibid.). This was indeed a counterrevolution (Bush 2002, 23). In other governorates of Syria, like al-Hassakeh, the Ministry of Agriculture and Agrarian Reform started to redistribute the land according to the abovementioned Decision 83. The distribution favoured Arab tribesmen over Kurdish farmers (Ababsa 2013, 55). Two tribal leaders and their families in particular benefited from the redistribution. These were Sheikh Mohammed al-Melhem of Jabbour and Sheikh Mohammad al-Fares of Tay.[13] The land blocks received by both sheikhs seem to have come as a reward for their role in crushing the Kurdish uprising in 2004.

This section shows that not only did the Syrian government during Bashar's reign fail in providing support to the tribes afflicted by the drought, but it also led to the rise of an upper class within the tribal community that

---

13. Interview with Mohammad Assaf of the Tay tribe.

From Reform to Revolt

benefited from the regime's selective reforms, while leaving the rest of the tribesmen facing their impoverished daily life.

Tribal clashes: The regime is losing its grip?

Although Hafez al-Assad's time in power included a major conflict with the Muslim Brotherhood spanning several years, the tribal regions of Syria were mainly stable, as discussed above. However, the era of Bashar al-Assad witnessed major instability, where clashes between different tribes, other sects and ethnicities erupted in different parts of the country, indicating that the regime had lost its leverage over the social dynamics within Syria. This section will briefly describe the major clashes that became a distinguishing feature of this period and will analyse the common themes underlying them.

The first important clash took place between a tribe of Jawabrah and the Druze in the southern governorate of Sweida. It was a result of a long-running dispute over grazing and property rights (George 2003, 6). The last straw came in November 2000 when Jawabrah tribesmen herded their cattle on land owned by Druze farmers.[14] This resulted in armed clashes between the tribe and the Druze farmers, leading to the death of a man from the Aawaj family in Sweida. The peasant union in Sweida sent a telegram to the President asking him to put a limit to the tribe's trespass on their lands, but the telegram was ignored. As a result, the people of Sweida turned to street protests asking the regime to end the problem. The regime responded by shooting at the protestors and arresting many of them. The regime was accused of siding with the Jawabrah tribe. The clashes between the tribe and the Druze continued and led to the death of twelve Druze farmers, which pushed the government to interfere militarily and arrest many people from the Jawabrah tribe. However, the government did not find a radical solution to the problem and continued to use violence as the only way to end it (Aljazeera Arabic 2011).

The second important clash took place between the Kurds and the Arab tribes in 2004 in al-Hassakeh governorate. On 12 March 2004, there was a football match between a local team from al-Hassakeh and another from Deir Ezzor in the town of Qamishli (Yildiz 2005, 41). Reports state that the problem was started by the fans of Deir Ezzor team, who are associated with the Arab tribes of Iraq and sympathised with the Iraqi regime (Savelsberg 2014, 91). The Deir Ezzor fans chanted slogans praising Saddam Hussein and insulting

---

14. Interview with Mus'ab Tahan of the Nuim tribe inhabiting the southern part of the country.

the Iraqi Kurdish leaders, Barzani and Talabani, for their role in toppling his regime (Tejel 2011, 115). The Kurdish team responded with chants praising President George Bush (Gambil 2004). Arab tribesmen from Tay and Jabbour in al-Hassakeh stood with their fellow tribesmen from Deir Ezzor and clashed with the Kurds. The Arabs used knives, stones and sticks (Danish Refugee Council 2007, 6). Syrian security forces opened fire on the Kurds and killed six of them (Tejel 2008). This clash was followed by violent protests and riots by the Kurdish population in different parts of al-Hassakeh (Danish Immigration Service 2010, 8). The Syrian army did not have a strong presence in the Eastern part of the country and could not therefore confront the angry Kurds on its own.[15] It sought assistance from the Arab tribes in the governorate (Savelsberg 2014, 92). The Jabbour tribe, which has a strong presence in Hassakeh, was entrusted to take up arms and surround the government buildings to protect them.[16] The Tay tribe, headed by Sheikh Mohammed al-Fares, was entrusted to defend the other major city in the governorate, Qamishli.[17] The Kurdish movement was suppressed with estimates that around forty people were killed plus over a hundred injured and more than 2,000 Kurds jailed (Lowe 2006).

The third clash took place between the tribes of Shammar and Jabbour in al-Hassakeh governorate in August 2005. It started when a Shammar tribesman killed another from the Jabbour tribe because of allegations of sexual molestation of a girl from Shammar (Aawsat 2005). In fact, the clash took place because the Shammar tribe sided with the Kurds during their riots in 2004,[18] The honour crime was just a pretext for a long series of troubles escalating between the two tribes. Seven thousand Jabbour tribesmen attacked Shammar and burnt their houses in al-Hassakeh.[19] This pushed the Syrian security forces to deploy 3,000 members to control the situation, eventually deporting all Shammar tribesmen from al-Hassakeh city and arresting many Jabbour tribesmen.

The fourth clash took place in April 2007 between the clans of Sabkha and Afadleh in the governorate of Raqqa (Donati 2013, 53). It started after objections from the Afadleh clan, whose sheikh Mohammad Faisel al-Hweidi lost his parliamentary seat in that year to Abdul Mohsen al-Rakan Sheikh of Sabkha (Syria News 2007). The Afadleh clan accused Sheikh Abdul Mohsen al-Rakan Sheikh and his followers of faking the election results (ibid.). They

---

15. Interview with Mekhlef Said of the Tay tribe in al-Hassakeh.
16. Interview with Sheikh Ahmad Sa'd Melhem of the Jabbour tribe.
17. Ibid.
18. Interview with Sheikh Ahmad Saad Melhem.
19. Interview with Sufian Meslet of the Jabbour tribe.

protested in the streets and chanted against the governor of Raqqa, who was accused of collaborating with the Afadleh Sheikh to fake the election results.[20] The Syrian security forces surrounded the governor's palace and used tear gas to disperse the protestors.[21] The governor came up with a conciliatory solution for both clans when both Sheikhs were given a seat in Parliament (Syria News 2007).

The fifth clash also took place in Raqqa governorate, where Ababsa narrates an interesting story of how members of the Walda tribe, whose former lands and homes were submerged by the Assad lake, protested against procedures that registered their traditional pasture land as state land, which was then illegally sold or rented out by the Raqqa Agriculture Direction to people who did not live in or know the village. The tribesmen started to shout 'Corruption is sucking peasant blood!' (Ababsa 2005, 41). The governor of Raqqa went to the village with some officials and asked the protestors to calm down but they started to throw stones at the officials, who had to retreat quickly to their cars and speed back to Raqqa. Many letters were sent to the president, minister of agriculture and Ba'ath Party Regional Command (ibid). Again, many tribesmen were arrested and brought to Raqqa political security branch, instead of finding a satisfactory solution to the problem.

Many common themes can be found from these different clashes that spread all over the country between the tribes. First, it is clear that the violence that occurred in different parts of the country had a certain 'irrational, spontaneous, expressive' dimension (Braud 1993, 28), which is the expression of an anger that had been accumulating for too long. These social groups were not able to express their anger or frustration for long time and when the regime started to show some signs of a soft hand towards them, they vented their anger at old grievances. 'Inability to preserve law and order further turned many tribes against the regime' (International Crisis Group 2004, 37). Second, the neo-liberal policies adopted by Bashar al-Assad reduced the amount of bribes and economic advantages provided by the regime and thus reduced the regime's ability to expand its patronage networks. During Hafez al-Assad's rule, tribal challenges were solved by distributing economic opportunities to the Sheikhs and their tribesmen. After 2000, reduced revenues from the state triggered different rivalries around grazing sources, parliamentary seats and economic advantages. 'As tribal conflicts were played out on the streets, people realised that the government's influence was waning' (International Crisis

---

20. Interview with Malkad Hamam from Raqqa.
21. Ibid.

Group 2004, 37). Third, Bashar al-Assad's regime continued to use the Arab tribes to counterbalance other ethnicities and religious sects just as his father had done, by using the tribes to reduce the growing Kurdish influence in the north and the Druze's calls for reform in the south. Fourth, the regime realised that it did not have enough military presence in the north-eastern part of the country. This led the regime to form the 17th Reserve Division in Raqqa in 2004 in an attempt to impose law and order and show its military capabilities.[22] Fifth, these clashes showed the disintegration of the social contract between the Syrian regime and its rural constituency in the periphery. The new social contract reversed the relationship with the tribes and replaced them with the bourgeoisie and the capitalist class of the cities.

Conclusion

Domestic security and social balance were the two most important pillars of the stability of Hafez al-Assad's regime from 1970 until 2000. Crime rates remained extremely low in comparison to many other Middle Eastern countries. The security apparatus was strong enough to keep all elements of the Syrian populace in check. Hafez al-Assad tried to guarantee that the majority of the security elite were all Alawite. Expanding the traditional patronage networks of Syrian society, he included other disaffected groups within the security structure, so that these services employed fifteen per cent of the country's total workforce (Chatty 2010, 43). Arab tribes that had high representation in the Syrian army were overrepresented in the security apparatus as well. Hafez al-Assad manipulated his confessional allies from the Arab tribes to protect his regime from the threat of military coups and maintain domestic stability. The regime also tried to maintain a balance between the different classes. The gap between rich and poor remained relatively tolerable in comparison to Egypt, for example, where a lot of people in the rural areas had to live in slums. Hafez al-Assad realised the importance of the tribes to the national economy because of the role they played in supporting agriculture and livestock. The government made credit available to the tribes wishing to invest in their herds. Emergency fodder stocks were created and fodder exports stopped, so as to have enough in time of drought. Artesian wells were dug and enclosures were constructed in flood paths to keep rainwater in different parts of the Syrian steppe to provide water for herds. Hospitals, schools and veterinary units were established in most of the tribal regions. 'Hafiz al-Assad understood that the

---

22. Interview with Mekhlef Said.

From Reform to Revolt

Alawites could not rule the country on their own so he cultivated Sunni allies from the Arab tribes, who were marginalised and despised by the city people as well' (Rubin 2008, 50).

Domestic security and social balance were jeopardised when Bashar al-Assad came to power in 2000. Bashar al-Assad is someone who grew up in the palace and so he had no contact with the rural community, unlike his father who grew up in the village and saw how the rural community lives and what it really needs. Bashar wanted to modernise the Syrian state and so he followed neo-liberal policies, not realising how destructive this would be to the regime's social base. The withdrawal of state services from the rural areas created great frustration among the tribes. These policies, accompanied by severe drought and the inappropriate actions of development agencies, polarised the tribes and endangered the socioeconomic conditions that had long stabilised the country. The government's liberalisation policies were also ignorant of realities on the ground. Ending the government's subsidies on agricultural products and fodder for livestock led to the collapse of the rural community in the tribal regions. According to the United Nations, sixty per cent of Syrian land and 1.3 million people, mostly in the eastern part of the country, were adversely affected by the drought (Mhanna 2014). In that part of the country, more than 800,000 people lost their entire sources of livelihood (ibid.). The drought displaced hundreds of thousands of people from the rural areas in waves of migration to the suburbs of the major cities. These new areas of settlement became Syria's first slums. The displaced people, who were mainly from the Arab tribes, were cut off from lines of governmental development and support and were left to face the challenges in the city on their own. In 2005, 5.1 million people were living under the poverty line, with two million Syrians unable to meet their basic needs (Haddad 2005, 5). All the factors mentioned above played an important role in eroding the domestic security and social balance that Hafez al-Assad had worked for decades to build, and thus triggered the civil unrest now underway in Syria. It was the tribal regions that had been marginalised and impoverished by the regime's policies where the spark of the uprising started and where its fiercest battles were waged later on.

References

Awsat, 2005. 'Bloody clashes between members of Shammar and al-Jabbur tribes'. Available at http://archive.aawsat.com/details.asp?article=319365&issueno=9766#.V8q22vkrLIW. Accessed 3 September 2016. In Arabic.

Ababsa, M. 2005. 'Privatisation in Syria: State Farms and the Case of the Euphrates Project'. European University Institute, Robert Schuman Centre for Advanced Studies' working paper series.

Ababsa. M., 2011. 'Agrarian counter-reform in Syria (2000–2010)', In R. Hinnebusch, A. El Hindi, M. Khaddam and M. Ababsa (eds), *Agriculture and Reform in Syria*. Scotland: St Andrews Papers on Contemporary Syria.

Ababsa, M. 2013. 'Fifty years of state land distribution in the Syrian Jazira: Agrarian reform, agrarian counter-reform, and the Arab Belt Policy (1958–2008)'. In H. Ayeb and R. Saad (eds), *Agrarian Transformation in the Arab World*. Cairo: The American Univeristy at Cairo Press. p. 33.

Ababsa, M. 2014. 'The end of a world: Drought and agrarian transformation in north-east Syria (2007, 2010)'. In Raymond A. Hinnebusch and Tina Zintl (eds), *Syria from Reform to Revolt, Volume 1: Political Economy and International Relations*. Syracuse, NY: Syracuse University Press. pp 199–226.

Abboud, S. 2015. 'Locating the "social" in the social market economy', In R. Hinnebusch and T. Zintl (eds), *Syria from Reform to Revolt, Volume 1: Political Economy and International Relations*. Syracuse, NY: Syracuse University Press.

ACSAD and ISDR. 2011. Drought vulnerability in the Arab Region: Case study; Drought in Syria – Ten years of scarce water (2000–2010). http://www.unisdr.org/files/23905_droughtsyriasmall.pdf. Accessed 31 January 2017.

Aljazeera Arabic 2011. Clashes between the Beduoin and the Druzes in al-Hassakeh. In Arabic http://www.aljazeera.net/news/arabic/2000/11/28/تجدد-الصدامات-بين-البدو-والدروز-في-السويداء

Batatu, H. 1999. *Syria's Peasantry, the Descendants of Its Lesser Rural Notables, and Their Politics*. Princeton: Princeton University Press.

Braud, P. 1993. 'La violence politique: repères et problèmes', *Culture et conflits* 9–10: 13–42.

Bush, R. 2002. *Counter-revolution in Egypt's Countryside: Land and Farmers in the Era of Economic Reform*. London: Zed books

Chatty, D. 2010. 'The Bedouin in contemporary Syria: the persistence of tribal authority and control'. *The Middle East Journal* 64: 29–49

Danish Immigration Service and Austrian Red Cross 2010. Human rights issues concerning Kurds in Syria, https://www.nyidanmark.dk/nr/rdonlyres/ff03ab63–10a5–4467-a038–20fe46b74ce8/0/syrienrapport2010pdf.pdf Accessed 31 January 2017.

Donati, C. 2013. 'The economics of authoritarian upgrading in Syria: Liberalization and the reconfiguration of economic networks'. In S. Heydemann and R. Leenders (eds), *Middle East Authoritarianisms: Governance, Contestation, and Regime Resilience in Syria and Iran*. Stanford, California: Stanford University Press.

Dukhan, H. 2014. 'Development-induced displacement among Syria's Bedouin', *Nomadic Peoples* 18: 61–79.

Ellis, C. and M. Flaherty. 1992. *Investigating Subjectivity: Research on Lived Experience*. London: Sage.

Gambill, G.C. 2000. 'Syria's night of the long knives'. Middle East Intelligence Bulletin, available at http://www.meforum.org/meib/articles/0006_s1.htm

Gambill, G.C. 2004. 'The Kurdish reawakening in Syria'. Middle East Intelligence Bulletin, available at http://www.meforum.org/meib/articles/0404_s1.htm

Ghadbian, N. 2001. 'The new Assad: Dynamics of continuity and change in Syria'. *Middle East Journal* **55**: 624–41.

Haddad, B. 2005. 'Syria's curious dilemma'. *Middle East Report* **236**: 4–13.

Heydemann, S., 2007. 'Upgrading authoritarianism in the Arab world'. The Brookings Institution. Washington D.C. Available at: http://www.brookings.edu/research/papers/2007/10/arabworld Accessed 11 August 2016.

Hinnebusch, R. 1989. *Peasant and Bureaucracy in Ba'athist Syria: The Political Economy of Rural Development.* Boulder: Westview.

Hinnebusch, R. 1990. *Authoritarian Power and State Formation in Ba'athist Syria.* Boulder: Westview.

Hinnebusch, R., A. El Hindi, M. Khaddam and M. Ababsa. 2011. '*Agriculture and Reform in Syria*'. Digest of Middle East Studies **20**: 326–329. doi:10.1111/j.1949-3606.2011.00102.x

Hinnebusch, R., 2012. 'Syria: from "authoritarian upgrading" to revolution?' *International Affairs* **88**: 95–113.

Ibrahim, L. and N. Razzouk. 2011. 'Syria starts $2.1 billion irrigation project on Tigris River'. Bloomberg, 7 March. Available at http://www.bloomberg.com/news/articles/2011-03-07/syria-starts-2-1-billion-irrigation-project-on-tigris-river Accessed 11 August 2016.

IFAD (The International Fund for Agricultural Development). 2011. 'Syrian Arab Republic: A country factsheet'. Available at http://www.ifad.org/events/gc/34/nen/factsheet/syria.pdf

IrinNews 2009. 'Drought driving farmers to the cities'. http://www.irinnews.org/feature/2009/09/02/drought-driving-farmers-cities

International Crisis Group. 2004. 'Syria under Bashar (II): Domestic policy challenges'. Middle East Report N°92– 11 February. Available at http://www.css.ethz.ch/en/services/digitallibrary/publications/publication.html/27426 Accessed 3 September 2016.

Khatib, L. 2011. *Islamic Revivalism in Syria: the Rise and Fall of Ba'thist Secularism: Routledge Studies in Political Islam, Vol. 7.* London and New York: Routledge.

Kilcullen, D. and N. Rosenblatt. 2014. 'The rise of Syria's urban poor: Why the war for Syria's future will be fought over the country's new urban villages', *PRISM*, National Defense University, Center for Complex Operations, Vol. 4, Syria Supplemental: 33–41.

Leverett, F. 2005. *Inheriting Syria: Bashar's Trial by Fire*. Brookings Institution.

Louhaichi, M. and A. Tastad. 2010. The Syrian steppe: Past trends, current status, and future priorities. *Rangelands* **32**: 2–7.

Lowe, R. 2006. *The Syrian Kurds: A People Discovered*. London: Chatham House

Macleod, H. 2011. 'Despite provocation, Syria's powerful tribes cling to peaceful protests', https://www.pri.org/stories/2011-08-28/despite-provocation-syrias-powerful-tribes-cling-peaceful-protests

Mhanna, W. 2014. 'Syria's climate crisis'. Al-Monitor http://www.al-monitor.com/pulse/politics/2013/12/syrian-drought-and-politics.html#

Moubayed, S. 2001. 'Syria loses its former ally in Lebanon, Druze leader Walid Jumblatt'. Washington Report on Middle East Affairs. Available at http://www.wrmea.org/2001-january-february/syria-loses-its-former-ally-in-lebanon-druze-leader-walid-jumblatt.html

OCHA 2010. 'Syria drought response plan 2009–2010'. Mid-Term Review. Available at http://www.unocha.org/cap/appeals/syria-drought-response-plan-2009–2010

Perthes, V. 2004. *Syria Under Bashar al-Assad: Modernisation and the Limits of Change*. Oxford: Oxford University Press.

Rubin, B., 2008. *The Truth about Syria*. New York: Palgrave-MacMillan.

Ruiz De Elvira, L. 2012. 'State/Charities relations in Syria: Between reinforcement, control and coercion', In L. Ruiz de Elvira and T. Zintl (eds), *Civil Society and the State in Syria: The Outsourcing of Social Responsibility*. Boulder: Lynne Rienner.

Savelsberg, E. 2014. 'The Syrian-Kurdish movements: Obstacles rather than driving forces for democratization', In D. Romano and M. Gurses (eds), *Conflict, Democratization, and the Kurds in the Middle East Turkey, Iran, Iraq and Syria*. New York: Palgrave-MacMillan.

Seifan, S., 2010. *Syria on the Path to Economic Reform*. St. Andrews: University of St. Andrews Centre for Syrian Studies.

Solh, M. 2010. 'Tackling the drought in Syria'. *Nature Middle East*, available at http://www.natureasia.com/en/nmiddleeast/article/10.1038/nmiddleeast.2010.206

Starr, S., 2012. *Revolt in Syria: Eye-witness to the Uprising*. London: Hurst and Company.

Syria-news. 2007. 'Riots in Raqqa are aggravating after elections', Available at http://syria-news.com/readnews.php?sy_seq=53032 Accessed 3 September 2016. In Arabic.

Syrian Human Rights Committee 2007. 'Wave of arrests against members of Damascus Declaration'. Available at http://www.shrc.org/en/?p=20477

Tejel, J. 2008. *Syria's Kurds: History, Politics and Society*. London and New York: Routledge.

UN 2010. 'Syria Drought Response Plan 2009–2010: Mid-Term Review' http://reliefweb.int/report/syrian-arab-republic/syria-drought-response-plan-2009–2010-mid-term-review

UNDP 2005. 'Macroeconomic policies for poverty reduction: The case of Syria'. Available at http://www.arabstates.undp.org/content/rbas/en/home/library/Sustainable_development/macroeconomics-policies-for-poverty-reduction--the-case-of-syria.html

Wieland, C. 2012. *A Decade of Lost Chances: Repression and Revolution from Damascus Spring to the Arab Spring*. Seattle: Cune Press.

Wieland, C. 2013. 'Assad's decade of lost chances'. In C. Wieland, A. Almqvist and H. Nassif (eds). *The Syrian Uprising: Dynamics of an Insurgency*. St Andrews: University of St. Andrews Centre for Syrian Studies.

Wright, R. 2008. *Dreams and Shadows: The Future of the Middle East*. Harmondsworth: Penguin.

Yildiz, K. 2005. *The Kurds of Syria: The Forgotten People*. London: Pluto.

Zisser, E. 2006. *Commanding Syria: Bashar al-Asad and the First Years in Power*. London: I.B. Tauris.

Radwan Ziadeh. 2013. *Power and Policy in Syria: Intelligence Services, Foreign Relations and Democracy*. London: I.B. Tauris and Co.

Chapter 5

HERDER PARTICIPATION IN MODERN MARKETS: THE ISSUES OF THE CREDIT LOAN TRAP

Gongbuzeren

Introduction

Providing access to financial services, such as micro-credit loans, to rural herders in developing countries has been a vital strategy in poverty alleviation, risk management and sustainable rural development (World Bank 1994, Anderson et al. 2002, Turner and Williams 2002, Addison and Brown 2014). Micro-finance gained popularity by challenging the traditional formal banking approaches' failure to respond to the multiplicity of unmet financial demands by the poor (Lakwo 2006). In recent years, governments, international and national NGOs and development agencies have provided pluralistic micro-finance services such as micro-credit, micro-saving, micro-insurance and micro-leasing supported by non-financial services to poor rural herders worldwide to address their needs (IFAD 2001).

Credit loans are also emerging in different forms in the pastoral regions of China, especially after China's promotion of market-based economic reforms in the west of China (Zhang 2014). In line with China's 'Opening up the West' programme, the rural pastoral regions of the Qinghai-Tibetan Plateau are seeing an ever greater scale of marketisation and social transition from traditional pastoral communities into a more commercialised society (Foggin 2008, Kreutzmann 2011, Wang et al. 2014, Gongbuzeren et al. 2016). In many pastoral areas, it is not just livestock commercialisation that is reconfiguring pastoralism, but rather the incorporation of these areas into other capitalist strategies of accumulation such as the introduction of financial markets, rangeland rental systems and the establishment of conservation areas

(Song 2010, Yeh and Gaerrang 2010, QPG 2011, Shi 2012). In this transition, micro-credit loans have been promoted as part of major financial interventions that tend to encourage herders to increase livestock production, better adapt to ecological crises and engage with alternative livelihoods. Such financial interventions are part of larger development frameworks that emphasise the positive role of markets in contemporary rural development strategies (Turner and Williams 2002, Lemos and Agrawal 2006). However, greater integration of pastoral regions into markets extends both opportunities and challenges for herder livelihood, including reshaping the structure of livelihood expenses, engagement in different financial markets and resource management costs (Wang et al. 2014).

There is a spectrum of studies on the role of credit loans in rural pastoral development. Some studies argue that credit loans from government or development agencies help local herders and women to engage with microenterprises that diversify their income sources, and empower marginalised groups (Mohammed 2006). In addition, many studies stated that credit loans, including micro-credit or livestock loans, could be an effective safety net to help herders to purchase livestock feeds and veterinarian services during disasters, so as to better adapt to ecological variability (McPeak and Barrett 2001, Barrett and Luseno 2004, Addison and Brown 2014). Especially, in the context of climate change, credit loans as a strategy for managing risks among rural herders living in dynamic ecosystems have received great attention, and many studies recommended that different financial institutions are needed to guarantee herders' access to credit loans (Turner and Williams 2002, Carter and Barrett 2006, Carter et al. 2006). However, there are opposing perspectives among research studies as well. These studies argue that the idea of financial self-sufficiency using micro-credit loans limits the focus of institutions to the financial performance of the loans rather than the impacts on the clients (Lakwo 2006), while the real question is how to get these financial resources into the hands of poor people who need them most (Steele et al. 2015). As a result of institutional objectives, the agenda of reducing poverty of the very poor is secondary to profit-maximisation attainable by redirecting support to the small or micro-business growth of the not-so-poor (Otero and Rhyne 1994, Hulme 1999, Devereux 2001, Lakwo 2006).

In China, most of the studies on credit loans focus on their impacts on agricultural regions. Some scholars have begun to discuss the credit loan issue in the pastoral regions, especially from the perspectives of financial institutions and the availability of credit loans. Credit loans are perceived to be effective in addressing herders' financial needs for better adaptation to climatic disasters, and intensification of livestock production systems (Song 2010). However, these studies state that the limited size of the credit loan, and lack of financial institutions that guarantee access to credit loans for herders, are major challenges (Liu and Gu 2014). In addition, there are many cases where herders were not able to repay the loan on time, affecting their credit in the future. Some studies pointed out that this is partly because herders use credit loans to purchase fodder during weather disasters to minimise livestock mortality, while very few herders are actually able to invest the loan in order to expand the number of livestock to gain profits (Han 2011, Zhang 2014). Similar issues are observed in Mongolian pastoral regions where herders use most of the loans to pay for goods that are consumed and are not able to increase productivity, while huge losses during disasters have pushed some families deeply into debt (Collier 2005, Sneath 2012). Therefore, some studies raise concerns about the effectiveness of credit loans in rural pastoral development, and argue that loans generate long-term and new risks when they are used for short-term emergencies in the pastoral regions (Li 2014, Zhang 2014).

As mentioned above, most of the studies regarding the role of micro-credit loans in rural pastoral development in China and other countries argued that, with effective financial institutions, micro-credit loans can help local herders better adapt to markets and address their poverty issues. However, these studies failed to consider the complex relationship between micro-credit loans and the socio-economic and ecological characteristics of rural pastoral regions, especially in the case of the arid and alpine steppes. Pastoralism in arid and alpine steppes is a complex and co-evolved social-ecological system (Li and Li 2012). The heterogeneity of resource distribution and constant variation of weather conditions, and the incorporation of rural pastoral regions into marketisation are all connected to affect the role of credit loans in pastoral regions. As Sneath (2012) stated, because of the seasonal nature of market income in the pastoral regions and the systemic risks posed by climate variations, herders' borrowing tends to reflect needs, not investment opportunities, which may indicate a major difference in the role of credit loans between pastoral and agricultural regions. Therefore, how features of the institutional and sociocultural environments of pastoral regions affect credit loan functions will help increase understanding of the true effects of the extension of credit loans in rural areas. Contributing to this discussion, this chapter will use a case study from the pastoral regions of the Qinghai-Tibet Plateau to analyse the current credit loan conditions in the pastoral regions, including how herders use and return the loans, and the key social-ecological factors driving herders to take different types of credit loan. In this case, credit loans include both micro-credit loans from government as well as other cash loans from individuals and other social groups such as local monasteries.

Case Study

The case study village, which we anonymised as AX Village, is located in Ruoergai County in the western region of Sichuan Province, Peoples' Republic of China (see Figure 1). We conducted over three years (2012–2014) of field data collection, using semi-structured interviews with pastoral households. A stratified sample was selected of thirty village households, standing for sixteen per cent of the total households in the village, with varying herd sizes, and the same samples were tracked over the three-year study period. As the author of this chapter is a native Tibetan who grew up in the nomadic area, no translator was needed for the fieldwork.

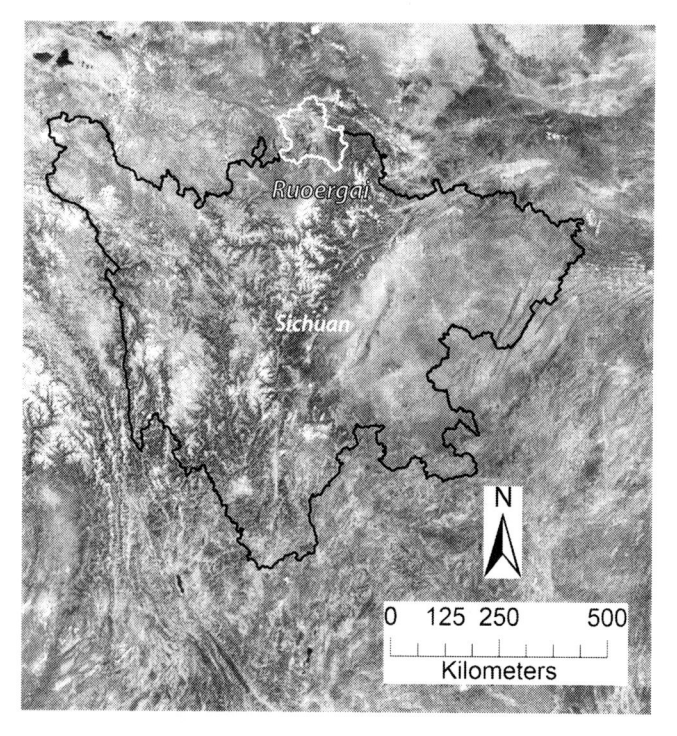

Figure 1. Map of Ruoergai County, Sichuan Province, China.

Herder Participation in Modern Markets

The pastoral regions of Ruoergai County have mosaics of complex landscapes including marshes, fens, bogs, wetland meadows, and shallow water, interspersed with low hills and sub-alpine meadows (Yan and Wu 2005). Ruoergai County has approximately 2,600 hectares of wetland region that provide habitats for rich biodiversity, including the black-necked crane. The area is also very important for the livelihoods of its local inhabitants. Such a complex and diverse cultural and ecological landscape becomes an opportunity for tourism. According to an interview with the country tourism bureau official, Ruoergai County government has been promoting the wetland nature reserve and pastoral regions of Ruoergai County for eco-tourism development since 2006. This has increased the scale of population movement in the region as well as the level of urbanisation and marketisation. According to AX village leader, in the last few years an average of 20,000 tourists per day have been visiting Huahu (a famous tourism destination) at weekends during the peak tourism season. A local hotel owner at the county seat stated that at present, over 200 hotels, including small guesthouses as well as big hotels, are established in the county seat. As the study site village is located between the county seat and Huahu, it is highly affected by the tourism development.

The rangelands in AX Village are a mix of alpine meadow and wetland pastures with average elevations reaching 3,500m and annual precipitation ranging from 490mm to 860mm. AX Village has experienced a number of institutional changes in rangeland management systems (Gongbuzeren et al. 2016). From 1958 to 1983, it was a state ranch where all livestock and rangeland were owned and used by the government, while herders worked for the ranch as a production team. The government also recruited rich pastoral families with high livestock numbers from other pastoral regions in Ruoergai County to join AX ranch. Starting from 1984, the livestock were privatised to individual households, while the rangeland was contracted to the community, which collectively used the rangelands with four seasonal livestock movements. AX was still a state-owned ranch so they had to pay taxes to the local government. In 2001, the state-owned ranch was dismantled and officially redesignated AX Village, so they did not have to pay taxes and maintained collective use of the rangelands as a community. In 2009, the herders in AX Village collectively decided to contract rangeland to individual households, with wire fences demarcating individual parcel boundaries (Gongbuzeren et al. 2016). Since then, the rangeland transfer system has gradually been gradually applied in AX Village, whereby some individual families rent grazing parcels from households with fewer or no livestock, in order to access more rangelands.

Gongbuzeren

Although some families are engaged in alternative livelihoods, extensive livestock production is still the main income source for herders in AX Village. They mainly sell sheep and yaks to a local slaughterhouse in the county seat, while livestock products such as butter and cheese are sold to business intermediaries.

Facing these larger socio-economic and institutional changes, we believed that AX Village could be an interesting case study site to address our research question, especially in understanding how the changes in characteristics of pastoralism affect the role of micro-credit loans. This chapter analyses the current situation of credit loans in AX Village, including how herders take, use and repay them, and the social-ecological factors that drive herders to take credit loans.

Results

Taking credit loans in AX Village

In the years from 2012 to 2014, among the total thirty households studied in AX Village, 24, 27 and 25 households had taken credit loans respectively. Herders took loans of various sizes from 0–20,000 RMB up to above 40,000 RMB per year. As Figure 2 demonstrates, among the households that took a loan, over fifty per cent, 41 per cent and 44 per cent respectively took loans above 40,000 RMB, while another major group of households' loans ranged between 1–20,000 RMB, with an increase from 25 per cent in 2012 to 36 per cent in 2014. This indicates that not only are high numbers of pastoral households taking credit loans, but the sizes of the loans among most households are high over the three-year period.

Among the households which took loans in AX Village, we further analysed how the amount of the annual loan relates to the total annual income of each household. Table 1 indicates that over 42 per cent, 44 per cent and 48 per cent of the households' loans ranged between one per cent and 49 per cent of their annual total income, and there is a trend of increase between 2012 and 2014. In addition, there is a major group of households (33 per cent, thirty per cent and 24 per cent) whose loans exceeded their total annual income, while a trend of decrease is observed between 2012–2014.

Based on the analyses of loan sizes and the comparison with household total annual income, it can be stated that even though a trend of small decrease in loan size is observed between 2012 to 2014, the number of households taking credit loans is still high, indicating high needs for credit loans to address their financial needs.

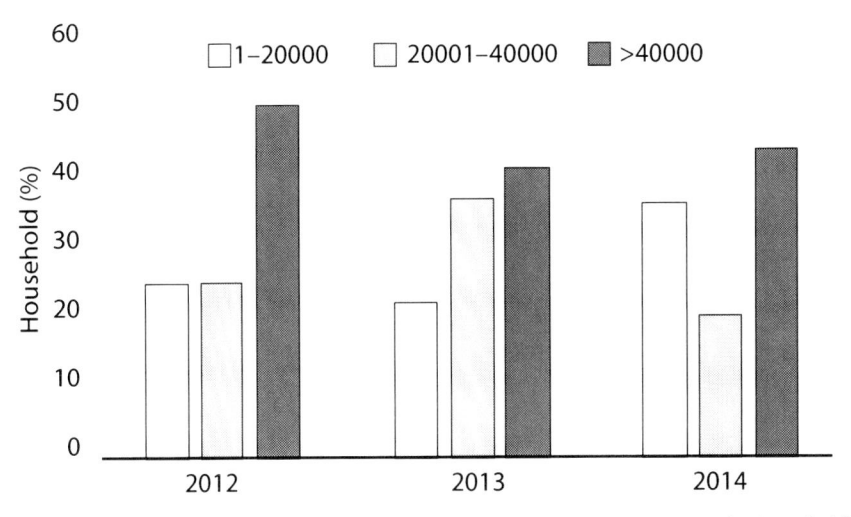

Figure 2. Percentage of herders taking different sizes of credit loan among the household samples (unit: RMB).

Loan/total income	0.01–0.49	0.50–0.79	0.80–1	>=1	Total household numbers
2012	42%	13%	13%	33%	24
2013	44%	22%	4%	30%	27
2014	48%	24%	4%	24%	25

Table 1. Analyses of percentage of credit loan from household total annual income.

According to our interviews, herders in AX Village got their loans from three different sources (Figure 3), and some families took loans from all three sources each year. First, over sixty per cent of the herders took loans from the government. However, herders said that government loans are very small, ranging from 5,000–20,000 RMB, not sufficient to meet their annual financial needs. Therefore, they had to take high-interest loans from individuals. Herders stated that they had to pay over twenty to thirty per cent interest on these loans. As Figure 3 demonstrates, over 56 per cent of the households in AX have loans from individuals, which seems to represent the second largest loan source in the village. According to local herders, these individual lenders include local herders from AX Village or other pastoral villages in the region, or intermediary business people from the local region or outside whose main

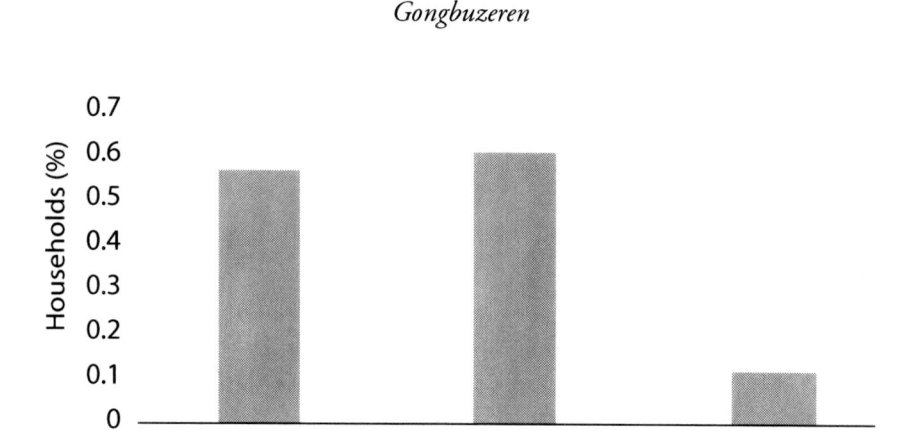

Figure 3. Sources of credit loan among the interviewed samples in AX Village.

business is high-interest loans. As financial markets become popular in the region, there are also a small percentage of households who take loans from local monasteries as well.

Returning the loans in AX Village

Based on the above analyses, it can be stated that herders rely heavily on microcredit loans, and the sources of loans vary from government to individuals as well as local monasteries. Therefore, we analyse how herders repay their loans. In AX Village, it appears that herders found two major ways to repay their loans over the years (Figure 4). First, they used income from livestock production such as selling livestock, butter and milk, and from non-livestock sources, such as tourism and government subsidy, to repay their loans each year. However, when the amount of repayment exceeds their income, they have to take further loans to repay their previous loan. In AX Village, over nine per cent of the households in 2012 stated that their income is insufficient to repay the loan, so they had to take further loans to repay the loan, and this percentage increased to 29 per cent in 2014. Based on this, it can be stated that, even though credit loans address the immediate cash needs of herders, many herders face a great challenge in repaying their loans. An increased percentage of households in AX Village are trapped in a vicious cycle of debt, where they have to take further loans to pay off previous loans.

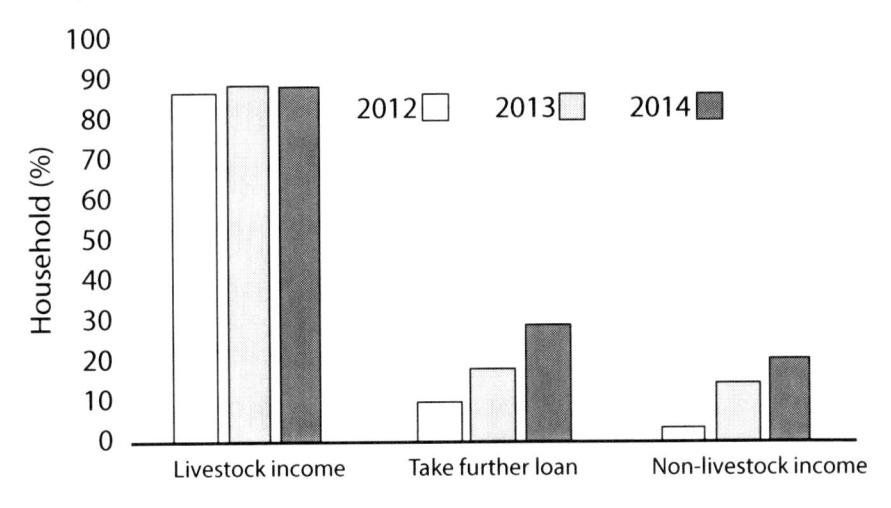

Figure 4. Ways of returning credit loans in AX Village.

Using the loans in AX Village

According to herders in AX Village, there are a number of major areas where the herders used the loans they took (see Figure 5). First, over 71 per cent, 67 per cent and 72 per cent of the herders between 2012–2014 stated that they took a credit loan to cover their living expenses, which include costs for food, clothes, health care, fuel and others. Second, another major percentage (63 per cent, 52 per cent, 64 per cent) stated they had to take loans to pay their rangeland rental fee. Herders stated that, after the implementation of the rangeland household contract system, the rangeland rental system became the only way to access other households' grazing parcels and facilitate livestock movements. Third, between 2012 and 2014, a certain percentage of households used the loans to expand their livestock numbers, though this percentage decreased from 29 per cent in 2012 to twelve per cent in 2014. In addition, a very small percentage of households used their loans to purchase assets over the three-year study period. Last but not least, an increased percentage of herders, from eight per cent in 2012 to 24 per cent in 2014, stated that they used loans to repay their previous loans.

Based on this, we can categorise the purposes of taking credit loans in AX Village into three major groups. First, the majority of the herders invest

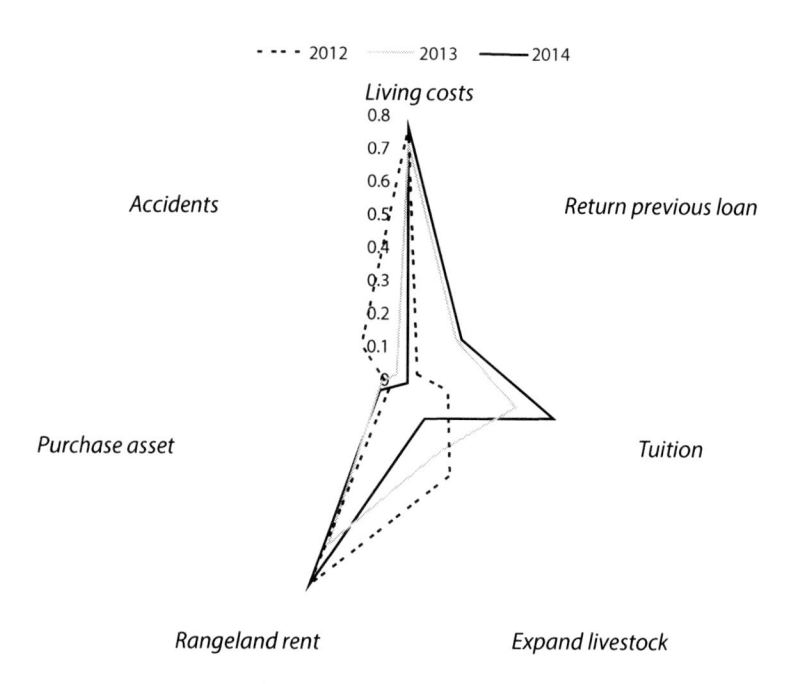

Figure 5. Purposes for which herders take credit loans in AX Village.

their loans in consumption-based expenses such as living costs, tuition and accidents. Second, herders used their loans to cover livestock production costs due to changes in rangeland management systems such as rangeland rental fees. Third, a small percentage of herders invested their loans in profit-generating activities such as expansion of livestock numbers or asset purchases. Therefore, from this analysis, we are able to observe that majority of herders in AX Village take credit loans from different sources to cover consumption-based activities, and cover livestock production costs due to changes in rangeland management system, while few are able to invest the loan in profit-generation activities to earn income.

Social-ecological factors pressing herders into loan traps

From the above analysis, we have observed that, while an increased number of herders in AX Village rely on credit loans to address their financial needs, many herders face great challenges in not being able to return the loans, and many pastoral households are trapped in a vicious cycle of debt. We further realised that most of the households used the loans they took to cover consumption-based activities while not so much was invested in profit-generation activities. According to our interviews with herders in AX Village, we realised that there are more complex social-ecological factors that interactively push herders into the loan traps.

Along with tourism and market development in the region, there has been an increase in population flow. For instance, one of the County Tourism Bureau officials stated in an interview that in the peak tourism season, daily tourist numbers reach over 30,000 in Ruoergai County. Public transportation is well developed in the region, including two domestic airports located within 150 kilometres of the county seat. Consequently, the integration of rural pastoral communities into such rapid development and marketisation has introduced great transformations in herder livelihood, especially herders' consumption behaviour and rapid changes in the price of goods. Among thirty households interviewed, all households owned motorcycles, while 65 per cent had either cars or trucks or tractors. Mr Kezhen said, 'When I was a village leader twenty years ago, we herded yaks and sheep on horseback, and used male yaks to transport goods during seasonal movements. At present, herders ride motorcycles to herd livestock and use trucks or tractors to transport goods.' Therefore, we observed that, although such development is convenient for the herders in many ways, it has also increased the need for a regular cash income for their living expenses. Consequently, credit loans have become a major part of household cash flow to address their daily needs in AX Village.

Livestock production constitutes the main source of livelihood for herders in AX Village, though the herders stated that they have very limited power over development of the livestock markets, including price regulation. For instance, one of the few local intermediary businessmen at the county seat told us in interview that they pay local herders around 30 RMB (4 USD) for a kilo of butter, and 3,500 RMB (550 USD) for a yak of average size, though they will sell these products for two or three times the price in the larger markets. Furthermore, the village leader stated in an interview that when they sell their livestock products in their peak livestock production season between September to October, the price of butter will be reduced to 25 RMB to 30 RMB, while the rest of the year, especially in Spring, the price increases to 30 RMB to 35 RMB though the herders do not have lots of dairy products to sell. Therefore, we observed that the herders are merely providers of raw materials, without the power to shape the markets to increase the values and prices of

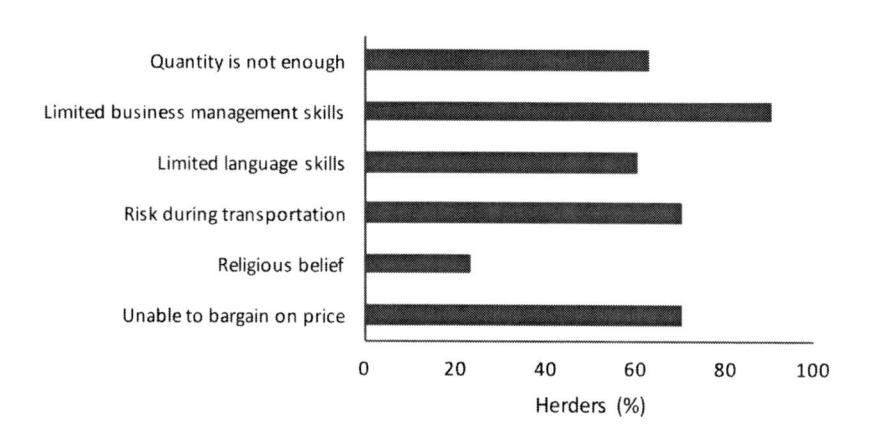

Figure 6. Factors that limit herders' participation in markets.

their eco-friendly products. In addition, even though different local markets are being established in the region, including rapidly developing tourism markets, the herders are not able to participate in the markets to diversify their income sources. Herders stated that they have many limitations in participating in these markets including limited business management and language skills, as well as low quantity of livestock production to meet the large market demands (see Figure 6). Consequently, the imbalance between the increased need for cash to cover their living expenses, and their inability to participate in the expanding markets to increase their income and diversify their income sources, pushed many herders into debt traps.

Before 2009, AX Village collectively used their rangelands to access different grazing areas at different times and to cope with weather risks (Gongbuzeren et al. 2016). However, after the implementation of the Rangeland Household Contract Responsibility system, all the previous seasonal pastures were combined and contracted to individual households, with each family receiving one large grazing parcel, so herders had to rely on a rangeland rental system to access more individual grazing parcels from individual households. Following this, livestock production costs have increased rapidly in AX Village. According to analyses of livestock production returns in AX Village by Gongbuzeren et al. (2016), the rangeland rental fees are the largest livestock production cost, with each household spending an average of 9,000 RMB per year, though their livestock production has not increased (Gongbuzeren et al. 2016). In addition, herders stated that the competition for renting individual grazing parcels had increased rapidly within AX Village, so that they have to pay higher prices to rent rangelands from other households within the same township or within Ruoergai County. Herders stated that, as demand for rangeland rentals had increased, families who rented out their rangeland demanded down-payment on all the costs at the beginning of the rental. Herders in AX village mostly rented rangelands during winter and spring, to access more grazing parcels in order to restore livestock health, though this is also a season where herders have limited income from livestock production. Consequently, they have to rely on credit loans, especially high-interest loans from individual herders within the region or local monasteries, to pay the rangeland rental fee.

It can therefore be stated that, even though various markets have been developed in the region with increasing movements of population, herders are not able to effectively participate in the markets to increase the value of their livestock products to increase income or diversify their income sources. At the same time, we also observed that market developments in the region rarely reflect the values of eco-friendly pastoral production, or take account of its seasonal nature or the low volumes of livestock produced. Consequently, the factors pushing many pastoral households in AX Village into a vicious cycle of debt go beyond the lack of financial institutions and the sizes of credit loans. The rapidly expanding markets in the pastoral regions without regard to the incorporation of the social-ecological values of pastoralism marginalise local herders, excluding them from the development opportunities and thus, while herders bear the costs of the market development, they rarely gain benefit from the market opportunities.

Discussion and conclusion

Our study results demonstrate that credit loans from both individuals and government have been a major part of household cash flow in AX Village, though herders use the loans to cover consumption-based costs, while few are able to invest the loans to generate profits, and thus many face great challenges in repaying the loans. Many pastoral households are trapped in a vicious cycle of debt where herders have to take further loans to repay previous loans. The results from AX Village demonstrate that these issues are not simply caused by lack of financial institutions or limited sizes of loan, but are also the result of market-based development initiated in the pastoral regions.

Swift (2007) stated that all herders depend on the market to a varying degree for their basic subsistence, though shortcomings in the market create a serious threat to livelihoods. Haq (1995) and other scholars stated that current market-based development focuses on how to increase economic growth, minimising the role of people as the agents of change and beneficiaries of development (Wang 2012). In addition, studies pointed out that the features of the institutional and socio-cultural environment of rural pastoral regions greatly shape market functions (Ribot 1998, Anderson et al. 2002, Turner and Williams 2002, Han 2011), though they are rarely taken into account in the dominant market-based economic framework. We believe these are some of the major factors leading herders in AX village into the trap of continuous debt through credit loan development.

First, different types of local markets are developed and promoted by the local government, including tourism markets, financial markets, the rangeland rental system and livestock markets. However, the income structures of AX village show that only a few herders from AX Village are actually able to participate in the markets to earn alternative income, such as tourism-based income and salary-based income. This indicates that current market development in the Ruoergai region only focuses on the creation of market environments and only limited attention is paid to the capacity building of the local herders so that they have the ability to participate in the market and take advantage of the opportunities to improve their livelihood. The analysis shows that lack of language skills and business management experience are two of the most important limiting factors that prevent herders from participating in markets. Consequently, herders have to rely more on credit loans to cover their expenses, while facing the great challenges of not being able to repay the loan.

Second, studies pointed out that pastoralism is a system that deliberately exploits the transient concentrations of nutrients that represent the most reliable feature of the dryland environments, and is geared at maximising the production of economic value while stabilising its performance in environments where 'uncertainty is harnessed for production' (Krätli and Schareika 2010). However, the government has sought to develop the livestock industry in the pastoral regions of the Qinghai-Tibet Plateau by encouraging rural livestock trade centres, inviting outside investors, and promoting yak meat sales that encouraged herders to increase their livestock off-take rate (Hayes 2008, Gaerrang 2012). Consequently, as the case of AX Village demonstrates, the seasonal nature and low quantity of livestock production in the pastoral regions do not fit the characteristics of contemporary livestock markets being promoted, and herders are further marginalised from the current market development through their limited power and skills to shape the markets and gain benefits.

Third, the rangeland resources of AX Village vary widely in location and seasonal capacity. After the implementation of the rangeland household contract system, herders have to rely on the rangeland rental system to access more rangelands. Even though this system may create certain income generating opportunities for poor families (Gongbueren et al. 2016), it also increases herders' livestock production costs and pressures herders to rely more on credit loans.

In brief, the case of AX Village indicates that credit loans have been a major part of pastoral household cash flow. An increased number of households in the pastoral regions rely on credit loans to address their financial shortages. However, herders also face the challenge of repaying the loans and many herders are pressured into a vicious cycle of loan traps. Based on the above analyses and discussion, it seems that the barriers faced by herders in participating in current market developments to improve their income, and institutional changes in rangeland management, are key factors driving them to take loans. The credit loan issue in AX Village is not simply caused by problems associated with credit loan markets or financial institutions, but rather is attached to larger issues of market-based economic development in the pastoral regions of the Qinghai-Tibet Plateau. It appears that current market-based development systems promoted by the government narrowly focus on the development of markets and pay little attention to the response capacity of local herders, who are supposed to be the main beneficiaries; the ecological conditions affecting their livelihood; and the socio-cultural aspects of their livestock production system. Consequently, higher reliance on credit loans without the ability to repay the loan becomes a critical result of failures of market-based economic development in the pastoral region, and rangeland management institutions that do not conform to the socio-cultural and ecological conditions of pastoralism. There are studies stating that countries need markets to grow, but they need capable state institutions to grow markets (World Bank 1997, Pieterse 2001). It is crucial for the state to play a facilitating role, encouraging and complementing the activities of private business and individuals, and establishing the appropriate institutional foundations for efficient market function. Therefore, this study recommends that government should take an active role to promote institutions to regulate local markets so that the ecological and cultural features of livestock production in the pastoral regions are acknowledged, and local people will have more opportunities to participate in the markets to gain benefits.

Gongbuzeren

References

Abdi, N. 2010. *The Role of Micro-finance in Strengthening Pastoral Household Food Security*. M.A Thesis, Addis Ababa University

Addison, J. and C. Brown. 2014. 'Multi-scaled analysis of the effect of climate, commodity prices and risk on the livelihoods of Mongolian pastoralists'. *Journal of Arid Environments* 109: 54–64.

Anderson, C.L., L. Locker and R. Nugent. 2002. 'Microcredit, social capital, and common pool resources'. *World Development* 30(1): 95–105.

Barrett, C. and Luseno, W. 2004. 'Decomposing producer price risk: a policy analysis tool with an application to norther Kenyan livestock markets'. *Food Policy* 29(4):393-405.

Carter, M.R. and C.B. Barrett. 2006. 'The economics of poverty traps and persistent poverty: an asset-based approach'. *Journal of Development Studies* 42(2): 178–199.

Carter, M.R., P.D. Little, T. Mogues and W. Negatu. 2006. 'Poverty traps and natural disasters in Ethiopia and Honduras'. *World Development* 35(5): 835–856

Collier, S. 2005. *The Spatial Forms and Social Norms of 'Actually Existing Neoliberalism': Toward a Substantive Analytics*. International Affairs Working Paper: New School University.

Devereux, S. 2001. 'Livelihood insecurity and social protection: a re-emerging issue in rural development'. *Development Policy Review* 19(4): 507–519

Foggin, M.J. 2008. 'Depopulating the Tibetan grasslands: national policies and perspectives for the future of Tibetan herders in Qinghai Province, China'. *Mountain Research and Development* 28(1): 26–31.

Gaerrang. 2012. *Alternative Development on the Tibetan Plateau: The Case of the Slaughter Renunciation Movement*. Ph.D. dissertation, Department of Geography, University of Colorado.

Gongbuzeren, M.H. Zhuang and W.J. Li. 2016. 'Market-based grazing land transfers and customary institutions in the management of rangelands: two case studies on the Qinghai-Tibetan Plateau'. *Land Use Policy* 57: 287–295.

Han, L.Y. 2011. *Grassland Logics*. Beijing: Beijing Science and Technology Press (Chinese).

Haq, M. U.1995. *Reflections on Human Development*. New York, Oxford University Press.

Hayes, J. 2008. *Environmental Change, Economic Growth and Local Societies: 'Change in Worlds' in the Songpan Region, 1700–2005*. Ph.D. dissertation, Department of History, University of British Columbia.

Hulme, D. 1999. 'Impact assessment methodologies for microfinance: theory, experience and better practice'. Manchester, University of Manchester, IDPM. Finance and Development Research Programme, Working paper No. 1

IFAD. 2001. *Rural Finance: From Unsustainable Projects to Sustainable Institutions for the Poor*. Rome: GMS Grafiche.

Krätli, S. and N. Schareika. 2010. 'Living off uncertainty: the intelligent animal production of dryland pastoralists'. *European Journal of Development Research* 22(5): 605–622.

Kreutzmann, H. 2011. 'Pastoral practices on the move-recent transformations in mountain pastoralism on the Tibetan Plateau'. In H. Kreutzmann, Y. Yang and J. Richter (eds), *Pastoralism and Rangeland Management on the Tibetan Plateau in the Context of Climate and Global Change*. Berlin: Federal Ministry for Economic Cooperation and Development.

Lakwo, F. 2006. *Micro-Finance, Rural Livelihoods, and Women's Empowerment in Uganda*. Leiden: African Studies Centre.

Lemos, C.L. and A. Agrawal. 2006. 'Environmental governance'. *Annual Review of Environmental Resources* 31: 297–325.

Li, Y.B. 2014. *Improvement of Carrying Capacity Management in Inner Mongolian Rangeland: Beyond the Non-equilibrium Paradigm*. Ph.D. thesis, Peking University.

Li, W.J. and Li, Y.B. 2012. 'Managing rangeland as a complex system: How government intervention decouples social systems from ecological systems'. *Ecology and Society* 17(1):9.

Liu, Q and R.Y. Gu. 2014. 'Micro-credit loan development and relevant policy recommendations in the pastoral regions of Tibetan Autonomous Region'. *Chinese Journal of Agricultural Economics* 7: 58–60 (Chinese).

McPeak, J.G. and Barrett, C.B. 2001. 'Differential risk exposure and stochastic poverty traps among east African pastoralists'. *American Journal of Agricultural Economics*. 83(3): 674-79.

Mohammed, N.A. 2006. *The Role of Micro-finance in Strengthening Pastoral Household Food Security*. M.A thesis, Addis Ababa University.

Otero, M. and E. Rhyne. 1994. *The New World of Microenterprise Finance*. West Hartford, CT: Kumarian Press.

Pieterse, N.J. 2001. *Development Theory: Deconstructions and Reconstructions*. London: SAGE publications.

QPG (Qinghai Province Government). 2011. Qinghai Province Government Standing Committee No 94 Document Qinghai Province rangeland transfer system. [online] at http://www.china.com.cn/guoqing/zwxx/2012–07/11/ content 25876548. htm

Ribot, J.C. 1998. 'Theorizing access: forest profits along Senegal's charcoal commodity chain'. *Development and Change* 29: 307–341.

Shi, H. 2012. 'Marginalization of farmers and herders through "land lost" in the ethnic regions of Qinghai Province'. *Human Resource Management*.

Sneath, D. 2012. 'The "age of the market" and the regime of debt: the role of the credit in the transformation of Pastoral Mongolia'. *Social Anthropology* 20(4): 458–473.

Song, H. 2010. 'Micro-credit loan situation and development the agricultural and pasoral regions of Qinghai Province'. *Qinghai Social Sciences* 4: 82–85 (Chinese).

Steele, P., N.H. Rai and I. Nhantumbo. 2015. 'Beyond loans: Instruments to ensure the poor access climate and development finance'. Climate Change, Policy and Planning, Policy Briefing. International Institute of Environment and Development.

Swift, J. 2007. *Institutionalizing Pastoral Risk Management in Mongolia: Lessons Learned*. Rural Institutions and Participation Service, FAO.

Turner, M. and T. Williams. 2002. 'Livestock market dynamics and local vulnerability in the Sahel'. *World Developmen* 30(4): 683–705.

Wang, R., J. Wang, S.C. Li and D.H. Qing. 2014. 'Vulnerability of the Tibetan pastoral systems to climate and global change'. *Ecology and Society* 19(4): 8.

Wang, S.Y. 2012. *Tibetan Market Participation in China*. Ph.D. thesis, University of Helsinki.

World Bank. 1994. Mongolia: country economic memorandum: priorities in macro-economic management. Report No. 13612-MOG, Country Operations Division, China and Mongolia Department, Asia and Pacific Regional Office.

World Bank. 1997. *World Development Report 1997: The State in a Changing World*. Washington, DC: World Bank.

Yan, Z.L and N. Wu. 2005. 'Rangeland privatization and its impact on the Zoige wetlands on the Eastern Tibetan Plateau'. *Journal of Mountain Science* 2: 105–115.

Yeh, E.T. and Gaerrang. 2010. 'Tibetan pastoralism in neoliberalising China: continuity and change in Guoli'. *Area*: 1–8.

Zhang, C.C. 2014. *Herders' Market-based Adaptation to Climate Change in Arid and Semi-arid Areas and Its Impacts on Local Social-ecological Environment*. Ph.D. thesis, Peking University.

Chapter 6

INDIGENOUS SYSTEMS OF ECOLOGICAL KNOWLEDGE AND CONSERVATION INITIATIVES IN JABAL AKHDAR MOUNTAIN, OMAN

Salah al Mazrui

Introduction

As an Arab Islamic society, Oman has a tradition of nature conservation based on two key elements: Islamic tradition and local Arab custom (*'urf*). The Qur'ān contains numerous verses that instruct Muslims to respect as well as be in harmony with nature. For example, in the *sūrah* called al-*Nāzi'āt* (Those Who Tear Out), it is written: 'And the earth, moreover, hath He extended (to a wide expanse); He draweth out there from its moisture and its pasture; And the mountains hath He firmly fixed; For use and convenience to you and your cattle', (Qur'ān 79: 30–33). But this comes with responsibilities: 'It is He who has appointed you guardians in the earth, and has raised some of you in rank above others, the He may try you in what He has given you. Surely your Lord is swift in reckoning; and surely He is All-Forgiving, All-Compassionate' (Qur'ān 6: 165) (Khalid n.d.) These two Qur'ānic verses are clear examples showing the relationship between humans and nature and how Islamic tradition fosters this connection.

As for *'urf*, the strategy to protect the environment in relation to customary laws depends on the context, but the hema system (*nidhām l'aḥmīya*) was formerly common in most societies of the Arabian Peninsula. Hema, which means 'land under protection', is an ancient conservation system practiced in Arabia that goes back to the pre-Islamic era and continued in Islamic times (Zahran and Younes 1990). Hema land is set aside and not cultivated or used for grazing for a period of time or until certain circumstance prevail. Prophet Muhammad encouraged the practice after seeing its 'importance for conservation of rangeland resources' (Zahran and Younes 1990, 21). As a system of control and environmental protection, hema is classified into three categories: tribal hema which is used and controlled by members of the same tribe, village hema used and controlled by village members and individual hema, which is 'smaller and is usually located next to the cultivated field of the owner' (ibid.). Zahran and Younes further explain that the hema system is 'closely integrated in the tribal tradition' and that anyone who violates this system is punished by slaughtering their trespassing animals, while in recent times, repeat offenders faced harsher penalties such as imprisonment (ibid.). As for the existence of the hema system in modern Oman, according to al-Busaidi this is 'mostly abandoned' (2012, 315).

Oman's traditional conservation system evolved over a wide span of time and was shaped by social, cultural and historical forces. An important social-cultural force that had a major role in developing Oman's traditional conservation is the country's unique tribal system. The Omani tribal system is based on concepts such as autonomy, territoriality (*bilaḍ*), honour (*sharaf*), alliance (*ḥilf*) and Ibāḍism,[1] the school of Islam dominant in Oman. Failure to grasp how these key notions function can lead to distortion or misrepresentation of the Omani tribal system, making it difficult to understand how the traditional grazing practice was envisioned. However, embedded in the tribal system is the concept of '*urf* (custom), which is key to understand because it influenced the conservation system. As Hakim explains, 'the 'Urf is dynamic, i.e. it changes with time' (1994, 113). It is useful to add, that '*urf* is culture- and context-specific as, mentioned above, and has to be contextualised. Furthermore, '*urf* can be understood in its relation to Islamic Law, which 'accords legitimation to and protection to a locality's custom and practices and thus contributes … to the identity of a place' (ibid., 117). Hema is part of '*urf,* as it is a customary practice which reponds to changing contexts over time.

In view of this, it is quite clear that Oman possesses an indigenous form of conservation, which can be deployed to protect the environment. Ironically, conservation efforts or initiatives in Oman have ignored indigenous methods when it came to instituting protected or reserved areas such as the Arabian Oryx Project in Yaaloni in the 1980s or the Jabal Akhdar Project managed by Earthwatch International that began in 2010. This paper therefore examines

---

1. Ibāḍī is the third largest Islamic *madhhab* (orientation or 'sect') after Sunni and Shia. It dates from the time of Fitnat l-Kubra (The Great Dissension) and the first major war at Siffin in 37AH/657 ad, which was a conflict over the office of the Caliphate (among other issues) between two opposing camps, one led by the Prophet's cousin and son-in-law, Ali bin Abi Talib, and other by Muawiya bin Abu Sufyan, the Governor of Syria.

two problematic areas in relation to conservation initiatives in Oman, namely the question of defining ecology and the role of the expatriate in conservation. The final section of the paper argues for the importance of community-based conservation and shows the usefulness of indigenous knowledge in relation to conservation initiatives. In short, what we are trying to do is to add socio-cultural and historical dimensions to the idea of conservation. Conservation needs to be understood not just in terms of how the wilderness is protected through the *hema* system, for example, but also the way local communities invented, adopted and adapted water irrigation technologies such as the *aflaj* system of underground channels and tunnels for moving water from distant sources, which has been in use for hundreds of years.

As Dumont (1970, 195) suggests: 'If history is the movement whereby a society reveals itself for what it is, there are in a sense as many qualitatively different histories as there are societies'. Following Dumont's insight and applying it to ecological conservation, one can propose that 'there are in a sense as many qualitatively different conservation processes as there are societies'. In this light, Oman's conservation initiatives should not be solely based on Western discourse practices (indeed, some like the Yaaloni case have proved a failure!), but will have to uncover indigenous methods of conservation that are not actually dead but dormant, simply because they have been neglected for various illogical reasons. A German botanist, Annette Patzelt, who conducted fieldwork in Jabal Akhdar saw the importance of indigenous knowledge and, therefore, wrote:

> Older people still have a wealth of indigenous knowledge about the uses of plants and traditional agricultural practices. However, the on-going transformation process of these oasis systems leads to rapid loss of this knowledge and it is, therefore, of crucial importance to document existing information (2009).

The importance of using indigenous sources when it comes to conservation is to try and capture how local tribespeople imagined and shaped their landscape. In other words, it will be difficult to undertake conservation if one is ignorant about the landscape, which is a social and cultural construct. McCabe (2002) reiterates the importance of involving indigenous knowledge in conservation initiatives. He explains that we should be 'proactive in trying to make our understanding of how local people use natural resources and how they view "conservation" useful to those who design and implement conservation projects' (2002, 65). This is because, 'the future of conservation will depend on how well or how poorly local communities are integrated in conservation projects and programmes' (ibid.).

McCabe's warnings when applied to Oman are quite telling. The failure of the Arabian Oryx Project initiated in the 1980s and the current problems encountered by Earthwatch in their attempt to conserve the woodlands of Jabal Akhdar can be attributed, to a large extent, to the practice of conducting conservation in a mechanical way, without a human face, which includes total neglect of the indigenous viewpoint and participation in the conservation process and decision making. In what follows we examine the idea of conservation without a human face in Oman in terms of the possible causes, as well as showing that one of the best methods of conservation is to involve the communities in what scholars and practitioners describe as community-based conservation.

Ecological setting: Physical and social aspects

Oman is made up of two major regions, the North (*shemāl*) and the South (*janūb*). In this chapter we will focus on the ecological setting of the North, where Jabal Akhdar (the focus of the chapter) is located. It is important to note from the onset that regions are 'diverse and tend to have their own history, culture and civilization structure, despite the homogeneity [*tajānus*] of the country' (al-Hāshimi (N.D.), 21). However, the North itself is composed of four distinct governorates: Ad Dakhilīya (interior), Ash Sharqiya (eastern), Ad Dhahirah (western) and Al Batinah (coastal). One common feature of the northern regions is that they are all mainly sand and gravel desert with rugged mountains. According to the observations of the geographer, John Wilkinson (1977, 12), the northern physical environment is 'divided into two major provinces, the mountainous fold zone and the flat desert foreland'. One of the key physical characteristics of the North is the Hajar mountain range that runs from the Musandam Peninsula, located at the northernmost part of the country, to Ras-Hadd, which is the extreme south-eastern part of the Arabian Peninsula. The Hajar, which cuts through all four northern regions, is generally regarded as comprising two parts: al Hajar al-Gharbī (Western Hajar) and al-Hajar al-Sharqī. The highest point of these mountains is the Jabal al-Akhdar (literally, the Green Mountain) massif, which is around 10,000 feet high (Peterson 1978, 16). Despite the fact that the country is largely desert and mountainous, pockets of arable land can still be found in the valleys and foothills of the mountains. Most of the villages, which are isolated from each other, are located in the larger valleys. Outside the major cities of Muscat and Nizwa, for example, it is in these villages that the majority of the population resides. For example, the 'largest settlement clusters in the mountains (like

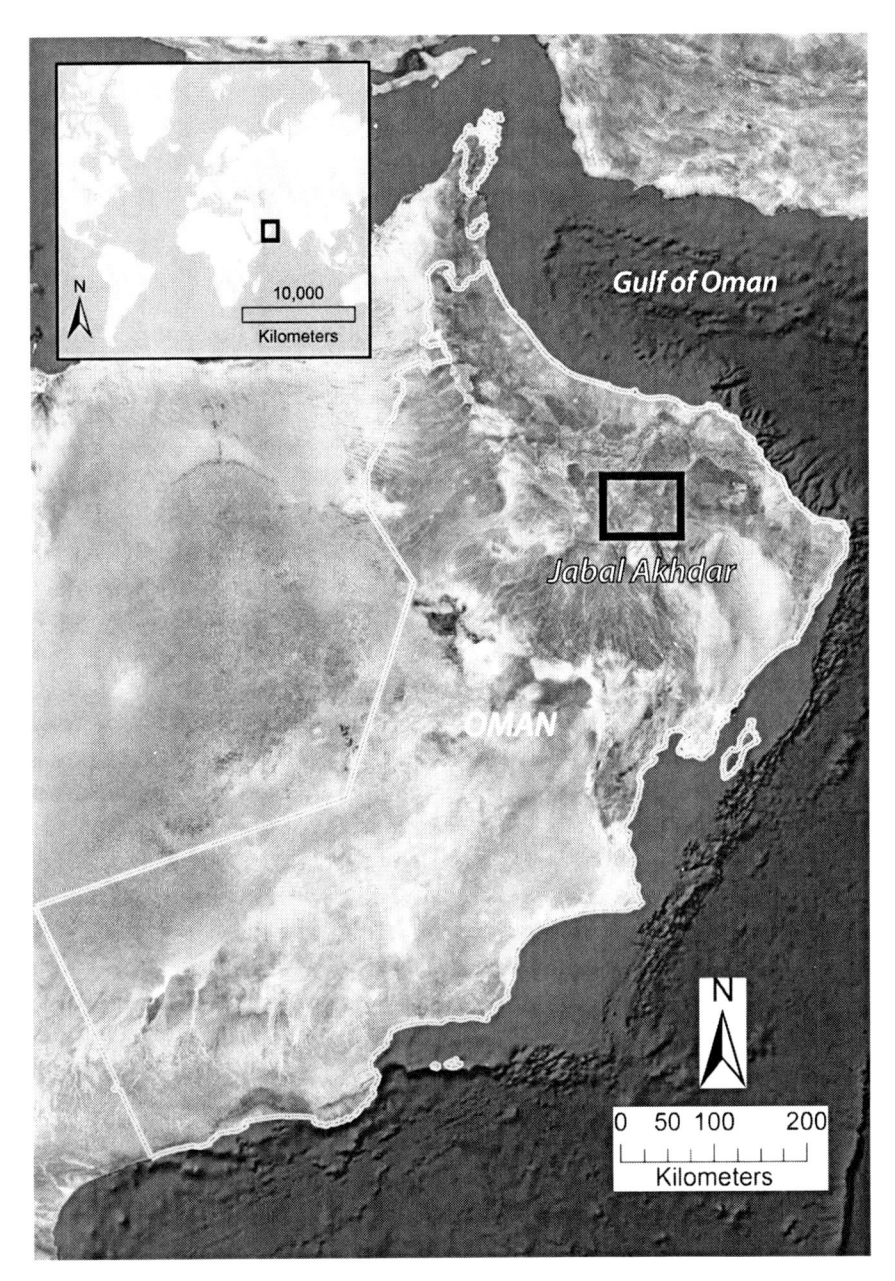

Indigenous Knowledge and Conservation Initiatives in Oman

Figure 1. Map of Jabal Akhdar region.

Sumāyil, Rustāq, and Nizwā) have total populations well under 10,000; for the most part the typical settlement has a population of between 500 and 2,500' (Wilkinson 1977, 17). However, we will now turn and examine only the Ad Dakhilīya region, where the Jabal Akhdar is located, in order to understand its unique characteristics and features.

Jabal Akhdar at the heart of Ad Dakhilīya

Jabal Akhdar is located at the heart of Ad Dakhilīya and has historically been an important trade centre because it supplied a variety of fruits and meat (in the form of goat and sheep) to the surrounding villages and towns. But first, it will be useful to describe Ad Dakhilīya both socially and physically. Ad Dakhilīya is bounded by the Ad Dhahirah region on the West, Ash Sharqiyah to the east and, to the north, Al Batinah. Ad Dakhilīya is inhabited mainly by tribespeople whose lifestyle is *ḥaḍar* (sedentary). Some of the pastoralist badu tribesmen own farms in some of the major settlements, however. Oasis agriculture, which involves cultivation and some livestock-herding, plays a major role in the economy and social organisation of Ad Dakhilīya. The aflaj system is crucial for irrigation since there is 'absolutely no rain-fed land (*ba'l*), and it is only the excess seasonal flow in the wadis and irrigation systems that is used for the growing of annual crops' (Wilkinson 1977, 28) such as wheat, barley, millet, sorghum and some vegetables. Situated in the middle of Ad Dakhilīya, the cool climate on the Jabal al-Akhdar mountain is totally different from the usually hot weather found in most of the towns and villages of the region. Temperatures as low as minus ten degrees have been observed in winter and in the summer the average temperature is around twenty degrees. The higher altitude also receives around 300 mm of annual rainfall. In this cool and relatively humid climate, temperate zone vegetables and fruits such pomegranates, peaches, apricots, figs, walnuts and grapes tend to flourish. Roses also grow in abundance, giving rise to a local industry producing rose water. Hence, it can be argued that Jabal Akhdar was once almost the bread basket of Ad Dakhilīya, or at least a principal supplier of food.

The key settlements in Ad Dakhilīya are in large towns such as Sumāyil, Rustāq, Nizwā, Nakhl, al-'Awabī, Izki and Bahla. Nizwa is the principal town of the region and has been the centre of Ibāḍī tradition and a seat for Imams and 'ulama (al-Hāshimi 2001, 105).[2]

---

2. Various tribes such as the Banī Riyām, Banī Ghāfir and Banī Hinā reside in Ad Dakhilīya. We must point out here that to name only certain tribes, stating that these are

Indigenous Knowledge and Conservation Initiatives in Oman

Jabal Akhdar: Analysis of Oman's unique ecosystem

The Jabal Akhdar is estimated to cover some 312,500 ha of rocky and stony rugged topography. According to Al-Mashakhi and Ahmed Koll, vegetation in Jabal Akhdar 'indicates that the rainfall is not less than 200–300 mm annually, which gives a vegetation cover with a higher proportion of grasses compared to that in other Northern areas' (2007, 14). The two authors add that, when compared to other Northern regions, the growing season is longer in Jabal Akhdar. A useful description of Jabal Akhdar's ecosystem is given by Katja Brinkmann et al.:

> The Jabal al Akhdar massif in the Hajar mountains of northern Oman has been classified as a local centre of plant endemism ... It belongs to the WWF's Global 200 ecoregion 'Arabian Highland Woodlands and Shrublands' occurring on the Arabian Peninsula, Yemen, Oman, Saudi Arabia and the United Arab Emirates with a total area of 470,000 km^2 and has an ecologically 'vulnerable' status ... Above 1500 m altitude, this area hosts about 33% of Oman's 1200 species of vascular plants, of which 14 taxa are endemic to Oman (2009, 1035–36).

Brinkmann also observed that 'pastoral livestock husbandry is the prevalent form of land use' (2009, 1036) in Jabal Akhdar, which Mashakhi and Ahmed Koll had noted as well and said that the 'Shawawi goat breeders' number nearly 10,000 people; thus, the total 'nomadic tribes which move along the northern and the southern range of mountains with herders in the Dhofar Mountains, are estimated at about seven to ten per cent of the country's population' (2007, 12). However, in terms of managing the rangeland ecosystem, Brinkmann explains that, 'it is important to study the relationships between environmental

---

'major tribes' inhabiting this particular area as historian John Peterson (1978, 16) and others have done, is, in our opinion, not a useful approach in explaining the spatial distribution of tribes. This is because there are so many tribes inhabiting these areas and to ignore most of them is to go against the meaning of 'tribalism', which is about territory, equilibrium, autonomy and *sharaf* (honour). In other words, not mentioning the areas that certain tribes inhabit (no matter how small the tribe) is by implication denying their existence. As a consequence, this will have an impact not only on their *sharaf* and autonomy but also on their space or landscape since tribes, as Dresch points out, are also 'territorial entities' (1989, 75); thus, also interfering with the existing equilibrium or balance of power. For example, the large town of Nizwa has more than 30 tribes, the town of Samail more than 20 tribes and the towns of Izki and Rustaq both have around 20 tribes each (al-Kharusi 2002, 325–363) and are all finely balanced within tribal ideology understood as Nizari and Yamani alliance tribal system and Ibāḍī ideology. The Dakhilīya also has non-tribal groups living in its region who are mainly the Bayasirah, Bayadir and Khuddam groups. By comparison these groups are the equivalent of Dhofar's *dhaʿif* (lit. weak) groups who historically had a subservient position

factors and vegetation' (2009, 1036). Remarkably, Brinkman does not highlight indigenous knowledge when it comes to studying the environment, whether by accident or design. For example in her data collection method she used 'GIS based analysis of GPS-tracked livestock grazing itineraries and animals' activity patterns classified as "resting", "grazing" and "walking" along the route. Further pasture areas of the surrounding settlements were defined by Dickhoefer et al. (submitted) based on farmer interviews' (2009, 1036). However, the interviews with the farmers that served as a basis for Dickhoefer et al. (2010), according to Brinkman, do not feature in the article. Said differently, we have read Dickhoefer et al.'s article carefully and still we could not get any information on these interviews in terms of hearing the 'natives speak', as it were. This does not mean that the interviews did not take place; it's just that the local voices were not included (even as a summary) in the academic text. Most anthropologists refer to the exclusion of indigenous narratives by saying the 'native's voice is muted'. Furthermore, we have read Dickhoefer's Ph.D. thesis (2009) and there is very little to gather on indigenous knowledge or local narratives on grazing, environment and so forth, even though she does refer to the importance of understanding and applying indigenous traditional knowledge.

Various other scholars who undertook studies on Jabal Akhdar's ecosystem have said little on how the local tribes that inhabited this unique terrain for thousands of years perceived or used their environment. For example, in an excellent article written by Schlecht et al., the authors observed the grazing itineraries of goats 'by means of Global Positioning Systems (GPS) during 4–5 days in each of the three villages' (2009, 357). Grazing behaviour was monitored in the morning when the goats were out for pasture by fixing a 'lightweight GPS collar … around the neck of one animal' and 'whenever possible, GPS raw files were differentially corrected using a Trimble ProXRS base station at Sayh Qatanah' (2009, 357). One cannot doubt the usefulness of this scientific method (including the use of electronic instruments) in an attempt to understand grazing behaviour, but this type of research should have been complemented or supported by understanding grazing from a socio-cultural perspective. Tribal communities – particularly herding communities – have ways to communicate with animals that are close to them, unlike an urban scientist who has been cut off from this human-animal interaction. Being among the *shawāwī* (goat-herders), one hears various stories such as goats knowing their the voice of their owners, finding their own way home and all sorts of symbolism and stories that show a close relation between man and beast, which would seem strange and unfathomable to an urban person whose instinct for

Indigenous Knowledge and Conservation Initiatives in Oman

and memory of dealing with non-human beings have been almost erased from his psyche, thanks to modernity. Thus, while the scientific method can record what animals actually do, people who have grown up with them can explain the reasons for their behaviour and even predict what they are likely to do in different circumstances.

Traditional notions and perceptions of territory

Neglecting indigenous knowledge will hamper our understanding of an ecosystem such as Jabal Akhdar whose territory has historically been defined as tribal lands, with each of the tribes knowing their boundaries from inside-out. The idea of the *dār* (homestead or tribal zone) is never doubted in principle, even though it is always contested and negotiated on the ground between the neighbouring tribes of Jabal Akhdar who inhabit almost forty settlements and whose livelihood still 'depends on traditional economic activities relating to agriculture, grazing, local trade, and handicrafts' (Busaidi 2012, 81). Therefore, the question of land or territory is another dimension that needs to be understood if management of rangelands and conservation is to be undertaken. In their insightful article, 'Customs excised: Arid land conservation in Syria', Rae et al. highlight the 'clash between formal and customary land tenure systems' (2002, 215) in the steppe area of Syria where for centuries 'tribal customary law held sway under the authority of local leaders' (ibid., 212). Even though this article is on Syria, it is relevant to Oman in terms of trying to understand territory based on *'urf* and *qanun*, laws under a modern nation state; 'the *qanun* is largely written, the *'urf* is largely unwritten' (ibid.) therefore creating problems whenever the question of ownership arises. In our own experience, we have seen several investment proposals for tourism projects in Jabal Akhdar fail to materialise because of land disputes between tribes based on *'urf*. In order to avoid any tribal backlash, the government treads carefully whenever the issue of land based on tribal ownership is concerned so as not to upset tribal equilibrium.

To further understand the importance of traditional territory, Wilkinson explains that:

> basic to the concept of *dar* (territory) are the notions about ownership … a starting point can be obtained from an examination of certain fundamental ideas concerning land organization in the *sharī'a* … in the Ibādi madhhab of Oman where the vast corpus of rulings concerning practical matters has very largely been harmonized with the local '*urf* (customary law) (1983, 303).

However, what is important for conservationists to note is that to the *ḥaḍr* (sedentary) and *bādū* (nomadic) tribes of Oman, the notions of territorial and sovereignty rights are linked with *dār* (territory generally associated with a specific tribe), which 'provides economic subsistence for the group and therefore one in which it has established exclusive and preferential rights over to others' (Wilkinson 1987, 129). Thus, neglecting this crucial concept of traditional territory is to do conservation a disservice. Management of rangelands will hardly be successful if one is ignorant of how local communities perceive and give meanings to their tribal territories, where ancestors have been born and buried, wars have been fought, identities have been formed, to name just a few of the reasons why people become so emotionally attached to their *dār*, besides being a place that 'provides economic subsistence'. As a social landscape, the *dār* is an autonomous *sharaf* – an imagined genealogical community. Throughout pre-modern Omani history, most tribal wars targeted the *dār* of one's rival, and men fought and some fell in protecting this 'sanctified' place. Thus, the emotional investment and sense of ownership of the *dar*, coupled with the Islamic obligation to act as guardians or stewards of the natural world mentioned earlier, make tribal organisation the obvious starting point for designing and implementing any conservation programme.

Another important element to understand is how the territory is perceived and narrated by indigenous intellectuals or leaders, be they poets, writers, *'ulamā'* (Islamic scholars) or tribal shaykhs. Landscape is not only about economics, politics or belonging, but also about aesthetics. Aesthetics can be a powerful tool to advance a cause; thus various Omani poets and writers have used poetry to praise landscape. For example, Sa'īd bin Alī al Mughārī, a prominent Omani scholar and historian captured nicely the perception of Omani Arabs when they first encountered the landscape of Zanzibar and its environs, which was once part of an Omani Empire. In drawing this literary picture of the landscape, al Mughārī creates a protagonist whom he calls *al musāfir* (the traveller): 'And from here the traveller gets nearer and catches sight of the four islands, after that he sees the country which appears as a splendid sight that merits Zanzibar as a garden of East Africa' (2001[1939], 76). The picture of this 'garden' becomes more vivid when al Mughārī describes *jazīyrat khadhrā'* (Green Island), which is the name the Arabs gave to Pemba island:

> And in this island, a person who settles here feels that time is always *'asr* (lit. afternoon; also, time before sunset) [whereby] the brilliance of its sun is a tender radiance (*'ishrāq raqīq*), illuminating its surrounding with its golden light (*bī'sha'tihā dhahbīyah*), sending luminous rays on its land and its trees and its

Indigenous Knowledge and Conservation Initiatives in Oman

wide array of plants. The hills set places apart [thus] hindering the describer in expressing and exploring (*istiqṣā*) this beauty; and from its green coast, there appears small [other] islands [made up] of emerald coral (*marjānīyah zamardīyah*), lying on the surface of the sea. (2001 [1939], 86; *translation from Arabic is mine*).

Al Mughārī's portrayal of the islands shows that Omani Arabs visualised these landscapes in terms of immense beauty usually expressed in poetic language that oscillates from secular poetry to Ibāḍī poetry. Painting an idyllic picture of these places should not come as a surprise, given that Omani Arabs originate from a country whose natural environment is a stark contrast to a tropical setting: an environment made up of formidable desert with chains of rocky, rugged mountains and scorching summer temperatures. It is therefore understandable that Omani Arabs portrayed their new abodes as beautiful gardens. Moreover, given the Arabs' penchant for poetry, it is not surprising that most of the descriptions of the landscape are articulated poetically. The point we are making is that landscape is also articulated aesthetically and this can draw people to settle in areas where they never thought they would. In this light, it is therefore also important to understand how landscape is portrayed through traditional arts such as poetry, music and literature, as all of these genres tend to evoke emotions and attachment to one's territory.

Having shown how imperative it is to understand traditional notions and perceptions of territory, we will now turn and examine how Oman, as a territory, has been defined by Western scholars as a dichotomous entity. This Western-derived image of Oman is so powerful that many Western scholars subscribed to it and, in my view, this image has also influenced Western conservationists assigned to undertake conservation programmes in Oman; in a sense, it has made those involved in conservation think that Western scholars are the final authorities when it comes to defining Oman's social and physical environment. Implicit in all this, is that the Western definition of Oman's ecology is 'superior' to or more 'scientific' than an indigenous description. In view of this, conservationists tend to refer to Western sources, as they are seen as authorities and, as a result, they neglect indigenous material and intellectuals. The only time an indigenous viewpoint is sought is through a controlled quantitative survey where respondents simply answer well-crafted questions, which are then used to justify that research is well-balanced as it incorporated a 'native viewpoint'. As a matter of fact, in such cases, the local people simply answered questions and ticked boxes and did not express any view! We are not belittling quantitative research, which is appropriately used by social scientists like geographers to study a wide range of topics including migration, settlement patterns, ethnic composition and segregation and so forth. The problem occurs when quantitative research is done in isolation without exploratory or qualitative work; that is, disregarding agency and the social cultural system and as a result, giving a false sense of objectivity by trying to separate the observer (scientist) from the observed (people) and by perceiving people as objects who lack meanings and values (Cloke et al. 1991). However, let us now turn and examine how the 'dichotomisation' of Oman has been conceived and justified, and then conclude this paper with a discussion on 'conservation without a human face' as it was (and is) practiced in Oman by Western consultants and NGOs.

The question that needs to be asked from the outset is, why do most of the Western scholars on Oman define the country in dichotomous terms? It is beyond the scope of this paper to answer this question, therefore, our focus is to highlight key literature and arguments on the 'dichotomisation' of Oman, which in our view, has influenced many researchers on Oman including conservationists and developers.

The 'dichotomisation' of Oman: A Western idea

One of the key examples that illustrates the dichotomisation of Oman by Western scholars comes from Wilkinson, who states that, 'Oman has a fundamental split personality, reflected in the title used until 1970 by the Al Bu Sai'd rulers, Sultan of Muscat and Oman' (1987, 1). Prior to Wilkinson, other scholars like Miles (1966 [1919]) and Landen (1967) have also described Oman in dichotomous terms but, in our view, Wilkinson's dichotomous analysis merits further investigation because his dualistic method has been adopted by various Western and Western-trained Arab scholars such as Peterson (1978), Skeet (1992), Ghabesh (2000), Kechichian (1995), Zahlan (1998) and many others. Oman, according to most of these scholars is a country of two great divisions: on the one hand, there is Ad Dakhilīya (the interior), which has usually been portrayed as a secretive, enclosed area, whereas, on the other hand, there is Al-Batinah (the coastal area), often described as open and outward-looking. For example, Peterson explained that 'the physical and psychological dichotomy between coast and interior up to the mid-twentieth century provided the most obvious division of Oman' (Peterson 1978, 16). Similarly, Skeet described the interior as tribal, Ibāḍī, mountainous and well known for its 'fundamental tribal and religious loyalties that were based on generations of historical tradition' (Skeet 1992, 33). Skeet described the coast as cosmopolitan, its people a mixture of indigenous farmers and sailors who had been infiltrated over the years by foreign merchants that gradually became indigenised. The inhabitants of the coast belonged to either Sunni or Shia sects rather than Ibāḍī (1992, 33). This last point expressed by Skeet is rather debatable: various major towns, given our own personal observation and familiarity with Al Batinah, consist of Arab tribes adhering to the Ibāḍī madhhab. However, what is interesting and unique and yet has not been examined is that one finds among Arab tribes two types of madhhab, the Sunni and Ibāḍī, which is rare in other regions of Oman. For example amongst the *banu shikel* from a town of Falaj al Qabail there are Ibāḍīs and Sunnis within the same tribe. The same occurs among the Mamamiry of Saham, the Jabri of Falaij al-Qabail and so on. Now this rarely happens (at least to our knowledge) in other parts of Oman. In Ad Dakhilīya, for instance, if the tribe is Ibāḍī (which is generally the case) the whole of it is Ibāḍī. In Dhofar, to take another example, if the tribe in Sunni-Shafi (as in most cases) than the whole tribe is Sunni-Shafi even if its members are dispersed in various areas of Dhofar. It is mainly in Al-Batinah that an Arab tribe can have both Ibāḍī and Sunni members, a point worth noting but beyond the scope of this study for further analysis.

Indeed, there are physical and historical differences between the coast and interior inasmuch as there are differences between the other main five regions of Oman, but our concern is to try and understand why scholars have been emphasising Dakhiliya/Batinah dualism when describing Oman. For instance, it is surprising to see Landen's description of Oman in dichotomous terms whilst at the same time he acknowledged that the country is 'cut into several distinct districts' (Landen 1967, 30). Why then place more emphasis on analysis based on dualism? In his work *Oman since 1856: Disruptive Modernisation in a Traditional Arab Society*, Landen states that, 'the coastal population has been more tolerant of foreigners and their differing habits and beliefs than have the isolated interior dwellers ... Ibadism of the coast in practice has been more moderate than the reserved, isolationist, conservative Ibadism of the interior' (1967, 38–9).

However a more analytical and in-depth understanding of dichotomisation of Oman comes from Wilkinson's study, *Water and Tribal Settlement in South-east Arabia: a Study of the Aflāj of Oman*. Wilkinson approaches the question of dichotomisation by first examining how the organisation of traditional economy contributes in 'creating the partial divorce' between Trucial Oman (what is now the United Arab Emirates) and non-Trucial Oman (i.e. the Sultanate of Oman). He explains that the relationship between local shaykhs who controlled the territory where pearling was conducted and the *tujjār* (merchants), mainly Indians from the sub-continent and indigenous traders, who controlled the finance of the pearl trade led to the development of an organised traditional economy. According to Wilkinson this 'international merchant' class came to acquire considerable power because they 'generated virtually all its foreign exchange' and 'more or less monopolized the means of contact with the outside world' (1977, 25). As a powerful and autonomous group, the merchants contributed in creating a political equilibrium between the rulers of these states: and that is, should one ruler 'try to gain control of a source of production or monopolize a sector in the communal industries by other than accepted commercial means, then his port was automatically ostracised' (1977, 25).

Although, Wilkinson described how traditional trade caused the split between Trucial and non-Trucial Oman, his main objective was to illustrate the point that the *tujjār*, particularly the Banian (Hindu merchants) whose commercial activities centred around port cities, also settled in Al Batinah (coastal Oman), which had a special locational advantage vis-à-vis commerce. As a result, local rulers and inhabitants came to tolerate the Banians who were also allowed to live according to their customs and practising their Hindu religion. Despite this tolerance of foreign customs, the fact remains that differences in attitudes and interests of these outsiders and local inhabitants have played a very important part in creating the split implicit in the title of the Sultanate, Muscat and Oman (Wilkinson 1977, 27). Based on this rationale, Wilkinson went on to explain that:

> Muscat represents the outward outward-looking, cosmopolitan trading society of the main port, frequently under foreign domination; Oman the independent inward-looking, predominantly tribal society of a subsistence economy. To some degree, the same kind of split existed throughout the rest of the Gulf, but there it rarely manifested itself in the form of territorial dichotomy because the economies of littoral states were predominantly maritime (1977, 27).

In this case, the main argument supporting Wilkinson's dichotomous analysis in relation to coastal and interior Oman is based on the development of traditional trade and the inter-relationship between local inhabitants and foreign merchants. Although these dichotomous phenomena clearly indicate oppositions, they are too few for one to make assumptions that Omani society is inherently dual or, to use Wilkinson's term, has a 'split personality'. In addition, there are too many paradoxes within Omani society, for one to argue that this is typically a 'coastal phenomenon' or this is a typically 'interior phenomenon' in order to justify the existence of the 'split personality'. So why has the dichotomisation

Indigenous Knowledge and Conservation Initiatives in Oman

of Oman been such a central topic to Western scholars even though this idea can longer be sustained as scientifically valid? In our view, the idea of 'theory' has played a major part in subdividing Oman, a country which was once so secretive that anthropologist Dale Eickelman dubbed it the 'Tibet of Arabia'. Theory has a special place in Western intellectual tradition because, as a form of 'systematic, scientific investigations into the foundations of human life', it also provides 'explanatory principles lying beneath immediate appearances, and behind what people might actually say are the reasons for their action' (James 2004, 18). So the dichotomisation of Oman, in our opinion, was theory-driven because scholars were searching for patterns that would explain hidden meanings in Omani society.

Conservation in Oman: A Western-expatriate domain

As noted above, conservationists who came to Oman, in our view, were influenced by Western writings on the country and therefore disregarded indigenous knowledge and interests, even if these were promoted by anthropologists such as Dawn Chatty, a point we will soon address. Some of these conservationists have read literature on Oman that was produced during the colonial era such as S.B. Miles, Bertram Thomas and Wilfred Thesiger, which all tend to exoticise Oman. In her essay, 'Colonial Archives and the Arts of Governance', Stoler highlights that colonial knowledge, including its categories, conceptual frames and practices, has been challenged and this includes its sources. Stoler writes:

> Questioning the making of colonial knowledge, and the privileged social categories it produced, has revamped what students of the colonial take to be sources of knowledge and what to expect of them (2002, 89).

The point to note is that documents written from the colonisers' perspective make it hard to discern the experiences and views of the natives. In other words, whatever the coloniser said was taken as unchallenged truth because it came from a dominant authority, one who was European. In *Colonialism and its Forms of Knowledge*, Cohn has stated that the relation between power and knowledge in the colonial state found its expression in the classifying and categorising efforts of colonial officials in their pursuit of control over the colonised masses. Seeing things from this point of view, we will come to understand, for example, why the conservationists who arrived in Oman in 1980 disregarded local knowledge or input. Let us now turn to one crucial example which is quite telling!

In her article, 'Animal reintroduction projects in the Middle East', Chatty explains that projects such as the reintroduction of the Arabian oryx in Oman in the late 1970s and 1980s regarded the 'local human population as obstacles to overcome … instead of partners in sustainable conservation and development' (2002, 228). Chatty goes on to explain that the failure of reintroduction of the Arabian Oryx in Yaaloni in the central Omani desert, can be attributed to several factors but key among them was the failure to involve the local tribes that inhabit the region where the oryx were introduced (ibid., 230). For example, when the Oryx sanctuary was set up in Jiddat Harasis, Chatty explains that the decision 'was made in Muscat by the expatriate advisor and the international consultants on hand' (211). The local tribes were 'summoned and informed' (231) after the decision had been taken. In fact, Chatty met the expatriate advisor of this project and asked him, 'how would he deal with the impact of his project' (231) and the advisor replied that, 'I am not interested in people, only plants and animals' (231). Chatty goes on to explain that, since the local tribal community was not consulted, the tribal community's 'hawta' (sanctuary) was impacted by this project. Consequently not only did the Arabian Oryx reintroduction totally fail as a project but the site was also removed from the World Heritage List. In order to implement a successful conservation programme in Oman, Chatty says, it is imperative to involve 'grass-roots, local-level approaches which emphasize co-ownership and management, and capacity building' (234).

Conclusion

The evolution of Oman's indigenous knowledge with regard to nature and conservation is a process that occurred over a wide span of time and was shaped by social, cultural and historical forces. An important social-cultural force that played a huge role in defining Oman's ecology is its unique tribal system. This is a phenomenon that can be broadly described in terms of autonomy, territoriality, honour (*sharaf*) and alliance system (*hilf*). Failure to grasp how these concepts function can lead to distortion and misrepresentation of the Omani tribal system, making it difficult to understand how indigenous conservation methods were envisioned since they are linked to the tribal system and other areas of socio-cultural organisation. As noted above, outsiders or expatriates seeking to protect natural ecosystems often attempt to do so by excluding indigenous inhabitants. This approach derives partly from ignorance concerning indigenous systems of ecological knowledge and practice. It thus falls to anthropologists, especially those interested in ecology, to interpret the 'insiders' ecology' to outsiders.

Indigenous Knowledge and Conservation Initiatives in Oman

This paper will later be augmented by incorporating two case studies undertaken through fieldwork and interviews with indigenous experts on plants (ethnobotany) and mountain pastoralists on grazing (traditional land use) in Jabal Akhdar.

References

Berkes, F. 2008. *Sacred Ecology. Traditional Ecological Knowledge and Resource Management*, 2nd Edition. Philadelphia: Taylor and Francis.

Berkes, F. and C. Folke. 2002. 'Back to the future: Ecosystem dynamics and local knowledge'. In L.H. Gunderson and C.S. Holling (eds) *Panarchy: Understanding Transformations in Human and Natural Systems*. Washington, DC: Island Press. pp. 121–146.

Brinkmann, K. et al. 2009. 'Vegetation patterns and diversity along an altitudinal and a grazing gradient inthe Jabal al Akhdar mountain range of northern Oman'. *Journal of Arid Environments* 73: 1035–45.

Buerkert. A. et al. 2009. 'Ecology and morphological traits of an ancient Musa *acuminata* cultivar from a mountain oasis of Oman'. *Genet Resour Crop Evol* 56: 609–14.

Al-Busaidi, M. 2012. *The Struggle between Nature and Development: Linking Local Knowledge with Sustainable Natural Resource Management in Al-Jabal Al-Akhdar Region, Oman*. Ph.D. thesis, University of Glasgow.

Callicott J.B. and M.P. Nelson (eds). 1998. *The Great New Wilderness Debate*. Athens GA and London: University of Georgia Press.

Chatty. D. 2002. 'Animal reintroduction projects in the Middle East: Conservation without a human face', in D. Chatty and M. Colchester (eds), *Conservation and Mobile Indigenous Peoples: Displacement, Forced Settlement, and Sustainable Development*. New York: Berghahn Books. pp. 227–44.

Cloke. P, C. Philo and D. Sadler. 1991. *Approaching Human Geography*. London: Chapman.

Cohn, B.S. 1987. *An Anthropologist Among the Historians and other Essays*, Delhi: Oxford University Press.

Dickhoefer, U. 2009. *Tradition and Transformation: Steps towards a Sustainable Goat Husbandry in Mountain Oases of Oman*. Ph.D. Thesis, Kassel; University Press, GmbH, Kassel, Germany.

Dickhoefer U., A. Buerkert, K. Brinkmann and E. Schlecht. 2010. 'The role of pasture management for sustainable livestock production in semi-arid subtropical mountain regions'. *Journal of Arid Environments* 74: 962–72.

Dumont, L. 1970. *Homo hierarchicus: the Caste System and its Implications*. Chicago: University of Chicago Press.

Escobar. A. 1998. 'Whose knowledge, whose nature? Biodiversity, conservation, and the political ecology of social movements'. *Journal of Political Ecology* 5: 53–82.

Fisher, M., S.A. Ghazanfar, S.A. Chaudhary, P.J. Seddon, E.F. Robertson, S. Omar, J.A. Abbas and B. Boer. 1998. 'Diversity and conservation'. In S.A. Ghazanfar and M. Fisher (eds), *Vegetation of the Arabian Peninsula*. London: Kluwer Academic Publishers. pp. 265–302.

Salah al Mazrui

Ghanzafar, S.A. 1991. 'Vegetation structure and phytogeography of Jabal Shams, an arid mountain in Oman'. *Journal of Biogeography* **18**: 299–309.

Hakim, B.S. 1994. 'The "Urf" and its role in diversifying the architecture of traditional Islamic cities'. *Journal of Architectural and Planning Research* **11**(2): 108–127.

Harmon, D. 2002. *In Light of Our Differences*. Washington, DC: Smithsonian Institution Press.

Al-Hāshimi, M.S. (N.D). *Imām Nūr Dīn al-Sālimī wā rāu' fi al-'ilahiyāt*. Sīb, Oman: Maktabat al-ḍāmrī.

Al-Hāshimi, S.M. 2001. '"Dowr 'ulamā" Nizwa as-siyāsī 'abr al-'uṣūr'. In *Nizwa 'Abr Attārīkh*. Oman: Wizārat turāth al-Qawmī wā thaqāfa.

Ibn Khaldun, A. 1958. *The Muqadimmah*. Translated from Arabic by F. Rosenthal. Princeton: Princeton University Press. Kelly, J.B. 1959. *Sultanate and Imamate in Oman*. London: Royal Institute of International Affairs.

Kelly, J.B. 1964. *Eastern Arabia Frontiers*. London: Faber; New York: Praeger

Kelly, J.B. 1956. 'The Buraimi oasis dispute'. *International Affairs* **32**: 318–26.

Kelly, J.B. 1972. 'A prevalence of furies: tribes, politics and religion in Oman and Trucial Oman'. In D. Hopwood (ed.) *The Arabian Peninsula: Society and Politics*. London: George Allen and Unwin

Kelly, J.B. 1976. 'Hadramaut, Oman, Dhufar: the experience of revolution', *Middle East Studies* **12**: 213–30.

Kelly, J.B. 1980. *Arabia, the Gulf and the West*. London: Weidenfield and Nicolson.

Khalid, F.M. (n.d.) *Qur'an Creation and Conservation: An Introduction to the ethical foundations of Islamic Environmentalism*, Islamic Foundation for Ecology and Environmental Sciences, http://www.ifees.org.uk/wp-content/uploads/2015/04/1380144345.pdf

Landen, R.G. 1967. *Oman Since 1856: Disruptive Modernisation in a Traditional Society*. Princeton: Princeton University Press

Kramer, R.A., and C.P. van Schaik. 1997. 'Preservation paradigms and tropical rain forests'. In R.A. Kramer, C.P. van Schaik and J. Johnson (eds) *Last Stand: Protected Areas and the Defense of Tropical Biodiversity*. New York: Oxford University Press. pp. 3–14.

Maffi, L. (ed). 2001. *On Biocultural Diversity*. Washington, DC: Smithsonian Institution Press.

Al-Mashakhi, M.S.A. and B.A.K. El-Hag. 2007. Country Pasture/Forage Resource Profiles: Oman. FAO.

McCabe. J.T. 2002. 'Giving conservation a human face: Lessons from forty years of combining conservation and development in Ngorongoro conservation area, Tanzania'. In D. Chatty and M. Colchester (eds) *Conservation and Mobile Indigenous People: Displacement, Forced Settlement, and Sustainable Development*. New York: Berghahn Books. pp. 61–77.

Miles, S.B. 1910. 'On the border of the Great Desert'. *Geographical Journal* **36**: 159–78.

Miles, S.B. 1919. *The Countries and Tribes of the Persian Gulf*. London: Harrison & Sons.

Al-Mughairy, S. 2001. *Juhaynat al-akhbār fi tārīkh Zinjibār*. Oman: Wizārat turāth al-Qawmī wā thaqāfa.

Nazarea. V. D. 2006. 'Local knowledge and memory in biodiversity conservation'. *Annu. Rev. Anthropology* **35**: 317–35.

Patzelt, A. 2009: *The Mountain Vegetation of Northern Oman: Al Jabal al Akhdar Initiative: Conservation and Sustainable Development in a Fragile Arid Mountain Ecosystem.* Research Report, Sultan Qaboos University, Muscat, Oman.

Peterson, J. 1978. *Oman in the Twentieth Century: Political Foundations of an Emerging State.* London: Croom Helm.

Peterson, J. 1987. 'Oman's odyssey: From Imamate to Sultanate'. In B.R. Pridham (ed.), *Oman: Economic, Social and Strategic Developments*, London: Croom Helm.

Pilgrim, S., L. Cullen, D.J. Smith and J. Pretty. 2008. 'Ecological knowledge is lost in wealthier communities and countries'. *Environmental Science and Technology* **42**: 1004–9.

Rae, J., G. Arab and D. Nordblom. 2002. 'Customs excised: Arid land conservation in Syria'. In D. Chatty and M. Colchester (eds) *Conservation and Mobile Indigenous Peoples: Displacement, Forced Settlement, and Sustainable Development.* New York: Berghahn Books. pp. 212–227.

Sauer, C.O. 1965. 'The morphology of landscape'. In J. Leighly (ed.) *Land and Life.* Berkeley: University of California Press. pp. 315–350.

Schlecht, E., U. Dickhoefer, E. Gumpertsberger and A. Buerkert. 2009. 'Grazing itineraries and forage selection of goats in the Jabal al Akhdar mountain range of northern Oman'. *Journal of Arid Environments* **73**: 355–63.

Schlecht E., U. Dickhöfer, M. Predotova and A. Buerkert. 2011. 'The importance of semi-arid natural mountain pastures for feed intake and recycling of nutrients by traditionally managed goats on the Arabian Peninsula'. *Journal of Arid Environments* **75**: 1136–46.

Skeet, I. 1992. *Oman: Politics and Development.* New York: St. Martin's Press.

Stefan S., N. Maher and A. Buerkert. 2007. 'Climate and irrigation water use of a mountain oasis in northern Oman'. *Agricultural Water Management* **89**: 1–14.

Stoler, A.L. 2002. 'Colonial archives and the arts of governance'. *Archival Science* **2**: 87–109.

Taylor, D.A. 2000. 'The rise of the environmental justice paradigm: Injustice framing and the social construction of environmental discourses'. *Am. Behavi. Sci.* **43**: 508–80.

Terborgh, J. 1999. *Requiem for Nature.* Washington, DC: Island Press/Shearwater Books.

Thesiger, W.P. 1983. *Arabian Sands.* London: Collins.

Thomas, B.S. 1932. *Arabia Felix: Across the Empty Quarter of Arabia.* London

Thomas, B.S. 1929. 'Among some unknown tribes of South Arabia'. *JRAI* **59**: 97–112.

Thomas, B.S. 1932. 'Anthropological Observations in South Arabia'. *JRAI* **62**: 3–11.

Thomas, B.S. 1937. 'Four strange tongues from South Arabia – the Hedara group'. *Proceedings of the British Academy* **23**.

Turner, N. and F. Berkes. 2006. 'Coming to understanding: Developing conservation through incremental learning in the Pacific Northwest'. *Human Ecology* **34**: 495–513.

Wilkinson, J.C. 1964. 'A sketch of the historical geography of the Trucial Oman down to the beginning of the 16th century'. *Geographical Journal* **130**.

Wilkinson, J.C. 1971. 'The Oman question: the background to political geography of South-East Arabia'. *Geographical Journal* 137: 361–71.

Wilkinson, J.C. 1972. 'The origins of the Omani state'. In Derek Hopwood (ed.) *The Arabian Peninsula: Society and Politics*. London: George Allen and Unwin.

Wilkinson, J.C. 1974. 'Bayāsirah and Bayādir'. *Arabian Studies* 1: 75–85.

Wilkinson, J.C. 1975. 'The Julanda of Oman'. *Journal of Oman Studies* 6: 97–108.

Wilkinson, J.C. 1977. *Water and Tribal Settlements in South East-Arabia: A Study of the Aflaj in Oman*. Oxford: Clarendon.

Wilkinson, J.C. 1981. 'Oman and East Africa: New light on early Kilwan History from the Omani Sources'. *International Journal of African Studies* 14: 272–305.

Wilkinson, J.C. 1983. 'Traditional concepts of territory in South-East Arabia'. *Geographical Journal* 149: 301–15.

Wilkinson, J.C. 1987. *The Imamate Tradition of Oman*. Cambridge: Cambridge University Press.

Zahran, M.A. and H.A. Younes. 1990. 'Hema System: Traditional Conservation of Plant Life in Saudi Arabia'. *Journal of King Abdulaziz University – Science* 2: 19–41. https://www.researchgate.net/publication/268428826_Hema_System_Traditional_Conservation_of_Plant_Life_in_Saudi_Arabia

Chapter 7

AFGHAN/PAKISTAN BORDER POLITICS:
WHAT FUTURE FOR KUCHI NOMADS?

Inam ur Rahim

Introduction

Pastoral systems occupy 25 per cent of the global land area and on marginal lands mobile livestock rearing is more advantageous than other land uses (FAO 2001) In general, the resource base of the mobile pastoralist is flexible and collective mechanisms for access and use of the resource base have been evolved through centuries of experience (Sandford and Habtu 2000, Thebaud and Batterbury 2001). In Afghanistan only five per cent of land is arable and most of the rest is either inaccessible and barren, or mainly suitable for supporting pastoral livelihoods and used for grazing (Wily 2013). The seasonal variation in forage availability has led to the evolution of mobile herding patterns of different scales and kinds.

Kuchi, an Afghan Persian word meaning 'those who migrate', is the common term used for Afghan nomadic pastoralists (Tapper 2008). Kuchi constitute ten per cent of the total Afghan population, but own up to fifty per cent of the national herd (Weijer 2005). Kuchi groups are found among all Afghan tribes; however, over eighty per cent are Durrani and Ghilzai Pakhtun. There are about 2.4 million Kuchi in Afghanistan, of whom around 1.5 million (sixty per cent) remain fully nomadic and dispersed through almost the whole of Afghanistan, with the majority using the central Afghanistan highlands for summer grazing. The rest have recently become partly or fully sedentary due to loss of livestock, restricted mobility, security threats and the conversion of pastures into agriculture land (WFP 2011).

Despite difficulties in maintaining a herding lifestyle, Kuchi provide a majority of the mutton supply in Afghanistan. Besides contributing to food security, Kuchi produce some of the world's finest carpets and rugs, as well as raw cashmere. Afghanistan is the third largest producer of raw cashmere (around seven per cent) after China and Mongolia (Weijer 2007). Kuchi are custodians of some of the finest animal genetic resources, including the famous Karakul sheep (Jacobs and Schloeder 2012). The four decades of war and insurgency since the 1978 coup have had a major impact on Kuchi livestock wealth, production practices and precise contributions to the Afghan economy, with different effects on different tribes.

Central Afghanistan's high pastures cover above forty per cent of its land surface. Millions of ruminants are brought there for summer grazing by Kuchi nomads (Robson et al. 2002). The lowland wintering areas lie all around the central highlands and extend up to the Amu River in the north, the Registan desert in the southwest bordering Iran and the western bank of the Indus River in the southeast in Pakistan. Thus, for many nomads their traditional transhumance routes involve crossing the Afghan/Pakistan border, commonly known as the Durand line.

The Durand line, that stretches 2,430 kilometres along the southern and eastern edges of Afghanistan, is its longest border. Different sedentary, semi-nomadic and nomadic Pakhtun tribes and other indigenous communities straddle the border. A special political administration was established to govern the native Pakhtun tribes resisting colonial rule, which still continues with little modification to date (Lewal 2010). For the past few decades, the areas on both sides of the line have been plagued by terrorism and extremist activities (UNHCR 2006), which have deeply impacted the resident population on both sides of the Durand line, as well as Kuchi using the mountain passes along the line (Khan 2010).

The Kuchi have been identified by the United Nation Assistance Mission in Afghanistan as one of the largest vulnerable populations in the country. During the past four decades, their movement across the Durand Line has been hindered. As Afghanistan's population grows, competing claims over summer pastures, both for rain-fed cultivation and for grazing of the settled communities' livestock, have created conflict over land across central and northern Afghanistan (Wily 2013). Despite the existence of border controls, many Kuchi were allowed to cross the border till 2016 as the relevant officials recognised the routine seasonal Kuchi migrations even in times of political turmoil. The border was once closed during the Pakistan-Afghanistan dispute during 1961–63, having a large-scale impact on Kuchi livelihood (Foschini 2011). More recently, the Pakistani government has embarked on the construction of a physical barrier and completed a trench along the Baluchistan portion of the Durand line in 2016. Once the trench is completed along the entire border, crossing will only be possible at official crossing points, which will reduce the already limited livelihood options of the Kuchi.

The context

Historical context

During the sixteenth and seventeenth centuries, Afghanistan was the focus of competition between the Persian and Moghul Empires. After the death of the Persian emperor Nadir Shah in 1747, Pakhtun soldiers returned to their tribal lands. They convened a Jirga, which established an independent government in Kandahar headed by the army commander, Ahmad Khan Abdali, belonging to the Sadozai line of the Abdali tribe (Munoz 2010). He subsequently took the name Ahmad Shah Durrani and his tribe became known as the Durrani tribe. The state established by Durrani included not only the Pakhtun traditional areas but the whole of present-day Afghanistan and Pakistan.

Though from 1747–1973, the country ,and a major portion of Pakistan, was largely ruled by Pakhtun tribes occupying the southwestern part, the population is heterogeneous, with Sunni Muslims (including most Pakhtuns) in the majority. The central highlands are occupied by the Persian-speaking Shia Hazaras, the north mostly by Sunni Tajiks and north-west by Turkic speaking Uzbek and Turkmen (Foust 2008). Figure 1 shows the distribution of different ethnic communities inside Afghanistan (Dorronsoro, 2009).

During the nineteenth century, the Afghan state came under pressure from the British Empire expanding northwards and the Russian Empire expanding southwards. Two Anglo-Afghan wars were fought before Afghanistan was established within its current boundaries during 1880–1901 and was officially declared a buffer state under the Anglo-Russian Treaty of 1907 (Grenville and Wasserstein 2001). It lost part of the Pakhtun traditional territory, stretching from the current border to the Indus River, to British India. During the early twentieth century, in return for support in World War One, the British offered to hand over the territories lost in the Second Afghan War (1878–1880); however, the then king of Afghanistan Habibullah declined (Smith et al. 1973).

Following the Russian-backed revolution of 1978, the new leaders' first priority was to impose a socialist system. They used violence as a tool and considered the traditional tribal leadership as the main hurdle to their ultimate objectives. This led to revolt everywhere in the country and the resistance of

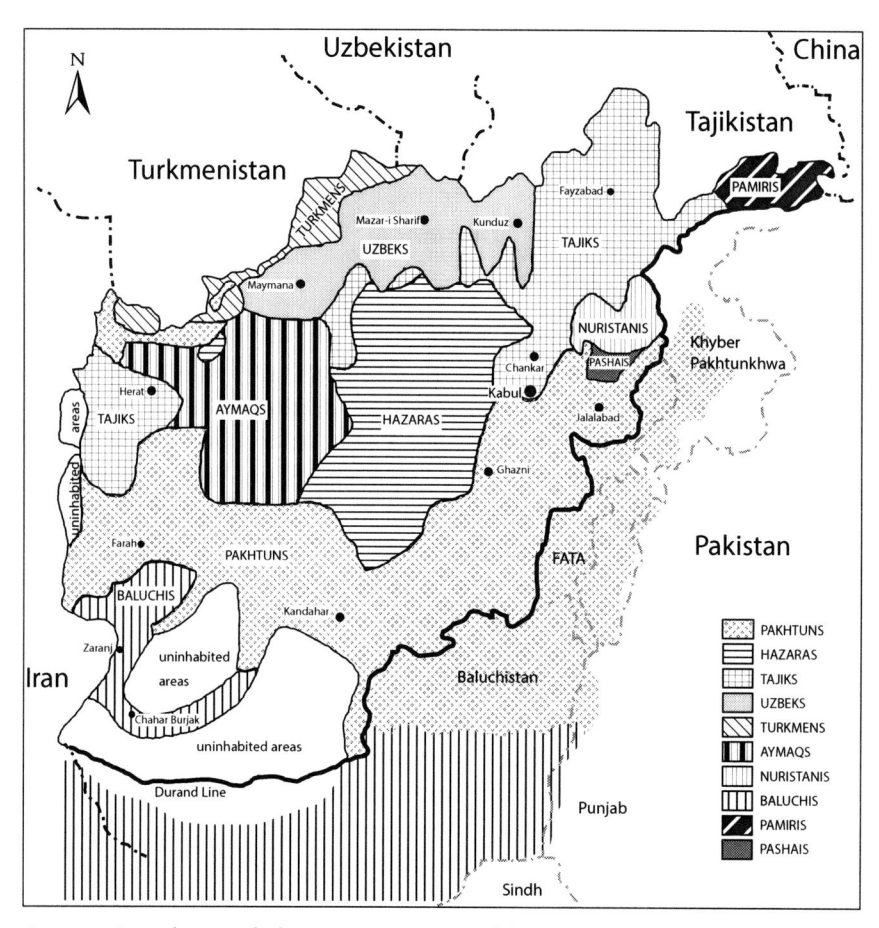

Figure 1. Distribution of ethnic communities in Afghanistan. Based on Dorronsoro, 2009.

a strong tribal society to protect its customs was further fuelled by the Soviet Army's invasion in support of the government.

Widespread opposition to the regime was supported by the US through its proxies (the Mujahideen). When eventually the Russians withdrew and the government fell, a power-sharing agreement collapsed and the country descended into a situation of civil war, with rival warlords seeking to extend control beyond their own tribal areas. The Taliban achieved dominance of the central and southern part of the country. But at this point the 11 September 2001 attacks in the US by Al-Qaeda terrorists based in Afghanistan and linked to the Taliban provoked an American invasion (Cronin 2002).

Afghan/Pakistan Border Politics

Since the American invasion in late 2001, the method of subduing hostile Pakhtun tribes by establishing small, safe militarised areas and then extending outward has obviously failed because of the social and ethnic fragmentation within the country. Stabilising one area in the south and south-east does not usually benefit its neighbourhood in a scenario where different groups and villages compete with each other for the spoils of a war economy. The competence of the bureaucracy to implement the rule of law and manipulate local politics for peace across the Pakhtun belt is very limited (Dorronsoro 2009).

Monopolising the use of force in such a fragile stratified society as Afghanistan is an extremely difficult task that takes time, and forcing the government to directly establish a modern state seems to undermine the effort of state-building (Brast 2012) During the last centuries, many attempts have been made to create a strong central state in Afghanistan, but all in vain. Periods of stability were rather during weak central government (Rubin 1995). Establishing a strong central government in a fragile and stratified Afghan tribal society would require an appropriate assembly of many interacting factors (Schetter et al. 2006).

Socio-political context

From the inception of the state in 1747, the central government co-existed with strong local Afghan tribal societies. Kuchi are interwoven in the Afghan tribal structures and organised into clans with a clear leadership structure (Weijer 2007). The dominance of local tribal governance structures has existed in Afghanistan since at least 500 BC when the Persian Emperor Darius was strongly resisted by 'small tribal kingdoms' during his campaign in the territory. The services of Afghan tribal warriors have also been repeatedly used by invaders during their successive invasions of Indian territory. With the establishment of the state, tribal structures were incorporated into the larger state framework (Guittard 2011).

Pakhtuns take collective action at the community level. The key actors in different tribes form alliances (*dalla*) within and across the tribes. Conflicts and cooperation within the tribe, across the tribes and with the outside world occur through these *dalla*s rather than tribes, hence the *dalla* is more relevant than the tribe. The *dalla*s also play an important role in preventing patron–client relationships with the state (Dupree 1980). A tribe may have disputes, but in a case of external aggression will unite until the aggression is over. Such an arrangement is called '*tiga*' and is symbolised by placing a stone at the site where an agreement is reached. The concept of collective Pakhtun tribal authority is also inherently opposed to any ambitions for being above the tribe. The society has even peacefully co-existed during periods with no centralised state authority; territories where such a system exists are locally termed '*Yaghistan*'. Leadership in a Pakhtun community is not hereditary but depends on the known ability and wisdom of the available contenders (Rahim and Viaro 2002).

Though the traditional communal mechanisms followed by Kuchi have been weakened by the continued war (Lamb 2012), they have also shown resilience. During the periods of relative peace in some regions, the Kuchi, who had been obliged by the war and mines to settle down, have again started a mobile way of life (Kreutzmann and Schütte 2011, Schütte 2012, Tapper 2008). In Afghanistan, the 'Pasture Law' of 1970 codified the property rights of the government to include all pastureland, with some amendment during the period of Taliban control in 2000. Currently, the pasture law is being redrafted to incorporate community-based pasture management systems (Kreutzmann and Schütte 2011).

Following the years of warfare, Afghanistan was one of the most heavily mined countries in the world. Efforts to remove the mines are prioritised according to the number of human and livestock casualties. As a consequence, the majority of de-mining efforts to date have focused on settlement areas, roads and infrastructure where there is regular, frequent human activity. The Kuchi remain vulnerable as a consequence, because of their reliance on rangelands and because it can take time to reach the critical threshold of casualties triggering a de-mining response, given that they tend to use most areas on a seasonal basis only (Jacobs and Schloeder 2012).

Kuchi have traditionally kept diverse livestock breeds to help them meet their diverse needs. These animals are well adapted to the prevailing environment and biophysical resources. They have better reproductive performance, higher fertility rates and short gestation periods, and are less susceptible to disease. They do, however, have a tendency to inbreeding and crossbreeding. Most of these indigenous breeds should be documented and information about their demographic trends made available; this information is very valuable to understand their sustainability needs and their biocultural identity, and thus to develop ways they can better respond to changes in their environment.

The Kuchi constitute a particularly disadvantaged group with respect to many social indicators like access to education, health and livelihood standards (Foschini 2011). The name 'Kuchi' indicates a mobile way of life, but different parts of the same tribe may follow a sedentary or a mobile life. Mobile tribe members are therefore in complementary social bonding with their seden-

Afghan/Pakistan Border Politics

tary relatives. In case of drought or some disease outbreak, they may opt to leave their animals with their sedentary relatives and, in return, help to graze their animals. They also lend money to sedentary crop producers in time of need (Engelen 2006). The Kuchi are mostly Pakhtun and follow the code of Pushtunwali. This code determines social order and responsibilities and acts as their constitution. It contains sets of values pertaining to honour, solidarity, hospitality, mutual support, shame and revenge, both for the individual and the tribe (Rahim and Viaro 2002).

Institutional context

Afghanistan has a Kuchi department that is solely dedicated to representing Kuchi interests at the governmental level. However, in Pakistan, there is no forum available for discussions between Kuchi and sedentary populations, to resolve issues critical to their survival. Relevant policymakers are unaware of the situation facing Kuchi and do not appreciate their valuable economic and societal contributions. Kuchi flocks are not counted in the routine livestock and agriculture census. The Kuchi have no access to public education and health services, mainly because of their constant migratory patterns and the fact that they live most of their lives in remote mountain areas. The literacy rate of this population is negligible and non-existent among women.

Kuchi also pose a number of problems for policymakers by their transnational mobility. Unlike sedentary farmers, Kuchi tend to cross borders in search of forage, regardless of national governments' policies (Blench 2001). Kuchi movement, with their animals, is tailored to the growth cycle of forage plants, and uses camels and donkeys to help in transport. They entirely depend on mobile livestock keeping for their livelihood (FAO 2003).

Livestock health and productivity services have not been extended to mobile landless herders, either for treating diseases or for preventive measures. The incidence of zoonotic diseases has never been investigated and documented, although there is a high risk that the mobile livestock could spread disease not only to the mobile herders but to the resident public and their livestock. Wildlife species are also prone to these diseases and epidemics have been reported. The annual livestock suffering diseases has the potential to reach up to 22 per cent. There is no efficient mechanism for quality control of veterinary medicines or vaccines in Afghanistan and Pakistan. The Kuchi have no access to quality diagnosis laboratories.

Local traditions and formal governance institutions related to grazing lands are either weak or dysfunctional. The traditional leadership pattern of experience in collective bargaining for fodder resources has gradually been eroded and more individualistic competition is occurring. The agreement between landowners and the Kuchi is not formal, but a tacit understanding between the two parties that has been in place for centuries. The custodian landlord or community does not limit stocking of livestock, but is concerned with bid money for the season. There is no long-term secure grazing tenure for herders and Kuchi feel little stake in the conservation and sustainable use of the range resources.

The mobility pattern

Kuchi were able to sustain their nomadic system during turbulent periods of Afghan history through close interactions with the resident communites on both sides of the Durand line, which like other international boundaries in colonial Asia, was drawn on a political basis without regard to the pastoral macro environment. Communities practicing cross-border mobile pastoralism are greatly affected during adverse interstate relations (Nori et al. 2005).

Kuchi are scattered through most of Afghanistan and part of Pakistan up to the western boundaries of the Indus. Weijer (2005) has classified Kuchi into the following broad categories:

- Long range pastoralists (LRP), travelling long distances between lowlands and uplands, including trans-boundary mobility between Pakistan and the Central Highlands of Afghanistan. They have large flocks of sheep, goats, and camels (800–1,200). All household members are involved in livestock management

- Short-range pastoralists (SRP), travelling short distances between lowland and upland, either in Afghanistan or Pakistan. They have medium sized multi-species flocks ranging from 150–300 animals and they are in the process of diversifying their livelihood.

- Recently settled agro-pastoralists (RSAP), with small primarily cattle herds, ranging from five to 25 animals and partly depending on cropping and transport services. For example, Nasar Kuchis are increasingly shifting their focus from livestock to transportation, provision of agricultural services through their tractors, wage labour, fuelwood sale and sale of clothes. Some of them have also purchased agricultural lands in Dera Ghazi Khan and Jacobabad in Punjab and Sindh and have shifted their dependency from mobile herding to cropping.

Afghan/Pakistan Border Politics

Generally, the bigger the flock, the longer the distance travelled between uplands and lowlands. Hence flocks numbering less than 300 animals occasionally cross the border and remain mobile either on the Afghan or Pakistani side of the Durand line throughout the year. Figure 2 shows the broader mobility patterns prevailing in different parts of Afghanistan (Barfield and Szabo 1991).

Mobility across the Durand line

During their seasonal migration, a large number of Kuchi cross the Durand line to spend their winter months in different parts of Pakistan. The Kuchi tribes crossing through different passes into Baluchistan include Kakarh, Achakzai, Tharakai, Sulaiman Khel, Nasar, Ghilji, Kharoti, Shinwari, Razakhel and Dur-

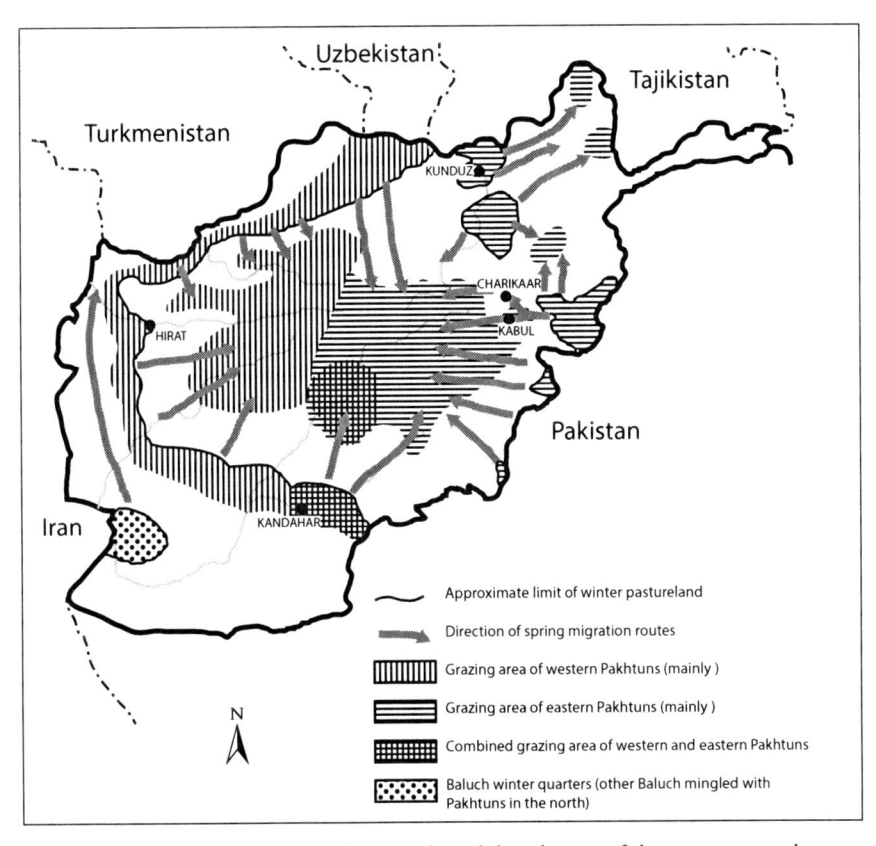

Figure 2. Mobility pattern of Kuchi nomads and distribution of their summer and winter areas in Afghanistan. Based on Barfield and Szabo 1991, 257.

rani. The Kuchi tribes visiting Khyber Pakhtunkhwa include Ahmad Zai, Khazar Khel, Sultan Khel, Haji Khel, Imran Khel, Tara Khel and Kharoti. The Kuchi visiting Naran valley belong to Ahmad Zai tribes, with sub-tribes, including Gulmat Khel, Sultan Khel, Mirali Khel and Akorh Khel. The composition of the tribes in the Pakhtun belt of Baluchistan is the same as that of the Kuchi tribes. In comparison, in Khyber Pakhtunkhwa, the tribal composition of the Kuchi differs from the resident Pakhtun population.

Owners of larger flocks, travelling between the highlands of Hazarajat and the lowlands of the Indus plains, also traded in clothes, rugs and carpets and food items before the 1970s when transport facilities were meagre (Weijer 2007). Some Kuchi households have partly or fully shifted their dependence from livestock to transportation and sale of fuelwood, while others have started farming fodder crops on rented lands for their livestock, along with stubble and road/canal side grazing in the rain-fed areas of the Potohar plateau in Northern Punjab. They also have access disputes in the Bamiyan Zone in Central Afghanistan, and with the permanent agro-pastoralist Hazara residents, who are reluctant to accept the Pakhtun Kuchi during the summer months. It is, however, not understood how the Kuchi have adapted to these access problems.

While crossing the Durand line every year, the Kuchi do not end their seasonal migration in Khyber Pakhtunkhwa and Baluchistan on the western side of the Indus River, but continue their journey to the areas east of the Indus all along the Western Punjab and Northern Sind provinces of Pakistan. The Kuchi people's livestock production system operates in 34 provinces of Afghanistan. As shown in Table 1, approximately five million animals enter Pakistan every year from Afghanistan via different trans-boundary passes and these are accompanied by 7,830 Kuchi families. Before the demarcation of the Durand line, these migration routes were formalised by Amir Amanullah Khan, the then King of Afghanistan, in consultation with the tribes currently residing on both sides of the Durand line.

The Kuchi flocks on average may contain 85–89 per cent sheep, five to eight per cent camels, four to eight per cent goats, two to four per cent equines and a few cows and dogs. In some flocks, particularly belonging to Imran Khel tribes, the number of camels has been indicated to be more than thirty per cent; however, in general, the number of camels is gradually decreasing, as the transportation of families is increasingly replaced by tractors. The Kuchi nomads spend the winter (3.5 months) in the plain areas of southeastern Khyber Pakhtunkhwa, northeastern Baluchistan, Western Punjab and part of northwestern Sind. The four summer months are spent in the central highlands of

Afghan/Pakistan Border Politics

Name of Pass	Number of Flocks	Average Size of Herd	Number of Animals
Ghazi	150	250	37500
Nawa	180	250	45000
Tirah Valley	350	300	105000
Piewar	450	550	247500
Ghulam Khan	300	550	165000
Shawal	550	600	330000
Makeen	650	500	325000
Qmardin Karez	2500	750	1875000
Baldini	1500	700	1050000
Toba Kakarhi	1200	650	780000
Total	7830		4960000

Table 1. Kuchi flocks and families crossing the Durand line during the annual migratory cycle, Spring 2015.

Figure 3. Kuchi family on the move with their animals. Photo: Tracy Hunter.

Figure 4. Herders on the way to high pastures in Buner Pakistan. Photo: Inam ur Rahim.

Afghanistan stretching from Zabul to Kunarh and Ghor to Bamyan province. The higher proportion of time (4.5 months) is, however, spent along the mobility corridors, where they cross ten different passes along the entire length of the Durand line as shown in Figure 5.

After the Soviet occupation of Afghanistan, some 350 Kuchi families shifted their migratory pattern during the summer from the central Afghan highlands to the Naran uplands in Mansehra and the Alai uplands in Batagram district of Hazara division in Pakistan. Those who succeeded in saving or re-establishing their flocks are today's successful mutton suppliers to the Pakistani markets.

The macro-environment of this trans-boundary nomadic system comprises almost all the Pakhtun areas in Afghanistan, Khyber Pakhtunkhwa, and Baluchistan. The names of the ten passes given in Figure 5 are the main representative passes of a series of multiple passes selected by different Kuchi herders to cross the border. Different Kuchi herders usually select multiple crossing points in the vicinity of the passes shown in the figure for their flocks to cross the border. The entire border along the Durand line is porous to their flocks;

Afghan/Pakistan Border Politics

however, they usually avoid the passes with a formal border control mechanism like Torkham and Spin Boldak to avoid complications.

Figure 5 shows the migratory pattern from the summer uplands in Central Afghanistan toward the winter lowlands in Pakistan. The Kuchi usually return along the same paths they took. The only deviation from this migratory pattern can be seen on the southmost Toba Kakarhi route. After crossing the Toba Kakarhi, the Kuchi visit Pishin and Noushki in Baluchistan and their flocks then re-enter the Shorawak lowland area located in Afghanistan (near the Pakistan-Afghanistan-Iran border) for their winter grazing.

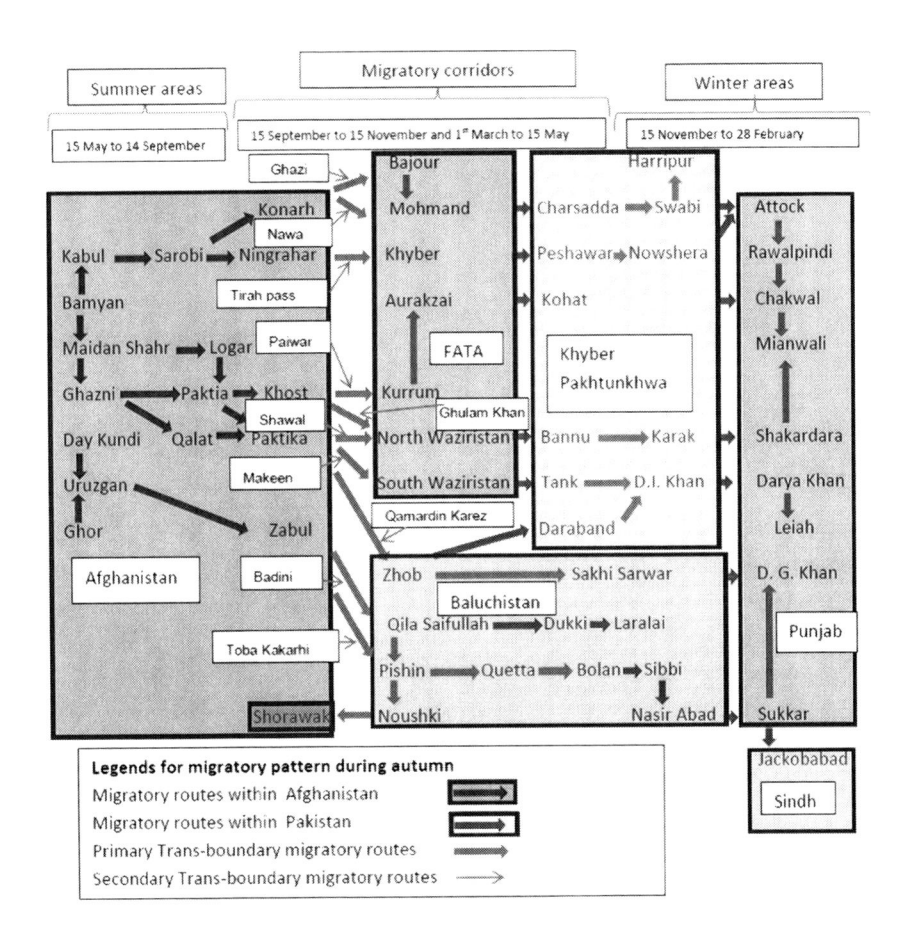

Figure 5. Mobility corridors across Durand line.

Inam ur Rahim

The issues

For centuries the Indus and its major tributaries have served as the natural wintering ground for nomadic peoples not only from Afghanistan, but also in Pakistan, in the form of the Ajar pastoral system in Malakand, Hazara and Kashmir. The increasing restriction on movement across the Durand Line is

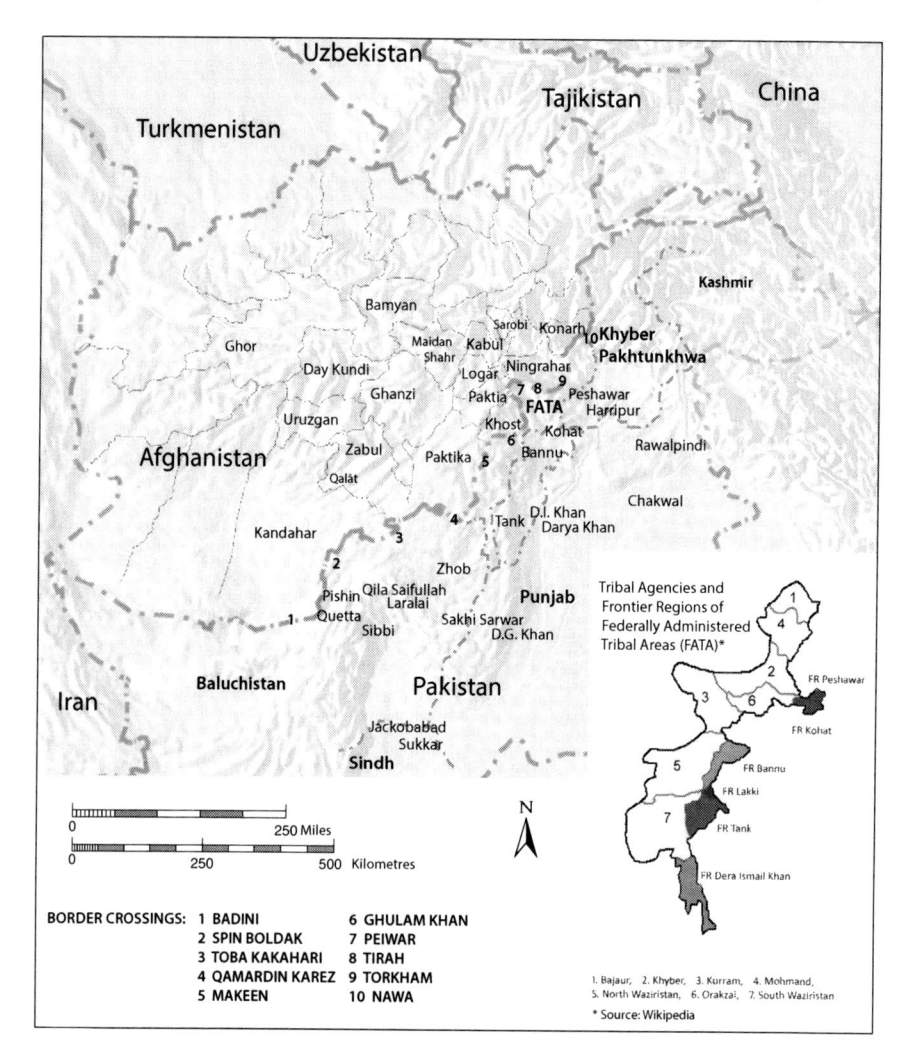

Figure 6. Map showing significant routes and destinations referred to in Figure 5.

Afghan/Pakistan Border Politics

gradually hindering Kuchi trans-boundary mobility and access to winter grazing grounds. Inside Afghanistan, they are facing resistance in obtaining access to their grazing resource base. The other hindrances include reduced access to their traditional summer pastures and takeover of pasture for cropping and mining in Afghanistan (Sweetser 1984).

Mobility issues

Forty years of war from 1978 onward transformed the social landscape in Afghanistan. The continued anarchy in Afghanistan severely disrupted Kuchi mobility through blocked access to the grazing areas, blocked mobility corridors, taxation by warlords and the snatching of livestock (Weijer 2007). Herders now experience frequent issues when migrating from traditional wintering lowlands to summer mountain grazing areas, due to the conversion of large tracts of rangelands to rain-fed agriculture. The Kuchi now move their animals by truck to bypass these areas or pay exorbitant fees to travel through what were once traditional migration corridors. Villages are also expanding into what once were deemed public rangeland areas, challenging traditional land-use arrangements with herders (Jacobs et al. 2009).

On one side the Kuchi have access disputes over the high summer pastures with the Hazara settled tribes in Central Afghanistan, who are reluctant to accept the Pakhtun Kuchis. On the other side, their access to winter grazing grounds has been curtailed through border issues between Pakistan and Afghanistan. Afghanistan's support for the Pakhtunistan campaign to return the Pakhtun tribal areas on the Pakistani side of the Durand line to Afghanistan led the Pakistani government to effectively close the border during 1961, causing many Kuchi to either abandon pastoralism or shift to other regions (Weijer 2007). After 1978, the Durand line remained open with little hindrance to Kuchi mobility till the ouster of the Taliban during 2001/2002. This was followed by a period of gradual rise in lawlessness on both sides of the Durand line. The Pakistani military has embarked on stricter measures to prevent militants infiltrating the area on the Pakistani side of the border, including the construction of a physical barrier which was partly completed in 2016. This period is also characterised by border mobility hindrances for Kuchi nomads.

In Afghanistan, the provinces where access to the preferred summer areas is constrained for large numbers of Kuchi flocks are Saripul, Faryab, Ghor, Wardak and Bamyan. Saripul province is the preferred summer area for approximately 12,000 Kuchi households, notably the districts of Kohistanat, Sang Charak and Balkhab. Kuchi come to these areas from the winter lowlands of Jawzjan and other districts of Saripul and Balkh province. Approximately 6,000 Kuchi households would prefer to visit Garzewan, Kohistan and Dawlatabad districts of Faryab province in summer but, due to tenure disputes, most of them are obliged to stay in other districts of the province (Weijer 2007).

A further 6,000 or so Kuchi households coming from Helmand, Logar, Jawzjan, Balkh and Khost provinces would prefer to visit Ghor province (notably Lal Sar Jangal, Chakhcharan and Pasaband district) during the summer months, but again are prevented by tenure disputes. Again, Wardak province (notably Behsood, Jalrez and Maidan Shar districts) is the traditional summer grazing area for almost 5,000 Kuchi households, but due to tenure disputes, they cannot move there. Similarly, 4,000 Kuchi households traditionally visited Parwan and Kapisa provinces during the summer period, from the winter areas of Takhar, Bagram district in Parwan province, and Kapisa province; however, due to tenure disputes their mobility is constrained.

Bamyan (notably Yakawlang and Panjab districts) is the preferred summer area for some 4,500 households, mostly from Logar, Nangarhar, Balkh, Khost, Samangan and Saripul provinces (Weijer 2007). In recent years, Kuchi households have tried to occupy upland areas in Bamyan during the summer, but this caused conflict with the resident Hazaras, who tried to move them on. The government was called on to intervene. The Kuchis are thus obliged to concentrate their flocks in Maidan and Jaliz areas during the summer. The area cannot support this level of flocks, and the hindered access to one pasture leads to overcrowding of livestock in the other and its degradation.

Meanwhile in Pakistan, the resident population in Baluchistan has no dispute with the Kuchi and does not demand rent money during the time they spend in the province on the way to Western Punjab. However, in Punjab, they pay a nominal rent to the landlords. In the Naran uplands of Khyber Pakhtunkhwa, they pay rent to landowners on a per household (tent) basis, while in the lowlands of Haripur and in the surrounding areas they pay rent on the basis of the size of the area they are occupying. The upland areas that the Kuchi frequent in Naran-Haripur include Chorh pastures in Batagram and Naran pastures of Mansehra (Basal, Saral, Burhawai, and Naran). The lowland areas include Fatehjang, Haripur, Mansehra, Rawalpindi, Abbottabad, Dangi Tool, Hassanabdal, Jari Kas, Rawat, Taxila and Pindi-Gap.

Livelihood issues

The Kuchi are one of the poorest and most marginalised communities in Afghanistan. They have been subjected to decades of war, insecurity and ethnic

Afghan/Pakistan Border Politics

Figure 7. The Kuchi herders, finding limited forage at winter lowlands, now increasingly purchase green forage for zero grazing. Photo: Inam ur Rahim.

tensions. This has severely disrupted their traditional patterns of land use and the relationships necessary for mitigating problems of a risk-prone lifestyle. In addition, several years of drought and bad winters in the main lowland areas have resulted in massive livestock losses. Thus the Kuchi are highly vulnerable to the combined effect of climatic variability and market fluctuations and are struggling hard to make a living out of a highly constrained and risky nomadic pastoral production system.

Winter is the main scarcity season for Kuchi flocks and, in order to keep their pregnant ewes alive, they must supplement their diet with wheat straw, wheat bran and maize grain, and with turnips and peas. In the lowlands, winter feed deficiency limits Kuchi herd size. Winter nutrition is the main limiting factor for livestock production. To some degree, supplementary feeding is practiced during the winter months, but not by all. There may be considerable scope for increased livestock production and improved livestock health through improving the quantity and quality of feed intake during the winter months.

Being landless, unlike agro-pastoralists, Kuchi have no fodder reserves from the fields or grassland reserves for winter stall feeding. Their livestock entirely depends on grazing. Furthermore, the lowland grazing areas are not able

Figure 8. A Kuchi herding his flock in the uplands of Naran with his tent in the background. Photo: Inam ur Rahim.

Figure 9. Herders re-establishing their lowland settlement after return from high pastures. Photo: Inam ur Rahim.

to support further grazing by the Kuchi livestock during the spring and early summer because of continuous grazing during autumn and winter. The fodder reserves of local agro-pastoralists are exhausted in late winter and the Kuchi have to pay a high price to get fodder. Their livestock must also compete with local livestock, and are often limited to riparian and other marginal agricultural vegetation. Flocks thus endure higher losses during this time of the year caused by malnutrition and a higher susceptibility to disease. This spurs the Kuchi to reach new grazing areas while finding limited pasture on mobility routes.

Over the last couple of decades, the population of agro-pastoralists has increased considerably and their settlements and agricultural fields have been extended, thus occupying large parts of the former mobility corridors and lowlands otherwise considered 'marginal lands'. The remittances of migrants have thereby acted as the main financial source for this extension. Commercial vegetables and orchards replaced staple cultivation as new cash crops in lowland areas and along the mobility corridors. As a direct consequence, many of the resting places along the mobility routes have been closed, leaving limited grazing surfaces for Kuchi herders.

With the shift from staples to cash crops, Kuchi are being discouraged from grazing their animals in these areas, mostly as a result of the herds' damage to these crops. This forces Kuchi to accelerate their movement, to make the journey from lowland to upland pastures in a shorter amount of time. As a result, the flocks reach the uplands and the lowlands significantly earlier compared to the traditional schedule.

Early arrival in the upland pastures because of mobility acceleration has a negative impact on pasture conditions. Animals start grazing on the young grasses sprouting in pastures still partially covered with snow, degrading the pastures. Re-establishing a slow mobility pace is hence a key measure that can contribute to restoring and protecting high altitude pastures (Rahim et al. 2011).

Finding a balance

Centuries of experience of using the ecosystem without external interference and the desire of many Kuchi to return to their traditional mobile life makes them a potential asset in the sustainable use of patchy resources (Degen and Weisbrod 2004). Historically Kuchi nomads have also played a role in Afghan nation-building; in the period of limited communication before 1950, the Kuchi played an important role in networking across the ethnicities residing in Afghanistan.

The Kuchi displacement has varied in space and time, but from southern Afghanistan, it was particularly high during the first displacement phase of the war (1978–88) (Schmeidl 2011). Despite their long stay and gradual integration in the Pakistan economy, they have not obtained refugee status on the basis of the 1951 UN Convention and its 1967 Protocol (Turton and Marsden 2002) but remain vulnerable to expulsion.

The roast mutton shops (*Shinwari Tikka*) starting up everywhere in Pakistan are heavily dependent on the availability of Kuchi sheep, thus diversifying the market for Kuchi livestock in Pakistan. More than 5,000 Balkhi sheep are weekly slaughtered in and around Peshawar and Islamabad alone. In this way the weight gained by a sheep in the central highlands of Afghanistan is helping in food security in the Indus plains and contributing to the Pakistani economy.

The trade in horses, sheep, fur, dried fruits and carpets in exchange for salt, sugar, clothes and household utensils by Kuchi nomads has continued through the centuries despite recurrent boundary changes in the sub-continent. After the creation of Pakistan and particularly during 1961–1963, the political dispute between Pakistan and Afghanistan led to closure of the border, preventing mobile Kuchi from crossing the Durand line and reaching the winter grazing grounds in the Indus plains. Though the control of mobility across the Durand line was gradually relaxed thereafter, however, the winter grazing and trade by Kuchi never regained its previous level (Foschini 2011).

During their time as refugees in Pakistan, a large proportion of Kuchis lost their livestock assets, and the gradual reduction in humanitarian assistance led to them drifting to the cities. In the repatriation process that began after the establishment of the Afghan government as a result of the Bonn agreement in 2001, millions of refugees have returned. However, returning Kuchi nomads, who have lost their livestock and grazing grounds, now have limited capital to recover the resource base on which they subsisted before displacement. They are ending up in urban sprawls around the cities in Afghanistan. The host country is no longer willing to accommodate them and the native country has no capacity to accommodate them.

The absence of land tenure policy and corresponding measures in Afghanistan has allowed tenure disputes to drag on and urban sprawls to multiply. After the gradual return of peace, the population of Kabul city has more than trebled during the last fifteen years and eighty per cent of its population resides in unplanned and informal settlements which cover 69 per cent of city land (MacDonald 2011).

Afghan/Pakistan Border Politics

Figure 10. Pastoralist children in Pakistan. Photo: Inam ur Rahim.

It is in the best interest of all the stakeholders, including Pakistan, Afghanistan and the Kuchi, to find a way of peaceful co-existence, allowing the Kuchi to enjoy their winter grazing grounds and sell their livestock in Pakistani markets. As the development of the China–Pakistan Economic Corridor leads to increasing growth and demand for supplies, this could make a win-win situation for all and contribute to regional peace and harmony.

REFERENCES

Barfield, T.J. and A. Szabo. 1991. *Afghanistan: An Atlas of Indigenous Domestic Architectiture*. Austin, TX: University of Texas Press.

Blench, R., 2001. *'You Can't Go Home Again': Pastoralism in the New Millennium*. London: Overseas Development Institute.

Brast, B., 2012. *Tribes, Warlords and the Rational Bureaucracy – Societal Differentiation in Afghanistan*. Paper presented at the ECPR Graduate Conference 2012, Jacobs University Bremen

Cronin, R.P., 2002. *Afghanistan: Challenges and Options for Reconstructing a Stable and Moderate State*. Library Of Congress Washington DC Congressional Research Service. www.iwar.org.uk/news-archive/crs/10093.pdf

Degen, A.A. and N. Weisbrod. 2004. 'Can pastoral nomads return to their traditional livelihood of raising livestock in the Registan desert of southern Afghanistan?' *Nomadic Peoples* 8: 214–229

Dorronsoro, G., 2009. *Fixing a Failed Strategy in Afghanistan*. Carnegie Endowment for International Peace 1779 Massachusetts Avenue, NW Washington, DC 20036. http://www.carnegieendowment.org/files/fixing_failed_strategy.pdf

Dupree, L., 1980. *Afghanistan*. Princeton: Princeton University Press.

Engelen, A., 2006. *Durable Solutions for Kuchi IDP's in the South of Afghanistan: Options and Opportunities*. UNHCR. http://www.unhcr.org/subsites/afghancrisis/46c993942/durable-solutions-kuchi-idps-south-afghanistan-options-opportunities-asia.html

FAO. 2001. *Pastoralism in the New Millennium*. Animal Production and Health Paper No. 150, Rome: UN Food and Agriculture Organization.

FAO. 2003. *The State of Food Insecurity in the World*. Rome: FAO. ftp://ftp.fao.org/docrep/fao/006/j0083e/j0083e00.pdf

Foschini, F., 2011. 'The social wandering of the Afghan Kuchis'. Conference Proceedings. The dynamics of change in conflict societies: Pakhtun region in perspective. 14–15 November, 2011. International Conference of the Department of Political Science, University of Peshawar. pp. 7–37.

Foust, J., 2008. *Afghan Tribal Structure Versus Iraqi Tribal Structure*. Cultural Knowledge Report. Human Terrain System, Research Reachback Centre. USArmy-Afghan Tribal Structure. https://www.info.publicintelligence.net/USArmy-AfghanTribalStructure.pdf

Grenville, J.A.S and B. Wasserstein. 2001. *The Major International Treaties of the Twentieth Century. A History and Guide with Texts*, Vol. 1. London: Routledge, Taylor and Francis. www.flagrancy.net-salvage-UNMappingReportAfghanistan

Guittard, A.C., 2011. *Qawm: Tribe-State Relations in Afghanistan from Darius to Karzai*. Boston College University Libraries. http://www.hdl.handle.net/2345/1975

Jacobs, M.J and C.A. Schloeder. 2012. 'Extensive Livestock Production: Afghanistan's Kuchi herders, risks to and strategies for their survival'. In V. Squires (ed.), *Rangeland Stewardship in Central Asia: Balancing Improved Livelihoods, Biodiversity Conservation and Land Protection*. Dordrecht: Springer.

Jacobs M.J., I. Naumovski, C.A. Schloeder and R.M. Dalili. 2009. *Empowering Afghan Herders to Build Peace and Improve Livelihoods*. Research Brief 09-01-PEACE. Global Livestock Collaborative Research Support Program, University of California at Davis.

Khan, S., 2010. 'Special status of tribal areas (FATA): An artificial imperial construct bleeding Asia'. *Eurasia Border Review* 1. Slavic Research Center. http://www.src-h.slav.hokudai.ac.jp/publictn/eurasia_border_review/no1/06_Khan.pdf

Kreutzmann, H. and S. Schütte. 2011. *Contested Commons – Multiple Insecurities of Pastoralists in North-Eastern Afghanistan*. Bonn: Erdkunde.

Lamb R.D., 2012. *Political Governance and Strategy in Afghanistan*. Report of Center for strategic and international studies. www.csis.org

Lewal, G., 2010. 'Areas between Afghanistan and Pakistan and the present turmoil'. *Eurasia Border Review* 1. http://www.src-h.slav.hokudai.ac.jp-publictn-eurasia_border_review-no1-07_Liwal

Macdonald, I., 2011. *Landlessness and Insecurity: Obstacles to Reintegration in Afghanistan*. Middle East Institute. http://www.refugeecooperation.org/publications/afghanistan/pdf/04_macdonald.pdf

Munoz, A.G., 2010. 'Pashtun tribalism and ethnic nationalism. Cultural and geographic research, Tribal Analysis Center'. Paper presented at 'Symposium on Afghanistan and Pakistan: The Challenges and Opportunities of Governance and the Role of Regional Actors.' 24–26 March 2010, University of South Florida

Nori M., J. Switzer and A. Crawford. 2005. *Herding on the Brink: Towards a Global Survey of Pastoral Communities and Conflict*. Occasional Paper from the IUCN, Commission on Environmental, Economic and Social Policy. Gland. http://www.iisd.org/publications/pub.aspx?id=705

Rahim, I and A. Viaro. 2002. *Swat: An Afghan Society in Pakistan – Urbanization and Trends in a Tribal Environment*, 1st Edition. Geneva, IUED; Karachi: City Press. https://www.archive-ouverte.unige.ch/unige:26453

Rahim, I., D. Maselli, H. Rueff and U. Wiesmann. 2011. 'Indigenous fodder trees can increase grazing accessibility for landless and mobile pastoralists in Northern Pakistan'. *Pastoralism: Research, Policy, and Practice* 1:1–20.

Robson B., J. Lipson, F. Younos and M. Mehdi. 2002. *The Afghans: Their History and Culture*. Center for Applied Linguistics, The Cultural Orientation Resource Center. https://www.eric.ed.gov/?id=ED482787

Rubin, B.R., 1995. *The Search for Peace in Afghanistan: From Buffer State to Failed State*. New York: Berghahn Books.

Sandford, S., and Y. Habtu. 2000. *On Emergency Response Interventions In Pastoral Areas Of Ethiopia*: Report Of The Pastoral Appraisal Team. DFID Ethiopia, Addis Ababa.

Schetter, C., R. Glassner and M. Karokhail. 2006. *Understanding Local Violence: Security Arrangements in Kandahar, Kunduz and Paktia* (No. 67). ZEF Working Paper Series. Bonn: Center for Development Research.

Schmeidl, S., 2011. *Protracted Displacement in Afghanistan: Will History Be Repeated?* East Institute. Fondation pour la Rechearche Strategique. https://www.refugeecooperation.org/publications/afghanistan/pdf/10_schmeidl.pdf

Schütte, S., 2012. 'Pastoralism, power and politics: access to pastures in Northern Afghanistan'. In *Pastoral Practices in High Asia*. Dordrecht: Springer. pp. 53–69.

Smith, H.H. et al., 1973. *Area Handbook for Afghanistan*. Fourth Edition. Washington: U.S.Government Printing Office.

Sweetser, A., 1984. 'Afghan Nomad Refugees in Pakistan'. *Nomads: Stopped in Their Tracks? Cultural Survival Quarterly* 8(1) https://www.culturalsurvival.org/publications/cultural-survival-quarterly/afghan-nomad-refugees-pakistan

Tapper, R., 2008. 'Who are the Kuchi? Nomad self-identities in Afghanistan'. *Journal of the Royal Anthropological Institute* 14(1): 97–116.

Thebaud, B. and S. Batterbury. 2001. 'Sahel pastoralists: opportunism, struggle, conflict and negotiation. A case study from eastern Niger'. *Global Environmental Change* 11(1): 69–78.

Turton, D. and P. Marsden. 2002. *Taking Refugees for a Ride? The Politics of Refugee Return to Afghanistan*. The Afghanistan Research and Evaluation Unit (AREU). Issues Paper Series. http://www.reliefweb.int/report/afghanistan/taking-refugees-ride-politics-refugee-return-afghanistan

UNHCR, 2006. The State of The World's Refugees: Human Displacement in the New Millennium. http://www.unhcr.org/publications/sowr/4a4dc1a89/state-worlds-refugees-2006-human-displacement-new-millennium.html

Weijer, F., 2005. *Toward A Pastoralist Support Strategy*. Background Document. USAID. http://www.mtnforum.org/sites/default/files/publication/files/1708.pdf

Weijer, F., 2007. *Cashmere Value Chain Analysis. Afghanistan*. USAID. http://www.afghanag.ucdavis.edu/other-topic/markets/marketing-reports/Rep_Cashmere_Value_Chain_USAID.pdf

WFP. 2011. *Drought Impact Emergency Food Security Assessment in Fourteen Affected Provinces of Afghanistan*. Second phase report. Islamic Republic Of Afghanistan. http://www.ochaonline.un.org/afghanistan/Clusters/FoodSecurityAgriculture/tabid/5582/language/enUS/Default.aspx

Wily, L.A. 2013. 'The battle over pastures: The hidden war in Afghanistan'. *Revue des mondes musulmans et de la Méditerranée* **133**|, http://www.remmm.revues.org/

Chapter 8

TRANSHUMANCE AND CHANGE AMONG THE RUNGS OF UTTARAKHAND HIMALAYAS

Nisthasri Awasthi

Introduction

Transhumance, once the mainstay of the Rung community, is now on the verge of disappearing. The Government of India does not consider transhumance a viable source of livelihood but rather an environmental threat due to overgrazing. To protect the environment, the government has set up thirteen National Parks and 59 wildlife sanctuaries across the Indian Himalayas, displacing transhumant herders from their rangelands. The irony is that only the older generation of the Rung community wants to continue with this practice, while the younger generation feel that it does not give them sufficient economic returns. As a result, the livelihoods associated with transhumance are under serious threat of disappearance. In this chapter, I will explore the socio-economic importance of transhumance with respect to the present state policies and the Rungs' attitude towards these policies. Ethnographic methods were used to study the Rungs of Darma valley in Kumaon for a period of three years. Against this backdrop, it is pertinent to study the economic and ecological viability of transhumance in the semi-arid region.

Transhumance is a kind of nomadism practised by using socially recognised routes in an annual seasonal cycle. The study of the community of transhumant pastoralists has two important connotations, ecological and socio-cultural. Transhumance, where herds and human beings subsist in an ecological symbiosis, is not solely a natural phenomenon but is culturally controlled. The herds supply the products such as meat and wool for the herders which they further trade with farming communities. This annual ecological cycle is reflected in the migratory pastoral rounds of Rungs, which are naturally, culturally and politically controlled.

Rungs send their herds to summer upland pastures for grazing from May to October. During this time, the herds are given into the charge of shepherds and are grazed in alpine meadows locally called *bugyal*, a term derived from the word *bug/bugi* meaning lush green vegetation. Here they can be moved from place to place according to where the pasture is best without the restrictions imposed by the state on grazing at the lower levels. Rung transhumance has also provided them with other opportunities for trade, agriculture and herb collection, and trade was a significant component of Rung transhumance in the past.

The importance of the physical and biotic environment in influencing the spatial and social organisation of pastoral society has been widely recognised since Evans-Pritchard's (1940) seminal book on the Nuer (Dyson-Hudson and Dyson-Hudson 1980). In the Indian context, pastoralists may be defined as follows:

> members of caste or ethnic groups with a strong traditional association with livestock keeping, where a substantial proportion of the group derive over 50 percent of household consumption from livestock products or their sale, and where over 90 percent of animal consumption is from natural pastures or browse, and where households are responsible for the full cycle of livestock breeding (Sharma et al. 2003, 3).

In India, pastoral ethnic groups vary in terms of size, location, ethnic identities, migration pattern and socio-economic organisation of pastoralism. The considerable local knowledge of pastoralists has not received any recognition in the policy domain and, as a result of the poor development in these regions, they remain socio-economically deprived. Geographically, nomadic pastoralism is most prevalent in the western regions of India on the Deccan Plateau, and in the Himalayan region of North India. In some communities, pastoralism serves as the primary economic base and other economic activities like agriculture, herb collection and wool production, complement this pastoral lifestyle.

The practice of transhumance among the Rungs is locally referred to as *kuncha* and is associated with alpine grazing, cottage industry in wool, settled cultivation, collection and sale of medicinal plants and a number of other smaller economic activities in different parts of the Indian Himalaya (Farooquee and Rao 1998). It is a grazing strategy in which livestock are taken care of during a long migration or transit over the course of the two seasons of the year, in search of pastures (Rinschede 1987). Among the Rungs, transhumance has been closely related to the trade economy (Prasad 1989, Dangwal 1997). According

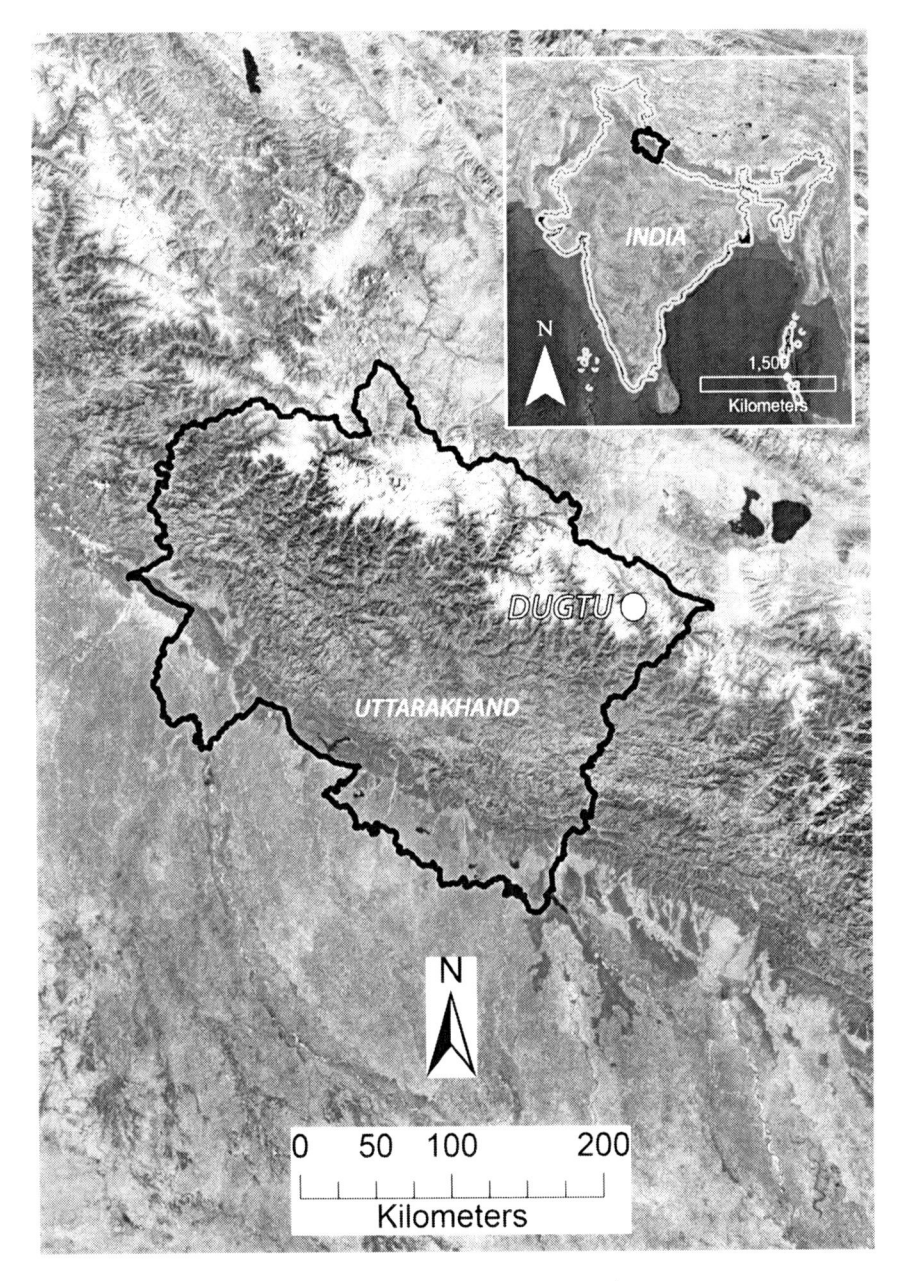

Figure 1. Map of Darma valley, India.

to Prasad (1989), the Rungs' seasonal movement has been a peculiar blend of greater and lesser transhumance, where they move between fixed destinations on fixed migratory routes. In earlier times, during summer they moved towards Tibet in the north along with their family, animals and belongings in search of pasture availability and agricultural land. Livestock (goat, sheep and yak) plays a significant role in the lifestyle of Rungs, as they breed animals for meat and wool production as well as using them as beasts of burden in rugged terrain.

Conceptual framework

Social constructivists argue that what is called 'nature' is far less universal and extra-human than is generally assumed by the realists. The debate over nature as a social construction can be clarified in terms of the two necessary concepts in any epistemological scheme: the knowing subject and the object of knowledge. The world of the 'knowing subject' is the world of ideas, of concepts, of values; the world of the 'object of knowledge' is the world of reality, of existence. The object of knowledge is 'out there' and given, in contrast to the conceptual space in which the subject exists. The social construction of nature argues that all concepts of biophysical nature and its associated ideas like wilderness, wildness, biodiversity carry cultural and political meanings reflected in everyday narratives. Foucault's idea that 'truth is a thing of this world ... each society has its regime of truth' (1980, 131), speaks about the political and cultural thread in the fabric of objective reality that we observe as we represent and evaluate it. The state conservation strategies and planning reflect a form of hegemonic governmentality (Foucault 1978), evident from the division of forest in Darma valley into reserved, civil and agricultural forests during the colonial era, which has been maintained by the postcolonial government. These official categories of forest are different from the locals' classification, which helps to map their surroundings and facilitate the use of the resources. Fletcher (2010) discusses neoliberal environmentality, using Foucault's concept of governmentality, which he describes as an environmental type of intervention. The exercise of categorising takes a biopolitical approach to conservation (Youatt 2008).

The constructivists not only look at the deleterious effects of environmental policies but also at those personal and interpersonal processes that are responsible for influencing livelihood and identity, leading to successful outcomes in terms of informing better policies. Moreover, this approach views individuals, not as passive targets of prejudice, stereotypes or discrimination who focus only on coping and avoiding negative outcomes of policies, but rather as active participants in society who seek to understand the social world through their own meanings and experiences.

This study explores issues of transhumance and identity among the Rung community of the Darma valley using a political ecology framework. The Rung habitat as well as the Rung community is fast changing and gradually giving way to sedentarisation. Therefore, transhumance as an ecological and social system needs to be studied as various exogenous factors, be it technology, values or policies, play their part. Broadly speaking, one of the most challenging issues in studies on transhumance emerges when researchers seek to articulate the real constraints that environment and livelihood issues create in local people's day-to-day lives. In doing so, they end up regarding the situation of transhumants as taken-for-granted and see no hope of betterment. Local meanings ascribed to transhumance are intricately linked to their experience of livelihood, forest ecology, grazing, pasturelands and policies. The findings of this study reveal that the meanings ascribed to transhumance and related livelihood activities are constructed in response to changes in environment and policies, as the Rungs grapple with the challenges they face.

The narratives obtained during fieldwork are also used to study the formation of identity among the Rungs, as the study adopts the idea that identity is formed and re-formed with respect to changing conditions of a community. According to Ricoeur (1991), identity is a function of a narrative, which becomes a medium of self-interpretation in various contexts. Identity formation is a process that unfolds in relation to the economic, historical and political contexts. In the context of the changing structure of Rung society, it becomes important to look into the concept of the existence of multiple identities, as mentioned above.

These perspectives would be in consonance with the study design: the use of narratives in studying transhumance, livelihood, and identity; and participants of the study comprising community members.

The Rungs

The Rungs are amongst many tribes of Uttarakhand in the Indian Himalayan Region who are identified as Bhotia. This identification refers to the Indian 'Scheduled Tribes' (ST) classification of 1967, which identifies groups and entitles communities to state benefits. However the term 'Bhotia' is contentious because it is a generic term encompassing several distinct ethnic groups across the Indian Himalayas, which share many features in common, at the

Figure 2. Bhotia woman. Photo: Nisthasri Awasthi.

same time as exhibiting certain distinctive features that may be unique to one or more groups and not shared by the rest. The first use of the term 'Bhotia' (by administrators during the British colonial period) signifies a somewhat confusing mixture of ethnic Tibetan and Bhutanese people (Brown, 1984). What is interesting about the Rungs is the multiple identities that community members ascribe to themselves. While the community has traditionally been identified as 'Bhotia' in official documents and literature, the Rungs define themselves by various other names based on local, regional and official contexts. In an apparent attempt to distance themselves from people classified as Bhotias who reside in other regions of the Himalayas, their association with their valley was evident from their narratives. With respect to their understanding of their 'tribal' status, most locals perceive that such a tribal status is meant only for those communities which are poor and backward. In spite of being labelled as ST, a lower status than the Hindu population, they are satisfied with their inclusion in this category as they get various state provisions and benefits in the form of education opportunities and government jobs. It is well established that identity construction is closely linked to changes in the wider society (Cerulo

1997). As cultures change, identities get redefined, formed and re-formed as people position themselves in their specific context. In the present study, when I asked the study participants *who are you?*, the unanimous reply came that *we are Rung people*. The assertion they are not Bhotias followed immediately after, as they worked to clarify the misconception that most people have about them.

Their habitat is spread across three valleys in Dharchula, namely Darma, Byans and Chaudans. The study was conducted in the Darma valley, which has twelve villages, three of which were focused on.

Research questions

The aim of this study is to explore the practice of transhumance among the Rungs of Darma valley of Kumaon in the Indian state of Uttarakhand. This will involve an examination of social, economic and ecological factors in transhumance and change. Secondly, the issue of identity is taken up with reference to different socio-economic transformations the society is undergoing. The study has two important implications for the social, economic and ecological understanding of transhumance: one, the impact on the local tribal population of the move away from transhumance and the turn to environmental politics; and, two, the impact on the social identity of pastoralists. The study employed unstructured in-depth interviews that would most truly represent the reality of the participants studied in terms of the aforementioned objectives. The study was carried out over a three-year period from October 2009 to May 2013 with repeat interviews during summer months, winter months and during the course of transhumance. Interviews were also conducted amongst members of the village who reside in cities such as Delhi and Haldwani. This method also attempts to answer some fundamental questions that evolved during the course of this research: i.e. what can be learned from informants and their lived experiences and used to bring out resilience and empowering narratives among the participants researched. These narratives help in understanding community empowerment with regard to how communities build on their abilities to act collectively on issues and make positive changes in their environment. I also ask, can this oral material be given a space and be included and seriously considered in the present day policy discourse on environment and ecology? This involves an ethnographically field-oriented rethinking of nature and, therefore, the dynamic narratives also require investigation of the historical perspective. This new understanding helps to rethink the nature–culture dichotomy that is fundamental to the dominance of central scientific knowledge about the environment in informing major policies. To link to the larger context of power (i.e. the state driven knowledge of the environment and the ecology), ensembles of meanings and local knowledge are documented.

Philosophical assumptions of the study

The ontological questions raised by this essay relate to the nature of reality and its characteristics. The study follows the constructivist paradigm in studying the social aspect of environment and identity; to an extent it also acknowledges its realism. In doing so, I take a critical approach to the taken-for-granted knowledge of transhumance that reality is studied through discourse. The meanings constructed through everyday narratives are seen as systems of knowledge in a particular discourse and how these discourses are articulated in production (by the speaker) and consumption (by the recipient) of texts (Fairclough 1992, 1995). Such discourses have dominated the present day policy on the environment, which finds reflection in the ideas of sustainable development and bio-diversity conservation adopted by the Forest Department. As a consequence, following the narrative of ecological degradation, restrictions on transhumance have been imposed. Local experiences of different sections of the community (old/young, male/female, migrants/non-migrants etc.) reflect a different understanding of transhumance and ecology, the way locals construe these processes in relation to their livelihood and everyday practice.

The study assumes that there are multiple realities – for example, the realities of individuals who experience transhumance and the difficulties associated with it. There is also the reality of the researcher that influences the study as well as that of the reader of the study. Hence, the basic purpose of employing methods like participant observation and unstructured interviews is so that, by studying research participants in their natural setting and reporting their narratives in their own words, these different realities can be presented, showing the different experiences of individuals in what is seemingly a homogeneous group. Narratives also included self-ethnographies, which are a powerful tool of resilience among Rungs. Therefore, the understanding behind employing these qualitative methods is the assumption that the realities of people experiencing apparently similar situations are not necessarily the same; and, in fact, it emerges that they are diverse and different. The interviews were guided by an informal conversational style in an unstructured format with minimal interference from the researcher.

Transhumance and Change Among the Rungs

This study was initiated with the broad aim of understanding the Rungs' experiences with respect to transhumance. I began the study with the naïve goal of learning the way of life lived by the transhumants and asking them how different sections of Rungs construct their experiences. In formulating the research objectives, the concept of political ecology was used as a starting reference. The different and varied information that the Rungs offered in the form of oral texts was carefully studied and examined. This led to the formulation of the tentative statements, conclusions and assumptions of the study. This approach was grounded in the context and experiences of the study participants; as such, the study contributes to the re-theorisation of certain ways of explicating transhumance and 'tribal' identity (as opposed to dominant theorisation of tribes in India). It is pertinent to provide a general understanding of the Rungs in the next section.

The Rung habitat

The Rungs live in the Darma valley of the Kumaon division of Uttarakhand, which in 1986 was recognised as Askot Musk Deer Sanctuary, under Wildlife (Protection) Act, 1972. The sanctuary encompasses an area of 600 square kilometres over a large range of altitudinal gradients, from about 560 metres to 6,904 metres at the summit of the Panchachuli range. It originally included 111 villages, Dharchula town, and a military cantonment within its boundaries, along with Reserved Forest (5.97 per cent), *Van panchayat*[1] (46.42 per cent), Civil Forest (45.23 per cent) and Agricultural Forest (2.31 per cent). This sanctuary was set up primarily with the object of conserving the musk deer. With various developmental projects coming to this region, activists and the state government both opposed expanding the sanctuary's boundaries and wished to restructure them. Additional land pressures include the construction of a road to Tibet and a project to tap this area's high hydroelectric potential. From the perspective of the Rungs and other residents of this area, these state programmes severely curtail their livelihood options. In 2007, the state filed a court case seeking permission to exclude the 111 villages (of Rungs and non-Rungs) from the sanctuary by redrawing the sanctuary boundaries and rationalising them. On 25 July 2013, the boundaries were redrawn and the 111 villages were excluded, after which it was rechristened the Askot Wildlife Sanctuary. As far as the dubious issue of the presence of musk deer in the region is concerned, the

---

1. Van Panchayats or Village Forest Councils are unique institutions for community management of forests.

Forest Department (interviews with their officials) maintains that though they are found in inaccessible areas, the surrounding forests act as buffer zones. Now, the Rungs have to abide by the forest rights regulations and the roads that are now being constructed to rural areas will be outside the sanctuary.

The total area of Dugtu village in Darma valley is 620,201 hectares with forest cover of 51,800 hectares. The total irrigated area is 10,808 hectares, which is the land in the vicinity of the village. Other than this, there are 134,037 hectares in the cultivable unirrigated land area and 387,084 hectares is usable land for purposes other than cultivation, such as grazing. The grazing land and forest is above the village and agricultural land lies below the village. A small patch of land is marked at the entry to the village which is used for grazing horses, mules and yaks owned by Rungs. It is important to note that these figures are according to the government records, and the actual data may vary a lot as the field observation revealed that agriculture is practiced in only thirty to forty per cent of this land. The field situation shows that a lot of land used for cultivation twenty or 25 years back is now left fallow due to non-availability of labour these days. The older population blame the young for their lack of interest in their traditional occupation, while the young population of the village consider it economically unviable.

The Rungs (both those still practicing transhumance and those who have stopped) stated that transhumance among communities is dwindling. Rungs that practice *kuncha* leave for the upper villages in May and they stay there till the end of October or early November, depending on the onset of snow. The decision to leave for transhumance is taken jointly by the families and accordingly three to four families leave together, along with their belongings. The rest follow them within a span of a few days. Their belongings and food are carried on hired horses and mules. In this way, they have to incur some cost to reach the summer settlement. Today, only older Rungs, usually above fifty years old, and children below seven migrate to the summer settlements and stay there for the whole summer period. The young members of the village keep coming to the summer villages for shorter periods during the time of cultivation.

According to the Census of India 2011, Dugtu village comprises fifty households, but field exploration reveals that only thirty households now inhabit the village. The other twenty households have stopped practicing *kuncha*. According to the 2011 census, the total population of the village was 243 persons; 128 males, 106 females and fifteen children. When sorted by age, 45 are aged one to twenty, 69 aged twenty to forty, 34 aged forty to sixty and the remaining 23 are aged over sixty. According to the same census, 138 are listed as Below Poverty Line (BPL) while the rest are Above Poverty Line (APL). The field observation however shows that there are 171 people in the village, of whom 76 stay in the summer settlement for the whole six months duration, 68 keep visiting for one or two months at a time and the remaining 27 do not come at all for *kuncha*.

The 1962 Indo-China war and subsequent closure of the border greatly affected the Rungs' economic activities. At this time, trade between Rungs and Tibetans stopped altogether. Before the war, the mainstay of this community was a well-regulated trade between the Tibetan community on the Chinese side and the Kumaoni community on the Indian side. Tibet is a land rich in rock salt, borax, gold dust, herbs, but not in agricultural land. While not strong agriculturalists, Tibetans are skilled at animal husbandry, producing both sheep and wool. This contrast in production gave rise to a system of mutual exchange and trade (Prasad, 1989). The war had an adverse effect on livestock numbers, production of traditional handicrafts (due to non-availability of high quality Tibetan wool) and practice of transhumance, to name a few. Though a couple of trade routes were reopened in 1992, very few families could benefit from this due to stringent regulations, as reported by older members of the community. Hence the Rungs gather herbs along their transhumance route and trade them with local communities. However, the transhumance practiced nowadays is different from the traditional practice, as it is restricted by state policies on forest and grazing land, and involves fewer people than before.

The changes in transhumance have resulted in changes to the use and role of livestock amongst the Rungs. With the introduction of motorised transport, the importance of cattle, which were earlier used for transportation, drastically declined. However, a few people still send their animals to neighbouring Nepal for the purpose of transportation during particular seasons. The remaining livestock, like sheep, is used only for breeding, meat and wool production.

As a result of the constitutional provisions for Bhotia as Scheduled Tribes, a split has occurred in the Bhotia economy, including the Rungs (Hoon 1996). On the one hand, a number of Bhotias benefited from the policy of reserved educational places and government jobs, and moved out of their traditional lifestyle. They travelled to other parts of the country to explore better opportunities in education and employment. On the other, a large proportion of Bhotias were left in the villages struggling to find employment and subsisting on available resources. It is this group of Bhotias who still carry on with transhumance and depend upon weaving and herb collection to earn income.

Added to the problems of the Bhotias is that the area has been opened up for state-controlled tourism. The local population has not been included and no initiative has been taken to provide facilities and training to them. The only way Rungs can participate in this industry is as tour guides, porters or mule owners who are exploited by non-Rung middlemen. Additionally, within the markets for woollen textiles and medicinal herbs, the Rungs are neglected by government agencies, and often exploited by non-governmental and private organisations.

In the light of the present situation of transhumance amongst the Rungs, it is important to note that the existence and continuation of transhumance depends on many factors and similarly various activities that are tied to this lifestyle. The decline in transhumance is also reported from Tibet (Goldstein and Beall 1989, Nautiyal et al. 2003). There has been very little understanding of the social life of pastoralist and transhumant communities and the value of ecosystem services provided by transhumance (Gonzalez et al. 2009). Policy makers have failed to make proper development plans for the Bhotias or other pastoral communities, due to lack of knowledge about their traditional lifestyle. Grazing of livestock during transhumance is seen by them as ecologically harmful, which has led to many kinds of restrictions. Sedentarisation has been promoted, rather than encouraging transhumant practice. The records show that there have been restrictions on grazing since the 1890s (the colonial period) and, according to the regulations in those times, annual passes were issued for grazing on payment of fees per animal (Pangti 1992). Though the British were in favour of the trade with Tibet because of economic and political benefits, they never encouraged pastoralists' traditional rights over forest and its customary usage.

Dependence of the Rungs on the Forest

Transhumant communities maintain a delicate balance with their natural environment. Nongbri (1999) writes that the state's control over forest resources is posing a threat to the livelihood of tribal communities. Rungs depend on the forest for firewood, grazing, wood for construction of houses, and medicinal herbs. When spending their summers at higher altitudes, Rungs can easily access forest resources. Most of the forest and pastureland is managed by the *van panchayat* and decisions are taken by the villagers collectively. Moreover, the area is far from the reach of the forest officials to carry out regular surveillance; thus, villagers do not fear much intrusion by the Forest Department. The villagers use a different area of forest each year and return to that particular area only after two to three years of regeneration. In the lower settlements, access to forests is difficult for them and grazing is impossible, so they leave their sheep with hired shepherds to be taken to the foothills till the winter recedes. At their winter settlements, most Rungs have other sources of cooking fuel such as gas cylinders or kerosene stoves. Therefore, fetching firewood for cooking, which is the primary source of fuel in the summer villages, is not a major concern for them.

Rungs depend on the collection and private sale of medicinal plants for income. Diversified production processes and a community survival culture helped them to protect the forest resources from over exploitation (Farooquee and Rao 1998). Worship of nature and a semi-nomadic lifestyle further add to the sustainable utilisation of the forest resources. Until the 1950s, government did not intervene in the extraction and sale of Medicinal and Aromatic Plants (MAPs). Later some state and private companies were set up for commercial exploitation of these plant species. It can be argued that the threat to nature is because of outsiders' intervention and the locals who have been using these resources wisely are not to be blamed. As roads and development projects make their habitat more accessible to outsiders, the threat to their livelihood is more pronounced now. Also, this occupation of the Rungs has been affected by government policy on forests and land. The locals, particularly the older ones, believe that the ban on seasonal grazing has reduced the diversity of traditional herbs, replacing them with extensive growth of other species.

Over the past ten years, some pharmaceutical companies have started purchasing these herbs from the Rungs, which has led to competitive commercial activity among the villagers. The trade in *keeda jadi*, also known as caterpillar fungus (a kind of parasitic fungus found in the alpine regions of the Himalayas), is becoming very popular among the Rungs and non-Rungs alike. Money earned through this trade, coupled with its no or low cost input, is attracting many locals, especially unemployed young individuals. Although locals are able to sell the fungus in the market to middlemen and agents, in the absence of any regulated trade, the Rungs seldom obtain market prices and their trade channels are not very clear. What is vaguely known to the locals is that the agents collect the material from them and sell at much higher price to other agents or directly to companies in China by way of Nepal.

The main objective of the Forest Department of the Pithoragarh Forest Division is to promote scientific research on the *bugyals* and medicinal herbs found there, exercise control on grazing activities and maintain the floral, faunal and agricultural bio-diversity of the region. In addition to this, other plans include eradication of weeds, prevention of forest fires, enhancing forest plantation, developing eco-tourism and establishing private-public partnerships in conservation, in order to provide locals with a better livelihood from the forest resources, while at the same time discouraging them from relying on forest resources (Management Plan of Pithoragarh Forest Division 2011–2022). The various forest laws and regulations imposed on the locals have not only reduced their dependency on the forest but also led to criminalisation of customary use by the locals (in terms of pasturelands and collection of medicinal herbs). This criminalisation of resource use was seen to be subverted by 'illegal extraction' of the herbs by the locals, particularly *keeda jadi*. The locals consider this an opportunity for those who can dare to take the risk of going to inaccessible and difficult regions for months to fetch this herb. Local communities redefine their rights and use by producing counter narratives (Peluso 1992) by saying that

> no officials come here to check and the area where herbs are found is so far, *keeda jadi* is just a *keeda* (insect) which appears after a long wait, it will not harm the environment.

The officials blame the locals for uncontrolled extraction, but, in spite of knowing such practice occurs, they admitted their inability to keep a vigil in these inaccessible places. It was also known from reliable sources, like social activists and respected members of the local population of Dharchula, that the same officials are also involved in illegal trade in the herbs. In fact, according to the locals, without the assistance of the officials it would not be possible for the people to carry on with the extraction. It was observed that there has been a change in the meaning of 'usefulness' (Robbins 2004) of landscape (forest and land). It is clear that, with fewer people practicing transhumance and going to upper settlements (in spite of diversifying agricultural crops in their agricultural land), labour-intensive agriculture has lost its importance. It is seen that the total area under cultivation is decreasing with time, resulting in large tracts of land lying unused. The commercial valuation of the land is also reflected in the narratives of a few young members who see their land as a fitting site for commercial cultivation of herbs. Many narratives pointed to the likelihood that opening up the region and removing the village from the sanctuary area would attract more of the village youth to go to their summer villages.

Transhumance and Change Among the Rungs

Response to development programmes

Several hydroelectric power projects are underway in the valley, including a 280 MW National Hydroelectric Power Corporation (NHPC) Dhauliganga hydro-power project in the area near Tapovan, Dharchula, which will supply electricity to India's Northern grid. Another, the Urthing-Sobla power project, is being developed by Reliance Energy. Besides this, other micro projects are also finding their way in the valley, sufficient for the production of electricity for a single village or a group of two to three villages. These projects are developed by Uttarakhand Renewable Energy Development Agency (UREDA), sub-contracted to small contractors for building the infrastructure, with labour being provided by villagers or people from surrounding areas.

The most significant development from the locals' perspective that came out during interviews is that roads should be built in the Darma valley so that more and more people from the village are encouraged to come to the summer settlements. This point confirms that the locals feel secure in their summer home and, given the facilities, would often like to go to their summer settlements. They see roads not only as an indicator of development in their village but also a means to bring them closer to their summer settlements. On the other hand, some villagers (mainly elders) are sceptical of the motor connectivity to the upper regions. They perceive the building of roads in the area as a threat to the peace in the valley and a risk to the essence of transhumance. The meaning associated with the coming of the roads is that this will lead to stringent checking and regular patrolling in their valleys by the forest guards: as a villager remarked, *they would show their power*.

In the light of the different responses from various sections of the Rungs, development is understood as a 'discursive power relation' (Escobar 1992) which sometimes takes the form of social movement. Though small protests in terms of requests for roads, electricity and other small amenities are seen, a larger social movement is conspicuously absent.

The changing kuncha (transhumance) experience

Transhumance is a discursive, material and cultural form of human-environment relationship. It is evident that the present practice of transhumance is a result of incorporation of biophysical sciences (scientific forestry) into history (in the form of forest laws) (Guha 1989, Escobar 1999) to produce laws that are then imposed upon the locals. Narratives of annual transhumance by the Rung during the study period can be juxtaposed with historic narratives of ideal transhumance practice. Rungs pointed out that this much-cherished activity would gradually disappear because of the changing conditions and loss of interest among the younger generation. The young Rungs (fifteen to 35 years) feel that transhumance has nothing to offer to the generations to come and therefore must be changed to provide economic stability. 'Downhill we get everything in the market. Here (i.e. in the higher settlement), it is a problem. We do not much like here (Darma) but make it a point to come for ceremonial rituals every year', remarked one of the female Rungs. A similar argument was also given by an elderly Rung, who was hopeful that their traditional transhumance activity would survive because of their deep reverence for their village deity. He said, 'that young people will have to come in future because there is something called spiritual power and religion, to offer prayers to the deity they will have to come some day or the other.' In making this argument, they seem to overlook the root cause of economic instability – undesirable state policies – and instead place the blame on the contemporary era. Moreover, the rhetoric of the economic unsustainability of transhumance or the pastoral way of life colours their experiences of ecology and livelihoods.

Not all families have been quick to accept changes in the pattern of transhumance. During my study, some families were seen to follow traditional practice in terms of caring for their livestock and finding pastures for them and understanding the importance of keeping them healthy to carry their loads, though others have stopped transhumance altogether. Moreover, motorable roads and the associated vehicles were said by locals to be a major factor leading to the disappearance of their annual migratory trading practice.

Rising prices have made keeping livestock costlier, further intensifying the problems faced by transhumants who depend upon others for transporting their load to their summer settlements at higher altitudes. Rungs have begun to depend upon other caste groups, identified by a community member as *harijan* (lower caste), who charged them 1,000 to 1,200 rupees in rent per yak to take care of their needs during their descent down to their winter settlement, as the yaks are kept where the motorable roads end.

Despite their deep attachment to the transhumant way of life, and deep longing for its continuity, Rungs acknowledged that exposure to education has brought about an intergenerational change in attitude towards transhumance. While the lure of education and the attraction of a more comfortable life makes settling downhill a preferred option for many youngsters, not all are willing to cut off their connection with their summer home. After trade stopped, education gained importance as a means to get stable employment. A similar

Transhumance and Change Among the Rungs

Figure 3. A shepherd in the process of transhumance. Photo: Nisthasri Awasthi.

situation of decline in transhumant activities and increasing trend of formal school education has also been revealed by Namgay et al. (2013) among the transhumant communities of Bhutan. At the same time, Avram (2009) talks about the revival of the legacy of transhumance through education, which is absent in the case of the Rungs. The modern education provided to Rung children has no place for transhumance, which further inspires them to take up other forms of employment available outside the region. This creates a divide between the community members, as some members of the community can afford education while some are not interested in studying. Also, the kind of education students in villages receive is different from the kind they get in cities.

The difference in climate in the summer settlement as contrasted with the climate in the winter settlement is a significant factor for the Rungs. For the generation that practised transhumance prior to 1962, it was clear that, in spite of other considerations (as experienced by the younger generation), they prefer to continue practising transhumance. Again, the notion of owning their land and property in Darma inspires them to continue transhumance, in spite of the physical vulnerability of the valley. The women of the village gave compelling accounts of their experiences of transhumance as they similarly commented on the better climatic and health conditions in the upper settlement. However, they are prevented from continuing with the practice of transhumance as they have to look after their school-going children in the lower settlement. In the absence of schools in the upper settlement, which was a matter of concern for the community, small children are not taken there and mothers are forced to stay back with them. The link between the decreasing importance and reducing viability of transhumance and the need for education is evident from the narratives where parents emphasise the importance of educating their children so that they do not have to live this *harsh life*. It can therefore be concluded that age, gender, proximity to the summer settlement and economic status all have a bearing on the propensity to go for transhumance (Childs 2012).

The Rungs emphasised that things have changed in comparison to the past when their occupation was closely linked to their natural surroundings and in turn influenced many local practices. In order to foster respect for their traditional life ways and encourage members to visit their summer villages, Rungs have instituted religious ceremonials on fixed occasions where people who are settled outside and even abroad have to come to their village every two to three years to pay homage to the village deity. These rituals are related to their landscape and give meaning to the vulnerability and importance of nature in their life. These rituals and the rules of essential attendance associated with them are seen to have promoted greater group solidarity among them, across economic groups.

Despite much scepticism among the Rungs regarding development projects, elderly Rungs feel that development in the region in terms of motorable roads will improve connectivity and facilitate communication between their villages and nearby towns, where the younger members are employed in different jobs. Further, it will become easier for them to reach their village when they travel. Many community members feel this could keep them connected to their families and also help them in continuing their practices of cultivation.

Although cross-border trade is a thing of the past, during the study period communities were seen to practise trade in their summer settlement at higher altitudes. However, this trade is more market- and product-oriented than before, when trade focused on exchange and ecology. Unlike in the past, when trade involved movement over long distances, today trade is localised and focused on selling consumer items to local consumers or herbs to agents, which is a result of increasing sedentarisation.

Transhumance and Change Among the Rungs

Apart from cultivating their land (which has considerably decreased), community members are also getting employment as construction workers in various government schemes to construct pavements and non-motorised roads.

Local constructions of conservation and ecology

Community members' accounts of climatic variation indicate locals' inquisitiveness about changes occurring to their climate. For example, the summer settlement at higher altitudes was preferred to their winter settlement at lower altitudes and was further perceived to be beneficial for one's health. While many still view the upper settlement as a *wonderful place with clean and salubrious air*, they are also aware of the dangers that surround them, which have hindered their practice of transhumance and trade. The locals consider the environment they inhabit to be indomitable, which is reflected in their stoic acceptance of the difficult conditions. This construction of the environment is reflected in the categories (Escobar, 1999, Robbins, 2004) with which they describe and order nature. This categorisation is reflected in their rituals, lifestyle, livelihood, management of resources and division of property in their communities. Transhumance is also a result of this classification of their landscape. It is inferred that the Rung identity is also a product of such categories. The narratives show that the locals classify their landscape as uphill (*malla*) and downhill (*talla*) and refer to both their homes in the same way. The transhumant routes are referred to as campsites (*padav*), which are considered as temporary settlements till they reach their destination. It is clear that transhumance comprises managing time and space. Space is seen as a cultural construct and its utilisation is culturally determined, often seen as a marker of identity that is tied to the space. The rights over pasturelands and the meanings people ascribe to the summer village in terms of peaceful life and better health, inscribe a sense of identity that is tied to the summer villages. Such attachment to their winter settlement is not seen because, though they own a house there, they do not have land for cultivation. Besides, their winter space is shared with non-Rungs and other settled Kumaonis, which leads to stiff competition for the scarce resources.

Being highly dependent on the forest and its resources, the Rungs have well-developed forest conservation practices, seen in the restrictions placed on felling of trees, especially in ecologically fragile areas. Thus, community members have their own rules restricting felling of trees as they regard their forest as very important and a protector and provider of their livelihood. Typical of this community which ekes out its living amidst harsh physical and climatic conditions, a collaborative and cooperative relationship appears to exist with communities in neighbouring regions within the valley.

Belief in climate change is demonstrated by this narrative that *it is getting warmer year by year, now the snow starts later than usual.* As a former *sarpanch* stated, *I used to keep myself updated regarding news of climate change through paper, radio and television.* The contrast of the past norms with the current situation suggests that, with time, there has been local internalisation of the state discourse promulgated through the mass media (Huber and Blackburn, 2012) and eventually of the need to take action. The villagers construct forest as their *guard* as opposed to the state's construct of forest as a reservoir of resources, which needs to be preserved.

The steps taken by the Forest Department are in consonance with the eleventh Five Year Plan, which in turn attempts to achieve the global Millennium Development Goals (MDGs), aiming to increase forest and tree cover in India by five per cent. The blame that has been placed on the locals for their 'irrational' use of resources led the Forest Department to impose bans and subsequently penalise the locals.

Interestingly, the government is trying to project the region as one of the centres of 'eco-tourism'. Needless to say, this objectification of landscape as a recreational site for the consumption of the city elite is in sharp contrast to the local idea of preservation held by Rungs. The government promotes forest as contributing to cultural services such as recreation, tourism, cultural identity and indigenous knowledge and articulates this with the broader discourse of sustainability. In this process they disempower and displace the local people. One of the priorities of the Forest Department, which has been clearly laid out in its ten-year management plan, is to reduce the dependency of the locals on their forest and displace those villages which are less inhabited, eventually incorporating the region into sanctuary.

State policy vis-à-vis transhumance and livelihood

The way in which local people experience and understand their environment is not reflected in government policy. Instead, it is presented as archaic and harmful for the environment, hence needing to be eliminated. The fact that policy documents use a particular language (English) and official terminology reflects the centralised and top-down nature of government initiatives. This needs to be seriously thought about in order to provide development to the locals without disturbing their livelihoods.

Transhumance and Change Among the Rungs

While the Rungs are aware of the importance of conserving their natural environment with well-established practices in place, they are not always in agreement with the model of conservation adopted by the government, which in their eyes is ill conceived and works against them. State policies that are intended to benefit the livelihood practices of hill communities such as the Rungs were seen to actually promote the illegal trade in herbs. Though many of the community members are aware that these practices are illegal, they seem to be ignorant about the exact nature of state regulations and restrictions demarcating regions falling under sanctuary areas. The shift in production to profitable medicinal herbs has become prevalent among the Rungs, which might lead to competition.

The women, however, seem to be unaware of policy developments, which can be attributed to the fact that their activity is restricted to their households. Women appear to take their situation for granted, as one said *we are fine … everything is going smooth*, occupied in her daily round of cooking, cleaning and caring for the young and the infirm. The remark that *if roads come, it would also be nice*, suggests that coming of the roads would make their journey easier and they could at the same time take care of their school-going children.

Discussion

In an attempt to examine the current transhumance practice among the Rungs in Darma valley and the process of identity formation in view of the changes in their society with respect to transhumance, the narrative accounts provided by the individuals helped in reconsidering certain concepts of transhumance, conservation and development, at the same time making a case for their legitimate needs and rights, which could go a long way in informing policies. The narratives clearly show that the change in society has been accepted as inevitable. The locals are accepting the change in a resilient way to adjust to new livelihood options available to them. Transformation in the practice of transhumance with time has changed the way the landscape has been constructed by the Rung community. The change in their livelihoods, changing structure of the family, their acceptance of development in terms of micro and macro hydro-power projects and the anticipated roads for better communication and facilities, all affirm the Rungs' resilience and readiness to change to overcome their challenging experiences. Therefore, as a result of changes in livelihood strategies and attitude towards transhumance, with the change in the worldview of the Rungs, the concept they have of their identity is also seen to have undergone a change.

The narrative approach that was grounded in the context and experiences of the study participants helped in reconceptualising certain ways of understanding transhumance and conservation. Narratives of the locals began by problematising transhumance and identity among the Rungs. This was followed by arguments on development, giving justification for some development issues and rejecting others. The conclusion of their narratives concerned the future state of transhumance and the inevitability of change.

Policies should be inclusive of the Rung community who have to live in this arduous region. What appears from this study is that there are a number of unmet needs of the locals, which the state government and the Forest Department are unable to address. Meeting these needs would go a long way towards providing the Rungs with a livelihood. There is a need to effect planning from the perspective of the locals, giving due respect to their views on development and at the same time providing a way forward for their traditional occupation. There is consequently a need for effective forms of governance that can accommodate local constructions of environmental change on one hand, yet also communicate forms of environmental protection on the other, in the light of the changing conditions of Rung society. Against the backdrop of providing livelihoods to the Rungs and preventing out-migration from the village, state policies need to look into the issues of development and livelihoods together and not see them as separate entities. The priority of the state government should be to focus on disaster management policies, considering the fragility of the region, while at the same time giving space to local knowledge of preparedness. At the same time, community participation in post-disaster relief and rehabilitation should also be considered. The local experiences in this area would help in framing better policies.

References

Avram, M. 2009. 'The legacy of transhumance in National Park of Abruzzo, Lazio and Molise (PNALM): Rediscovery and exploitation', *GeoJournal of Tourism and Geosites* 4: 153–59.

Brown, C.W. 1984. *The Goat is Mine, the Load is Yours*. Lund: Lund Studies in Anthropology.

Cerulo, K.A. 1997. 'Identity construction: New issues, new directions', *Annual Review of Sociology* 23: 386–409.

Childs, G. 2012. 'Trans-Himalayan migrations as processes, not events: Towards a theoretical framework'. In T. Huber and S. Blackburn (eds) *Origins and Migrations among Tibeto-Burman Speakers of the Extended Eastern Himalaya*. Leiden: Brill. pp. 11–32.

Dangwal, D.D. 1997. 'State, forests and graziers in the hills of Uttar Pradesh: impact of colonial forestry on peasants, Gujars and Bhotiyas'. *The Indian Economic and Social History Review* **34**: 405–35.

Dyson-Hudson, R and N. Dyson-Hudson. 1980, 'Nomadic pastoralism'. *Annual Review of Anthropology* **9**: 15–61.

Escobar, A. 1992. 'Imagining a post-development era? Critical thought, development and social movements'. *Social Text* **10**: 20–56.

Escobar, A. 1999, 'After nature: Steps to an antiessentialist political ecology'. *Current Anthropology* **40**: 1–30.

Evans-Pritchard, E. 1940, *The Nuer: A Description of the Modes of Livelihood and Political Institutions of a Nilotic People*. Oxford: Clarendon Press.

Fairclough, N. 1992. *Discourse and Social Change*. Cambridge: Polity Press.

Fairclough, N. 1995. *Critical Discourse Analysis*. London: Longman.

Farooquee, N.A. and K.S. Rao. 1998. 'Transhumance: an adaptation for survival and strategy for conservation of natural resources'. In *Research for Mountain Development: Some Initiatives and Accomplishments*. Nainital: Gyanodaya Prakashan.

Fletcher, R. 2010, 'Neoliberal environmentality: Towards a poststructuralist political ecology of the conservation debate'. *Conservation and Society* **8**: 171–81.

Foucault, M. 1978. 'Governmentality' (Lecture at the Collège de France, Feb. 1, 1978)', in G. Burchell, C. Gordon and P. Miller (eds), 1991, *The Foucault Effect: Studies in Governmentality*. Hemel Hempstead: Harvester Wheatsheaf Hemel Hempstead. pp. 87–104.

Foucault, M. 1980. *Power/ Knowledge: Selected Interviews and Other Writings 1972–1977*. London: Harvester Press.

Goldstein, M. and C. Beall. 1989. 'The impact of reform policy on nomadic pastoralists in Western Tibet'. *Asian Survey* **29**: 619–24.

Guha, R. 1989. *The Unquiet Woods: Ecological Changes and Peasant Resistance in the Himalaya*. Delhi: Oxford University Press.

Hoon, V. 1996. *Living on the Move: Bhotias of the Kumaon Himalaya*. New Delhi: Sage Publications.

Namgay, K., J. Millar, R. Black and T. Samdup. 2013. 'Transhumant agro-pastoralism in Bhutan: Exploring contemporary practices and socio-cultural traditions'. *Pastoralism: Research, Policy and Practice* **3**: 1–26.

Nautiyal, S., K.S. Rao, R.K. Maikhuri and K.G. Saxena. 2003. 'Transhumant pastoralism in the Nanda Devi Biosphere Reserve, India'. *Mountain Research and Development* **23**: 255–62.

Nongbri, T. 1999. 'Forest policy in North-East India'. *Indian Anthropologist* **29**: 1–36.

Pangti, S.S. 1992. *Madhya Himalaya Ke Bhotiya Janjati: Jauhar Ke Shauka* [in Hindi,

Bhotiya Tribes of Central Himalaya: Shaukas of Jauhar]. New Delhi: Takhsila Prakashan.

Peluso, N.L. 1992. *Rich Forests, Poor People. Resource Control and Resistance in Java*. Oxford: University of California Press.

Prasad, R.R. 1989. *Bhotia Tribals of India: Dynamics of Economic Transformation*. New Delhi: Gian Publishing House.

Ricoeur, P. 1991. 'Narrative identity'. In D. Wood (ed.), *On Paul Ricoeur: Narrative and Interpretation*. London: Routledge.

Rinschede, G. 1987. 'Transhumance in European and American mountains'. In N. Allan, G. Knapp and C. Stadel (eds), *Human Impact on Mountains*. Lanham: Rowman and Littlefield. pp. 96–108.

Robbins, P. 2004. *Political Ecology: A Critical Introduction*. USA: Blackwell Publishing.

Sharma, V.P., I.K. Rollefson and J. Morton. 2003. *Pastoralism in India: a Scoping Study*. Indian Institute of Management, Ahmedabad- League for Pastoral Peoples, Germany- Natural Resources Institute, University of Greenwich University Collaborative Report for the DFID (Department for International Development), UK.

Youatt, R. 2008. 'Counting species: Biopower and the global biodiversity census'. *Environmental Values* 17: 393–417.

Chapter 9

FROM STEWARDS TO TRESPASSERS: PASTORALIST MANAGEMENT OF FOREST RESOURCES

Aman Singh

Introduction

This chapter describes the community forests in Rajasthan known as *orans*, which historically have been maintained by local people as an essential resource. Today, however, areas have been taken over by the Forest Department as reserves, excluding local people. Considerable degradation of the forest has been observed. The chapter looks at the reasons for this in a case study in the buffer zone of the Sariska Tiger Reserve in Alwar District of Rajasthan.

Orans are community forests dedicated 'to some deities and spirits by the local people, both tribals and non-tribals … preserved [and] maintained through people's participation'. (Sekhar 2004) Acknowledging their connection and dependence on the water, flora, and fauna of these forests, local people sanctified them by performing ceremonies to honour the deities that inhabit them, as well dictating a strict set of rules about the use of the resources (Singh and Bahl 2006). Each *oran* has its own set of established customs to ensure the protection of its specific combination of resources. These vary from completely banning the collection of any materials from the forest floor to only prohibiting the felling of particular species of trees (Malhotra 2001).

Also known as *devbanis*, these local forests vary in size from 100 to 500 *bhighas* (about 100 hectares), and in our study area are found nestling in the foothills of the Aravalli range. Most *orans* have sources of water, either small springs or rivulets running through them or a variety of ponds and *nadis* in their midst. A large collection of such forest patches is known locally as a *chhind*. 'Chhind' in the local dialect means a landscape used largely for grazing. These can cover fairly extensive areas across interspersed habitation. The well-known Sariska Tiger forest reserve close to our study area is in fact one such collection of *orans* that together formed a substantial forest tract. To this day it is possible to identify the various *orans* that comprise the Sariska Tiger Reserve.

At the heart of every *oran* is a deity, whose domain has at some point in time been marked out by a ritual, usually consisting of the pouring of Ganges water or saffron-milk around the grove. Taking care of the shrine is a *sadhu* (monk), whose own modest needs are met by local communities. The *sadhu* is an interface between local community concerns and the preservation and wellbeing of the *orans*. These *orans* are a source of natural wealth like fodder, fuel, timber, berries, roots and herbs and, moreover, play an important role in promoting a flourishing livestock-based economy and growth of livestock rearing communities.

Singh and Bahl (2006) report that co-management of the *orans* by villagers and pastoralists contributed to a greater species diversity in cultivated and wild plants as well as guaranteeing sustainable access to all members of the community. If the sacred groves are to be preserved, traditional knowledge and cultural practices need to be included in the policies that determine who is allowed to utilise the natural resources found within them, and to what extent. Given the diverse academic and institutional backgrounds of those currently working on forestry in India, it is perhaps unsurprising that essentialist portrayals of 'traditional' ecological relations endure alongside more critical, historically and politically nuanced, readings. Rangarajan (1996) and Sivaramakrishnan (1999) have drawn attention to the multiple and divergent 'internal' pressures on colonial forestry, from the ideological anxieties of foresters to relations with local communities. Guha (1983) discusses the imperial interventions which were everywhere a malevolent force, disrupting the delicate, symbiotic balance between forest dwellers and the land that had evolved over many hundreds of years. Rather than introducing stability, Guha argued, imperial forestry succeeded only in dismantling age-old livelihood systems and replacing them with unsustainable, market-driven management models. Guha's work has had a profound influence on studies of colonial-era environmental relations, both in India and beyond. In Rajasthan, ideas about indigenous conservation and the 'ecologically noble savage' (Redford 1991, 46) are alive and well. The last few decades have seen a dramatic surge in interest in traditional ecological knowledge and 'environmental ethics' originating from this arid and semi-arid region. Much of the current concern with indigenous knowledge and practices stems from the pioneering work of Jodha (1985, 1992) and Brara

From Stewards to Trespassers

Figure 1. Modernising pastoralism: Gujjar pastoralists with GPS, Bakhtpura Village. Photo: Aman Singh.

(1989, 1992) on common property resources in the state. Both argued that the introduction of land reforms in the 1950s disrupted traditional institutional arrangements for managing common resources – forests, wastelands, community pastures, etc. – leading to the current decline in the quantity and quality of such lands. Gold and Gujar (1989), for example, have employed collaborative oral histories to explore radical changes in the 'politics of nature' (Gold and Gujar 1989, Robbins, Gold and Gujar 2003) in pre- and post-Independence rural Rajasthan. Based on fieldwork in the erstwhile Kingdom of Sawar, their works interweave political economy, environmental history and folklore studies to chart the changing relations between state, subject and 'nature' from a subjective, subaltern standpoint. Critically, these studies call attention to the multiplicity of historical realities and the crucial role of memory – 'symbolic and embodied, hence neither individual nor collective' (Robbins, Gold and Gujar 2003, 88) – in configuring these.

The two major social groups living in this area that utilise as well as worship the sacred forest groves are the Meenas and the Gujars. The Meenas are settled agriculturalists and make up forty per cent of the population while the Gujars are nomadic pastoralists and constitute around 32 per cent of the population (Sekhar 2003). Both depend on the *orans* for fuel, medicinal plants, fruits and fodder for their livestock. According to the pastoralists, the *orans* provide them with indispensable vegetation to feed their cattle. In addition to grazing grounds, shady *orans* afford a resting spot and a refuge from the scorching Rajasthani sun to both livestock and the herders (Singh and Bahl 2006). In addition, cultivated and medicinal plants are often planted in their drip line since the leaf litter contains nitrogen, a practice 'embedded in the local knowledge' (Jodha 1986). The forest resources most often collected by the Meenas include mango, timru and kikoda fruits for household consumption as well as honey, soapnut, neem and jamun which are used for consumption as well as trading purposes (Chaudhry et al. 2008). Although the Meenas and Gujars have co-existed in the same spatial and social context for generations, the government has generated a conflict between them by classifying the Gujars as a backward caste and the Meenas as an indigenous, scheduled tribe, thereby giving the Meenas exclusive territorial rights over certain *orans*.

Orans in context

Orans are situated in dry environments across western India. This makes them important water sources in Rajasthan; though the largest state (ten per cent of the country's total area) it has only one per cent of the country's water resources. Here *orans* protect springs and aquifers, and host centuries-old water storage facilities. Most sources are small springs or rivulets or a variety of ponds. Several *orans* have large perennial springs used year-round for irrigation. Gopal Das ki Devbani has a very old and architecturally ornate 'Oran talab' (rainwater harvesting structure). Jugrawar ki Rundh Bani, Gujjawas ki Bani, Bherunath ji ki Bani and several other *orans* likewise have large ponds which serve as water harvesting structures for the catchment area and are usually located to collect maximum run-off and serve the important purpose of providing water for irrigation and drinking. The need for a dependable water supply, such as from wells, has been a major incentive for communities to use *orans* in a sustainable manner.

Orans are very important to the lives of different resource users, meeting economic, social, cultural and spiritual needs of the community. Strong internal social control within *oran* communities enables effective sanctions to be imposed on violators, reflecting their importance to resource users. *Orans* generally have a well-defined boundary and are governed by an egalitarian system, with respect to all users. Normally, every *oran* has a mechanism for conflict resolution among its resource users with simple and clear rules for all users, and significant commitment from all resource users (for example annual contributions for maintenance). Strong religious beliefs also support the Oran; for respect for the Devbani stems from strong faith in God.

Many species are found within the *orans*; local societies use them for a variety of livelihood needs including traditional non-timber forest products (e.g. *kair* pickle, *ber* fruit, honey collection, *panni ghas/jhunda* handicrafts, clay, *chapun* for baskets). Some of the plant species that have been preserved or reintroduced in *orans* have medicinal value, such as *adusta*, which is used as a cough syrup. Other species, notably the *jharber, satavari, kuri, saava* and certain other wild grains, are valuable for home consumption and market sale. In addition, these species, along with minor forest produce such as honey, pottery (from the clay) and baskets (from grasses), can be sold at market, providing a supplement to village incomes which is invaluable during times of hardship (drought, poor harvest, blight, etc.).

There are some specific social norms with regards to the *oran* in the community. In and around some, noone is allowed to carry an axe. Alternatively, axes may be allowed but only for the lopping of branches, not to cut down the whole tree. However, the villagers in our case study indicated that community enforcement of the norms is no longer very strong, and said that some of the women are carrying axes into the forest. It was stated that there are no regular meetings regarding the forest and a meeting is basically only held when a prominent person is present. Earlier they used to have monthly meetings, but with the change in the number of people following the social norms, this has decreased. When they do have a meeting, fines and rules are agreed upon, and they usually invite a forest-guard to discuss management efforts in the forest. The members of this committee are not elected, but shifts and membership are based on the individual's performance.

The resilience of pastoralists regarding *oran* is reflected in legends about a people's tenacity in preserving their inheritance. This oral tradition was based on a curious mix of community folklore and the kind of official support they received from the traditional rulers of the region, known as the Rajputs, during the colonial period. An oral tradition of customary rules, still active in several villages, regarding access, use and decision-making in these groves is highly dependent on the historical circumstances of their foundation and on the strength of the culture and collective beliefs. The names of the *orans* provide a clue to the historical origins of the woodland, for example 'Kakad bani' is an *oran* consecrated to 'Kakad Devta'. Then if the woodland is within the common boundaries of a single village it would be 'Rakhat bani' and so would be the responsibility of that village alone. Likewise, the *oran* served as a common resource for the village livestock and a source of medicinal herbs, which was protected by the villagers collectively. Sometimes several villages shared such a woodlot and dedicated it to the deities whom they worshipped. Similarly 'Dharadi' symbolism attached to planting and protection of plants. Many *gotras* (clans) have a tree as a totem. The people belonging to the *gotra* regard this particular tree as sacred.

Orans also serve as socio-religious medicine – if disease breaks out in livestock then villagers gather in one place and promise the deity a feast if the disease is mitigated. The practices of the resident *sadhu* also have a preventative dimension; he is called upon to ensure that livestock are protected from sickness and other evil forces, 'anointing' the animals with twigs from the *neem* tree (the *jhara dena* ritual). Specialist knowledge of this sort is not limited to the *sadhu*; most of the older generations are aware of various plants used to treat, among other things, sore throats, migraines, open wounds and osteoarthritis. And, in many villages, tribal communities still gather once a year for the *dudh ki dhar dena* ritual, during which milk is collected from each household and then drizzled around the sacred grove with the whole village following in procession. This practice is thought to ward off evil spirits for the coming year.

Introducing the Bhaktpura field site

Grounded in research over two decades covering 900 *orans* in several districts of Rajasthan, this chapter focuses on the example of one *oran* – Bherunath Bani – in Bakhtpura village, located in the buffer zone of the Sariska Tiger Reserve, approximately twenty kilometres from the city of Alwar. Agro-pastoralism is the main livelihood activity undertaken in Bakhtpura. In attempting to understand the diversity of pastoralists' roles in relation to natural resources and the institutions that mediate access, Bakhtpura appeared to be a promising site. Bakhtpura covers an area of approximately 346 hectares, of which around 150 hectares are recorded as agricultural land (irrigated and unirrigated) and a further 148 hectares are classified as Protected Forest (Census of India 2001, District Census Handbook (District Alwar)).

Local people had a good and precise understanding about the boundaries of the Bakhtpura village commons and the different areas of land. The

From Stewards to Trespassers

Figure 2. Pastoralist woman and her buffaloes, Lilunda village, Sariska Tiger Reserve. Photo: Aman Singh.

boundaries of the commons have a very long and well-known history in Bakhtpura village since the days of the Mughal Empire. Although the Forest Department has extended the area of the forest that comes under its control over the last fifteen years, this has only affected the total village commons to a very small degree, as the land has simply shifted category from Revenue Wasteland to Forestland. Given the religious significance of the *oran*, similar to the *orans* in Jaisalmer district, rules and norms of usage and access are very well respected in the community. But the areas within the forest reserve have become increasingly degraded.

Historically, the upkeep of the *oran* in Alwar district has been the responsibility of a traditional local institution in the village going by the name of 'Thain'. Comprising a group of five to seven village notables, the Thain appointed the *sadhu*, as well as having the power to dispense with his services. They also decided on the rules for use of the *oran* and the penalties for breaking the rules, including fines. This arrangement played an important role in mediating the community's interests and those relating to the preservation of the *oran*. Around twenty years ago in Bakhtpura, there was a pass system in place, for entering the forest for grazing purposes and collection of fuelwood. The amount paid for passing into the area was determined by the number and species of livestock and/or by the number of axes taken into the forest, based on a calculation of how much wood one person with one axe would collect in a day. Thereby, it was a taxing system where the amount paid was determined by the amount of resource a household took from the commons.

In 1985 the area was turned into a Tiger Reserve and the village lost the majority of their grazing rights in the area, though they still have the rights for grazing within a distance of three to four kilometres from the village, in the periphery of the reserve. After 1985 a system of fines for breaking the rules in the reserve was set up by the Forest Department, but the number of fines registered is very low. The villagers believe that the Forest Officials are usually bribed by the trespassers; therefore a very low number of fines are given.

Robust institutions are necessary to counteract the profit-maximising actions of individual actors. This requires transparent systems with strict rules, graduated sanctions, clear incentives and such like. Rather than allowing people to make decisions (e.g. about resource use) based solely on narrow, economic/productive considerations, but instead including history, political concerns, beliefs, etc., institutional theory (and, as such, much development discourse), such systems will lead to individuals who conform to the logic of local standards. Our study depicts the following institutional design principles (Table 1).

Table 1. Considerations in oran *institutional design.*

Structures of authority	Different authority systems (traditional village institutions, elders, deity, Panchayat, Government) side-by-side, development players, religion
Internalised social norms	Rules contested, negotiated
Dynamic leadership	Village institutions and elders are important
Simple rules	Rules are presented differently between people, variations on a theme. Institutional inertia needs to be overcome in setting new rules
Accountability	Deities are not accountable in any conventional way, whereas the traditional village institutions are but Panchayats (constitutional village institutions) are not
Government policy	For management of orans, a committee of local people and trustees can be constituted

Figure 3. Bhagwana Gujjar: a pastoralist with herd of goats from Binak village. Photo: Aman Singh.

Bakhtpura village has an ongoing conflict with the nearby village of Binka over the grazing. In 2010, one member of the Bakhtpura community was beaten up by members of the other village, and this resulted in a major fight between members of the two communities, where both sides used weapons, such as axes, stones and clubs. The police came and arrested some members from both communities and held them for several days. A settlement was made, to follow the traditional grazing rights and boundaries. In 2014, a group of twenty to 25 women from a nearby village often came to cut the trees. The members of the village community stated that it was very difficult for them to control this, and especially to do it without creating a new fight. But at the same time some damage was done to the forest because of this as the neighbouring villages have over-exploited their own forest and are now coming to collect forest resources from Bakhtpura's protected resource. This change in behaviour of the neighbouring village developed slowly over three years. The first two years they came and did some lumbering in the community forest, they took only a little and there was no real reaction from Bakhtpura community. However in 2014 the

Figure 4. A woman Gujjar pastoralist with her herd of goats from Vijaipura village. Photo: Aman Singh.

quantities they were taking increased due to the lack of earlier resistance. The community was of the opinion that inter-community cohesion was pretty strong and that over the last 25 years they have had good control of their own village members with regards to grazing, harvesting of wood and protecting the *oran*.

Similarly, a case in Bherunath *oran* reflects the local values. A Gujjar individual settled in this village and did not follow the rules and regulations about this *oran* but one day started chopping down trees. Villagers told him he could not do that, but he was very adamant and also physically very powerful, so he did not listen to the other community members. When he went back to his house with the logs, after a few days something happened so that he had to sell his whole land and leave the village; so the punishment is very severe if anything happens within the boundary of this *oran*.

Bhaktpura

The *oran* of this village has been cut into two parts, one that is community controlled and another that has been enclosed as a forest reserve. The result of this has been that the reserved forest has been stripped bare – presumably by the local community – whereas the community controlled forests retain fairly thick stands of trees. There is also a very good *johad* (water reservoir) in the *oran*. With the onset of rains in late July, the *johad* swells to its maximum, meaning that water will be retained in the forest for the dry season. Here, tree cover is extensive, the understorey dense and diverse. From March to October, the lush *bani* scintillates crimson then chrome with the flowers of *dhak* (*Butea monosperma*) and *khair* (*Acacia catechu*); in the dry winter months, the same trees offer shade to languid children and goats.

Bakhtpura is dominated by Gujjars (54 households). Jatavs (a Scheduled Caste) are the second most populous group (thirty households), with Rajputs (four households) and Bhil (three households) also represented, though in much smaller numbers. The total population of the village is 686 (Census of India 2001, District Census Handbook (District Alwar)). All the households in Bakhtpura kept livestock. Goats were by far the most common (846 in total, with an average holding of roughly a dozen head per household), followed by 274 buffalo and 34 cows (KRAPAVIS 2009). Villagers are also considered pastoralists, using the terms interchangeably.

In Bakhtpura, Dhok (*Anogeissus pendula*) is the dominant tree species. Grass species like Satavari, Kuri, Saava, and certain other wild grains are found. Other tree species found are Babul (*Acacia nilotica*), Ber (*Zizyphus mauritiana*), Giant Milkweed (Calotropis procera), Kair (*Capparis decidua*), Kala Khair (*Acacia catechu*), Hingota (*Balanites egyptiaca*), Neem (*Azardirachta indica*), Peepal (*Ficus religiosa*), as well as creepers and fig species. A total of 404 indigenous and naturalised plant species belonging to 272 genera under 87 families are found in the Sariska Tiger Reserve area. According to Champion and Seth (1968), Dhok is an edaphic plant in tropical, dry deciduous forests. Dhok is a prominent tree species often found in pure stands in the middle slopes of the hills; its leaves are good fodder and this is the principal species growing in the reserve. The main niches of vegetation for village livestock grazing are:

- Hill top plateaus called *maalas*, where pastures of good quality are to be found
- Community protected scrub forests along the foothills
- Riverbeds and streams, where the riverbeds are also used for sand collection and reed production for sale in the nearby region
- Fallow fields in the tract and nearby areas.

Aman Singh

Research approach

The role of *orans* in pastoralist livelihoods was studied using a structured survey format, and field visits to get information both on the larger community and on individuals. This gave an indication of people's perceptions. This was cross-checked against other data sources: archival records; *shilalekhs* (stone tablets) on the *orans*; Government Census and Gazetteers; related website searches; NGO reports (including KRAPAVIS), and published case studies (Patwa 2013, Singh, A. 2010, Singh, A. and Gupta 2010, Singh, A. and Jobanputra 2009, Singh, R. 2009, Sisodia and Singh, A. 2002).

Information was also gathered through community meetings. Oral histories were sought on the issue, not only in meetings but discussing on-the-site, and in people's homes; through this process the community become more informed on the vital issues of *orans*. Initial inquiries in the villages focused on the practical aspects of resource use. The timing, spacing and major methods of resource extraction were established through semi-structured interviews with pastoralists and farmers. Investigators also spoke with women about water and wood collection and learned of the labours of livestock-rearing, from fodder and dung collection to veterinary practices.

Research culminated with a comprehensive survey conducted in Bhaktpura village, which recorded human and livestock demographics, agricultural practices and production, natural resource extraction, approximate area of the *oran* site, ownership, statement of significance, special or unique features of the site, biodiversity, present condition, threats, traditional practices followed for conserving *orans* and their unique values of sacredness, priority (for conservation management), agency/person/community (if any, involved in preservation and usage, names and contact addresses, including those of the key persons), particularly those who could be involved in future preservation and management of the site and could provide leadership in this regard.

The surveys registered villagers' opinions about the relative importance of institutions, the efficacy of rules and punishments, informal responses to rule violations and other analogous issues. They also sought to establish the nature and extent of participation in public decision-making forums by different individuals and groups. The behaviour of individuals vis-à-vis natural resources and formal institutions could not be understood apart from the social, historical and political context. Why people cut some trees while conserving others and avoided Forest Department trees was contingent on a range of factors that could be discerned only through enduring ethnographic engagement. In addition to those methods, oral histories were recorded from several older community members in order to gain some sense of the region's social and political past, in particular the frequent episodes of conflict between state and subjects over claims to natural resources. This process went hand-in-hand with archival research, the findings from which spurred further productive discussion in the village. Data on medicinal plants was also collected. The area under investigation was searched for veterinary medicinal plants used by the Gujjars and other pastoral communities of Alwar district. The field survey was carried out covering different seasons over a period of one year. As a first step we conducted a four-day workshop with local educated youth and pastoralist elders to understand their local medicinal system on animal health.

Findings

The viability of the *oran* lies in its role in fulfilling real needs of local people. *Orans* are critically important pasture tracts for local livestock. Geared mainly to the needs of cattle, they provide a rich reserve that is invaluable especially in times of environmental stress. Other animals use the *orans* and at times these cater to the needs of migrating herd owners. In addition to pasture, the *orans* are a year-round source of fuelwood. Thus while standing trees cannot be cut down within the *oran*, fallen branches can be collected. *Orans* often provide valuable medicinal herbs and plants for people and animals. What is more, they are a refuge for wildlife in an otherwise densely populated landscape. Finally, the *devbanis* and shrines are a locus for community gatherings at festival times. In a nutshell, *orans* and *devbanis* are a living and active part of the socio-ecological landscape of local communities.

Social factors

Regarding the level of dependency on the village commons, interview groups stated that about fifty per cent of their income was produced through the commons during normal monsoon rains. In the summer, pastoralists migrate for grazing or for manual labour. For approximately three months during the winter they depend on their private and often irrigated lands for crop residues and agriculture, and for about six months during and after the monsoon their livelihood is partly dependent on the village commons. In times of drought the village commons can sustain their livelihood for two to three months. The villagers will migrate with their buffaloes to the *Nogawa* plains, around ninety kilometres from the village, to graze the livestock. One member of the interview group said that during the last drought he lost fifty to sixty per cent of his livestock as not enough fodder was available. He came back to the village with his remaining buffaloes and started using mustard plants, char berries and leaves from a specific tree that grows in the *oran* as fodder. He stated that the leaves from the tree are only used during severe famines; with this poor quality fodder he made it through the drought. Some special rules come into effect during drought. Some land is allotted to each household from the disadvantaged category for grazing, and no grazing in the forest is allowed so that the forest vegetation can regenerate. The villagers indicated that some households do break the drought rules, but not often.

'Yadi hamara devbani thik to sab kuch hai; yadi yah thik nahi to chara, pani aur bhojan ke lale.' [If our *oran* is intact we have everything, if not, we suffer from lack of fodder, water and wood] said Badri Gujjar, a sixty-year-old pastoralist, from Bakhtpura village. In rural Rajasthan, poverty and vulnerability to climatic changes (drought, famine) are common. Villagers highlight their dependence on *orans* for wood for fuel and timber, fodder for their animals, water and medicinal plants. *Orans* are critically important pasture tracts for local livestock and meet the real needs of local people; productive *orans* result in less poverty and more livelihood security in communities. People of Meena ki Dhani, a tribal village, said that

> the driving force of our livelihood is the *oran* 'Adaval'; we are all aware how useful it is for us, for if we need anything we take it from there. We have our animals to graze over there. So the binding force is our own livelihoods, and we recognise all people from this area. We understand that if we destroy the *oran* our lives will be compromised, and that is why we organise this way, have the Samiti [village organising body].

Even though the *oran* is geared mainly to the needs of cattle, other animals also use it. At times *orans* cater to the needs of migrating herd owners as well as the 7.5 million pastoralists residing in Rajasthan and their 54.4 million livestock, out of which 14.3 million are sheep.

As communities in Rajasthan are predominantly mobile and pastoral, they depend to a great extent on the grazing grounds provided by the *orans*; for example, 41 per cent of livestock in Barmer district depend on them for fodder. With grazing there is flexibility – as long as there is grass or leaves, animal graze. At other times people only use the *oran* for shade and water. For other forest produce, people may take as much as falls to the ground when the tree is shaken. And only a limited quantity can be taken home. This results in better grazing for livestock and increased availability of medicinal plants

From Stewards to Trespassers

and other minor forest produce. According to our survey of 72 residents, the significance of Bakhtpura's *oran* can be summarised as follows.

Table 2. Oran *significance to the local community.*

	Not Important	Somewhat important	Important	More Important	Most Important
1) How important is the Oran to you?	0	0	0	0	72
2) How important is Devi to you?	0	1	0	0	71
3) How important is the Samiti to you?	0	1	5	4	62
4) How important is the Forest Department to you?	31	14	20	2	5
5) How much conflict over private land is there in village?	1	51	14	3	1
6) How much conflict over the Oran is there in the village?	69	2	1	0	0
7) How much conflict over other land is there in the village?	0	22	48	2	0
8) How is the state of the local environment now compared to the past?	0	46	22	3	1
9) How is the state of religious belief now compared to the past?	9	34	18	4	7

Environmental factors

The diverse *oran* water sources are very important for communities in terms of providing water for their livestock, irrigation and drinking purposes. Research into *oran* water resources suggests that these potentially provide a permanent solution to water scarcity and degradation in the area (Krishna and Singh 2014). They ensure a continued supply of water even after the monsoons and greatly benefit local livelihoods through the increased availability of water for livestock and crop irrigation. For example, Garuba ji Devbani and Adaval ki Devbani districts in Alwar irrigate about 200 hectares. According the potter community from the Dehlavas village, 'Clay from the *oran's johad* is considered good for making pottery'.

Many trees found in *orans* are useful for a number of purposes. They are harvested in a sustainable manner and are by and large protected by all the sections of tribal society, having a sort of revered and totemic status. Even when the forest is destroyed in the quest for agricultural land by the local population, these multi-purpose tree species are generally left unscathed. A list of such trees is given below.

Table 3. Trees found in local orans. Source: KRAPAVIS 2009.

Local Name	Botanical name	Purpose
Dhok	*Anogeissus pendula*	Fodder, shade
Jamun	*Syzygium cumini*	Fruit, shade
Gular	*Ficus glomerata*	Fruit, shade
Khajjur	*Phoenis sylvestris*	Fruit, male trees harvested for timber used in construction, leaves for mat and broom making
Neem	*Azadirachta indica*	Medicinal importance, shade, oil
Bans	*Bambusa arundinaceae*	Used in house construction, for mat, furniture and broom making
Khejari	*Prosopis cineraria*	Fruit for cooking and fodder, shade
Peepal	*Ficus religiosa*	Fruit, fodder, religious importance, shade
Bargad	*F. benghalensis*	Fruit, leaves for making plate and bowls, religious importance, shade
Imali	*Tamarindus indicus*	Fruit, shade
Kair	*Capparis deciduas*	Fruits for food; making vegetable pickle, medicines etc
Ber	*Zizyphus mauritiana*	Fruits and fodder
Salar	*Boswellia serrata*	Fodder, shade

Climatic change: Variability and reduction in rainfall

There are indications – based on both formal and folk knowledge – that changes are taking place in the local climatic conditions. Whether these form part of changing global scenarios is a subject for further research. What is clear, however, is that these changes have had important consequences at the local level on important aspects of the production system. Some of the more striking changes that are reportedly taking place at the local level are as follows.

From Stewards to Trespassers

- *Declining annual rainfall:* The average annual rainfall of the district is stated to be 600 mm (Census of India 2001, District Census Handbook (District Alwar), 21). Over the last ten years it appears that only in two years has the rainfall reached 600mm. For the most part total precipitation has been well below the annual average. Popular local perceptions strongly support the view that there has been a fall in the annual rainfall.

- *Shortening rainy season:* there is a perception that the number of rainy days in the monsoon has decreased. Chaumasa, the local term for the rainy season, means 'four-months' etymologically. Today the rainy season rarely stretches beyond three months. There is also the impression that the frequency of light showers has fallen.

- *Unpredictable winter rainfall:* There is a local perception that winter rainfall has become irregular and delayed.

- *Changing seasonal succession:* although the region is in characterised by a stable three-season succession, there has been a perceptible shift in the duration of each. Traditionally the two major festivals of Divali and Holi mark the beginning and end of winter. An informal measure of this change is when people sleep indoors and outdoors in the rural areas. Traditionally they would move out a week or so before Holi. Today people continue to sleep indoors well after Holi.

The reported changes in local rainfall and seasonality have had clear consequences on the status and biotic composition of the *orans*. The most apparent change has been in the decline of large plant species. Alwar *orans* were renowned for their bamboo; now its numbers have fallen sharply. A Bamboo Cooperative Society formed as early as 1952 is now defunct, largely due to low availability of bamboo. Another large plant species know locally as Kala Khair has visibly decreased in presence. The Googal tree, which was widespread, has now virtually disappeared. A most important species of the *oran* in terms of its grazing utility is Dhok. There are few young specimens of this tree available today.

The picture is similar for grasses and shrubs. For instance, the species of millet locally known as Sawan, mentioned above, is an excellent fodder grass and its grain is used to make *kheer*. Its peculiarity is that it needs sustained light showers to grow optimally. The shortening of the rainy season has directly affected its growth, and there is today a severe decline in its availability. In contrast a grass that has spread recently is Laumpla. This grass grows under dry conditions, and indicates the spread of aridity.

Similarly it was reported that some twenty odd species of bulbous plants of medicinal value were formerly available in these *orans*. Today these have become hard to find. Last but not least, most *orans* have water sources in the form of tanks known locally as *johads*, *talav* and *bawri*. Many of these have now run dry. The natural springs found in some *orans* now have reduced water flow or no longer flow throughout the year.

Orans also serve as ethno-medicinal centres. When livestock (buffalo, goats and cows) become ill, traditional healers are able to identify and apply plant medicines (in the form of a paste or powder) that have anti-bacterial, anti-inflammatory or pain-relieving qualities. Based on previous study (KRAPAVIS 2009), the ethno-medicinal functions of certain plants are as follows.

Table 4. Ethno-medical significance of the plants in the oran.

Local Name	Botanical name	Part used	Condition treated
Chapun	*Grewia hirsutae Vahl*	Root	Retention of placenta
Neem	*Azadiracta indica*	Stem, bark leaves	Fever, diarrhoea, skin diseases
Peelu	*Salvodora oleoides*	Leaves	Constipation
Chhila/ Dhak	*Butea monosperma*	Stem bark	Fever
Desi akda	*Calotropis gigantea*	Stem bark	Swellings, bloat
Kair	*Capparis decidua*	Fruit	Stomach
Sur kand	*Saccarum spontaneum*	Tuber	Poisoning
Jhad desi	*Zyziphus mauritiana*	Root	Foot rot

Conclusion

Orans evolved as a social mechanism to safeguard the livelihoods of some of the subcontinent's most economically vulnerable people by ensuring their access to water and other vital resources even in times of political or climatic instability. In the last sixty years, Rajasthan's *orans* have undergone a steady decline in both quantity and quality. Villagers are now facing not only an acute scarcity of resources and greater vulnerability to economic and climatic changes, but also, due to the dismantling of traditional institutions and entitlements, a weakening of customary social bonds of cooperation and reciprocity. There has been a serious depletion (up to fifty per cent) of some NTFP (non-timber forest products) species in the Aravali region in comparison to the situation fifteen to twenty years ago, including Khair, Salar, Paneer bandh and Bamboo (Chaudhry et al. 2008).

Figure 5. Pastoralism in Kraska (Sariska Tiger Reserve), where human and livestock use the same source of water 'rain water harvesting'. Photo: Aman Singh.

The potential economic value of the *oran* is immense and significant for the economic well-being of the people. There is an urgent need to make an assessment of the annual financial value, and support the role of NTFPs from *orans* in the rural economy. At a more specific level, the diversity of the vegetation in the forest canopy as well as the under-storey is deteriorating. In particular, species that were useful for pasture and NTFPs have reduced and some have reportedly altogether disappeared. As a result, the perceived value of the *oran* is diminishing, and the community is reluctant to invest resources and energy in its upkeep. The easy availability of groundwater today thanks to mechanised borehole digging has also made redundant the traditional sources of water available in the *orans*. Over time water sources such *bawries* and *johads* have become neglected, and there is in general less interest in the management of community water resources.

It is quite surprising that, despite the critical importance of *orans* for local livelihoods and biodiversity conservation, there remains considerable ambiguity regarding their legal status and ownership. This ambiguity has resulted in *orans* being neglected by all relevant parties. When the Forest Department wishes to take an *oran* over for its own purposes, it does so without hesitation; likewise when local administrations want to distribute *oran* lands they do so without a thought; when local farmers choose to encroach upon *orans* they do so legally. Local entrepreneurs have also disturbed *oran* lands for mining purposes. As a result, the fate of these community forests has been decided by everyone other than the local community.

It is evident that the *orans* are operating today in something of an institutional vacuum and indeed it is not clear at the present time what agency enjoys jurisdiction over them. As stated earlier, their upkeep was the responsibility of a traditional village institution (e.g. Thain). Today the traditional institutions have disintegrated. Modern institutions that have supplanted them, such as the official village Panchayat, have displayed little interest in the management of *orans*. Unlike the Thain, which represented community concerns pertaining to the use of the *oran*, the Panchayat is not in any way oriented to these ends. At the level of the village community, there is often tension between those who wish to preserve the *oran* and those who would rather turn it over to agriculture. This is nowhere manifested more clearly than in the weakening of village institutions that held the community together.

Local populations have been increasingly excluded from management of their resources. The Forest Department can easily restrict access to *orans* for government plantation purposes, or declare the grove an inviolable reserve. This has led to two consequences, one being the alienation of local people and the second being the deterioration of natural resources due to mismanagement. The village of Bakhtpura in our study area illustrates the difference a community's involvement in an *oran* can make. The *oran* of this village has been divided into two parts, one governed by the community and the other enclosed as a forest reserve. The results of this division have been that the reserved forest has been stripped bare, presumably by the local community, whereas the community-controlled forest retains fairly thick vegetation.

Another cause of alienation could be the relationship between the loss of the people's faith in the spiritual relevance of *orans* and the consumerist mentality of the private sector. The role of the state in promoting the growth of industry without heeding the concerns of local communities, as well as the lack of employment in the rural paradigm, results in out-migration and further weakening of socio-cultural and spiritual ties.

Encroachment is a recurrent problem affecting every *oran*. Cultivators living on the margins of the groves surreptitiously expand their farmlands into the *orans*. Substantial tracts of *oran* land have been distributed for cultivation,

From Stewards to Trespassers

most recently for jatropha. This benefits a few people, mostly entrepreneurs from outside the local community, yet significantly contributes to the heightening of local tensions. In such instances local communities are formally deprived of access to the *oran*, although often enough grazing continues secretly. These processes (Box 1) have resulted in villagers transitioning from stewards to

Box 1. Changes to orans.

Institutional vacuum: Government jurisdiction over *orans* is unclear. Previously the upkeep of the *oran* was the responsibility of a village institution (e.g. Thain). Today traditional institutions have disintegrated and been supplanted by the village Panchayat (village level legislative body) that has little interest in Oran management. At the village level there is often tension between those who wish to preserve the *oran* and those who would rather cut it down.

Community alienation: Bakhtpura residents have been increasingly excluded from management of their resources. The Forest Department can restrict access to the *oran* or declare a reserve, alienating locals and mismanaging resources. The village *oran* has been cut in two, with one part governed by the community and the other enclosed as a forest reserve. The reserved forest has been stripped bare, presumably by the local community, whereas the community-controlled forest retains fairly thick vegetation. There has been a loss of faith in the spiritual relevance of the *oran* and increasing consumerism, reflecting the promotion of industry over local concerns and a lack of employment. This results in out-migration and weakening of the socio-cultural and spiritual ties to the *oran*.

Encroachment: Land on the margins of the *oran* has been allocated for cultivation, most recently for jatropha plants, benefiting outsiders and heightening local tensions. Often local communities are deprived of access to the *oran*, though some grazing continues secretly. Villagers transition from being stewards to trespassers overnight, damaging the link between communities and their *oran*.

Changes in the production system: The *oran* had historically served as pasture for cattle. The species composition had consequently evolved in response to the grazing requirements of cattle. Today buffaloes use the *oran* for grazing and wallowing, especially during the lean parts of the year, and grazing by goats and sheep has increased, yet the species composition is not well-suited for buffaloes, goats or sheep.

Decline of flora and fauna: Among several ecological changes has been the decline of large plant species, grasses and shrubs. For instance, *sawan*, a type of millet, is an excellent fodder grass and its grain is used to make *kheer* (milk pudding). Shorter rainy seasons have affected its growth and there has been a severe decline in its availability. Over twenty species of medicinal plants in the *oran* are now threatened.

Perceived value of the *oran*: There is a mismatch between animal needs and *oran* pasturage. Moreover, the vegetation in the forest canopy and undergrowth is reducing in diversity. Species that were once useful for pasture have decreased or disappeared in some cases. As a result the perceived value of the *oran* is low and the community is reluctant to invest resources and energy in its upkeep.

trespassers overnight, as government actions and laws affect local behaviour. These factors all contribute to the larger deterioration of the relationship between communities and their *orans*.

References

Brara, R. 1989. '"Commons" policy as process: The case of Rajasthan, 1955–1985.' *Economic and Political Weekly*: 2247–2254.

Brara, R. 1992. 'Are grazing lands "Wastelands"? Some evidence from Rajasthan.' *Economic and Political Weekly*: 411–18.

Census of India 2001, District Census Handbook (District Alwar), available at http://www.censusindia.gov.in/2011census/dchb/DCHB_A/08/0806_PART_A_DCHB_ALWAR.pdf

Champion, H.G. and S.K. Seth. 1968. *The Revised Survey of the Forest Types of India*. New Delhi: Manager of Publications.

Chaudhry, P., R.L. Srivastava, A.S. Apte, P. Kumar and S. Rao Narayan. 2008. 'The role of non-timber forest products in the rural economy and their quantitative assessment in the Aravali mountain range of India'. *International Journal of Green Economics* 2: 427.

Gold, A.G. and B.R. Gujar. 1989. 'Of Gods, trees and boundaries: Divine conservation in Rajasthan'. *Asian Folklore Studies* 48: 211–229.

Robbins, P., A.G. Gold and B.R. Gujar. 2003. 'In the time of trees and sorrows: Nature, power, and memory in Rajasthan'. *Geographical Review* 93: 277–279.

Guha, R. 1983. 'Forestry in British and post-British India: A historical analysis'. *Economic amnd Political Weekly*: 1882–1896.

KRAPAVIS. 2009. Household Survey.

Krishna, N. and A. Singh. 2014. *Ecological Traditions of India- Rajasthan*, Volume X. CPREEC (a centre of the Ministry of Environment and Forests, Govt of India).

Jodha, N. 1985. 'Population growth and the decline of common property resources in Rajasthan, India'. *Population and Development Review* 11: 274–264.

Jodha, N.S. 1986. 'Common property resources and the rural poor in dry regions of India'. *Economic and Political Weekly* 21:1169–1181.

Jodha, N.S. 1992 'Common property resources: A missing dimension of development strategies', Discussion Paper, No. 169. Washington, DC: The World Bank.

Malhotra K.C. 2001. 'Cultural and ecological dimensions of sacred groves in India'. Indian National Science Academy.

Patwa, S. 2013. 'Ahinsa ki Shakti, Prayavaran aur Samaj'. *Jansatta*, Hindi daily newspaper.

Rangarajan, M. 1996. 'Fire in the forest'. *Economic and Political Weekly*: 4888–4890.

Redford, K.H. 1991. 'The ecologically Noble Savage'. *Cultural Survival Quarterly* 15: 46.

Sekhar, N.U. 2003. 'Local people's attitudes towards conservation and wildlife tourism around Sariska Tiger Reserve, India'. *Journal of Environmental Management* 69: 339–347.

Sekhar N.U. 2004. 'Local versus expert knowledge in forest management in a semi-arid part of India'. *Land Degradation and Development* **15**: 133–142.

Singh, A. 2010. 'Community manage Orans for protecting their livelihoods', Strengthening People-led Development, MISEREOR.

Singh, A. and R. Bahl. 2006. 'Oran land issues: A livelihood concern for pastoralists in Rajasthan'. Available at SSRN: http://ssrn.com/abstract=981506

Singh, A. and A. Gupta. 2010. 'Conserving Orans for sustainable livelihood'. *Magazine LEISA India* **12**: 18–20.

Singh, A. and D. Jobanputra. 2009. 'Embedded conservation'. dry-net.org

Singh, R. 2009. 'Action Plan for saving sacred groves'. *Times of India Jaipur*, 25 June.

Sisodia, P. and A. Singh. 2002. 'Devbani- Oran', in Hindi, KRAPAVIS.

Sivaramakrishnan, K. 1999. *Modern Forests, Statemaking and Environmental Change in Colonial Eastern India*. Stanford: Stanford University Press

Chapter 10

CONSERVATION OF TANGIBLE AND INTANGIBLE PROPERTIES OF THE TENT IN JORDANIAN BADIA

Wassef Al Sekhaneh

A tent that flutters in the wind is more comfortable to me than a great palace. A morsel of food in the dish from my tent is tastier to me than a chunk of bread. The sound of the wind coming from all sides is more pleasant to me than the plucking of tambourine.

Attributed to Maysoun, wife of the Umayyad Caliph, Mu'awiyya.

(Chatty 1996)

Introduction

The Hashemite Kingdom of Jordan is situated on the east bank of the river Jordan. It is bordered by Iraq in the east, Saudi Arabia in the south and east, Israel and the West Bank in the west and Syria in the north. (Map 1) The territory of Jordan covers about 92,000 square kilometres. Eighty per cent of the Jordanian area is arid. Most of the Bedouin are settled this area (Oxford Business Group 2011)

Jordan is usually described as a tribal nation-state ruled by a tribal leadership dominated by tribal affiliations and loyalties. Bedouins constituted and continue to constitute a large segment of the total population about 35 per cent of the Jordanian Population. Over the years, the government and Bedouin tribes have developed a unique symbiosis. The government has depended several times on the tribes and Bedouin elements in the army to crush external as well as internal enemies. This symbiosis, however, came after a period of hostility in the early days of the nation-state (Anderson 2009, Layne 1994, Massad 2001).

This article will describe the relationship between the Bedouins and their environment in the Jordanian state. This begins with their dwellings, from

Tangible and Intangible Properties of the Tent

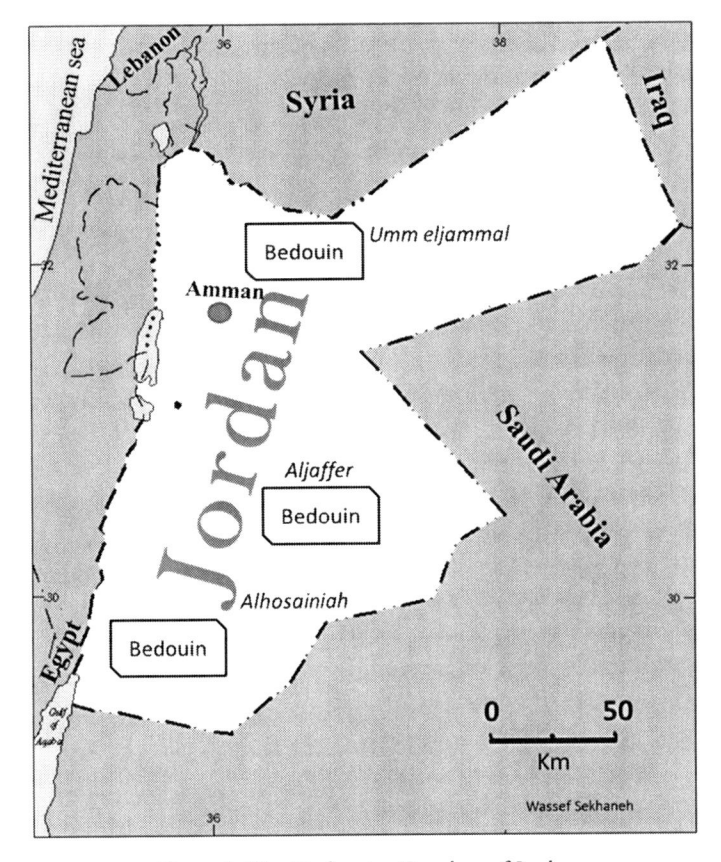

Figure 1. The Hashemite Kingdom of Jordan.

Bedouin tent to stone house. It concentrates on the concept of the Bedouin traditional tent as a form of architecture and social space, which has become a quite complex choice in the changing social and cultural context of the Bedouin in Jordan. The aim of this research is to study the socio-cultural anthropological contexts of the tent as intangible heritage, which generate and define the tangible parameters by which Jordanian Bedouins organise their lives and their houses; and to explore to what extent anthropological concepts apply to these data through the whole meaning of the tent, both substantial and insubstantial. The concept of intangibility has become tremendously significant in heritage studies, particularly concerning intangible practices and debates over authenticity (Churchill 2006, Silverman 2011). The concepts of tangible and intangible heritage are intimately linked. Intangible heritage has received much recent attention with the passage of UNESCO's Convention for the Safeguarding of the Intangible Heritage in 2003 (Ruggles 2009).

This study is based on fieldwork carried out between 2012 and 2014, in Umm eljammal in the northern Badia, and Aljaffer and Alhosainiah in the southern Badia of Jordan and a review of the published ethnographic literature on Jordanian Bedouin society. The three villages are selected to represent the three types of Badia in Jordan, the southern, quasi southern and northern region.

The interactions between Bedouin cultural practices and the physical environment are strong. In the twentieth century, concern with people's impact on the natural environment has led to many conservation efforts based on romantic notions of pristine wilderness (Stevens 1997, Chatty and Colchester 2002). As such, many conservation projects have created land reserves that exclude human use of natural resources. To conserve both nature and culture, one has to understand the interaction between culture and nature in the Jordanian Badia. In this way, the indigenous people can be empowered to conserve their ecosystem based on their already-existing traditional conservation practices.

Family and tribal customs sometimes surpass the civil and personal law implemented by the government. They play a significant role in people's everyday lives and their interactions with bureaucratic and judicial procedures. Tribal customs focus on the wholeness of the social system rather than on its individual characteristics and this system is becoming more and more incorporated into the modern state bureaucracy. When a crime or a dispute (i.e. killing, accident, honour etc.) occurs, both civil law and tribal law work hand-in-hand to reach a settlement. In most cases, tribal law takes care of the problem before civil procedures even take off. The Bedouins' tribal law is a balanced scorecard based on concepts of 'honour', decency', 'dignity' and 'respect'. The Bedouins are governed by tribal law and the tribal law is essential for understanding the Bedouin culture and norms. The interactions of Bedouins on a daily basis are determined by the concepts of 'honour', decency', 'dignity' and 'respect'. An understanding of these four concepts is necessary to understand relationships among the Bedouin (Abu-Lughod 1999, Al-Sekhaneh 2005, Katakura 1973). None of the four values can be measured separately or independently; these values help the Bedouins organise their life.

National identity construction and interest in Jordan has always been intermingled with other forms of collective identity and tribal representations such as pan-Arabism, pan-Islamism and tribalism. Thus, local patriotism or tribe belonging has competed against other local, regional and trans-regional

Tangible and Intangible Properties of the Tent

identities, whether national, religious or otherwise. The existence of such countless forms of identification is not peculiar to Jordan; it is indeed common to many other countries in the Middle East like Syria, Iraq, and Saudi Arabia (al Sekaneh 2016). These constituent elements are not mutually exclusive, for they often overlap with and complement one another; they are cumulative features of Jordanian Bedouin culture. The priority and significance given to each of these forms of identity by individuals is therefore rooted not only in the tribe interests, but also in shifts that can be understood in relation to the historical and political climate dominant at a particular time and space. The Bedouins today have to shift from the 'glocalised' state and in doing so they have moved from hair houses (tent) to stone houses, each with their own intangible properties.

The tribe in the Bedouin society in Jordan constitutes a shielded time-space that offers protection to those who stay within it. Hence, one of the worst crimes in the Bedouin society of Jordan is to 'blacken a man's face' by breaking 'the law of the Tent' (*haqq elbait*) or cut the face (*taqtee alwajeh*), i.e. by injuring a person who is shielded by its protection. The proverb derives from the 'black' tent used by Arab tribes and is from the recent past (Al-Sekhaneh 2016).

The Bedouin tent as a tangible structure is called *bait asha'* or literally 'hair house'. It is woven from goats' hair by the senior woman of the *bait* on a simple drop spindle (*maghzal*). The tent is owned by the woman (*sahbat el bait*) as her individual personal property. It is undoubtedly from this meaning that the term *bait* was adapted to refer to the stone house as well (Al-Sekhaneh 2005).

In order to understand the architecture and meaning of the permanent Bedouin houses and/or permanent settled population, one must first examine the forms and meaning of the traditional Bedouin housing – i.e. the tent – in terms of an intangible asset or phenomenon. There is, unfortunately, very little literature existing specifically about Bedouin domestic architecture, particularly in the different Provinces of Jordan. The houses in the Jordanian Badia are modelled on traditional Jordan Bedouin black tents. Nowadays traditional and modern housing are considered to be different, but both reflect deeply rooted basic values in the Bedouin culture and their cultural heritage.

All buildings in the Bedouin area of Jordan contain symbolic architectural elements rooted in Bedouin culture. The buildings were constructed and modelled according to local socio-cultural setting, which provides a skeleton model for the design and construction processes and the separation between males and females that reflects the central reality of modern life, conserving the full diversity of Bedouin cultural heritage. In 2016, three types of dwelling are

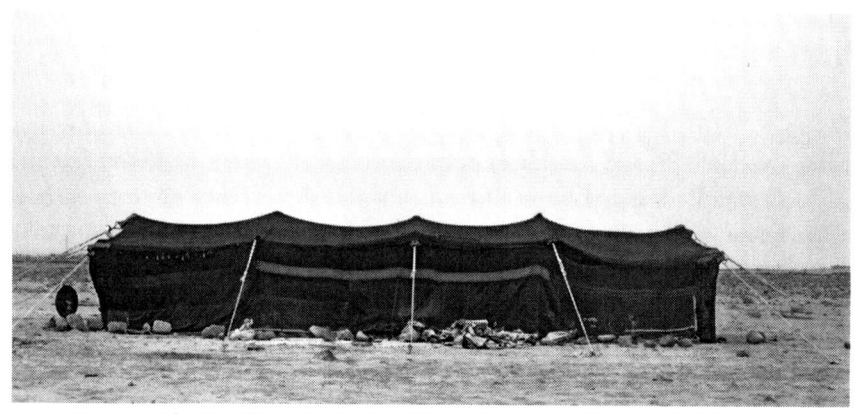

Figure 2. The Tent from the back in Umm eljammal. *Photograph: M. Hazza.*

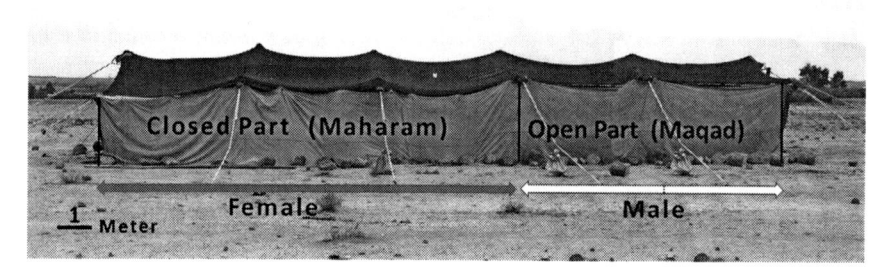

Figure 3. Tent in Umm eljammal *with 'protected' maharam and 'open' maqad. Photograph: Author.*

used by the Bedouin: the tent, traditional buildings made of natural building materials and modern housing made up largely of man-made materials.

Traditional housing is associated with simple building methods, which are arranged to express both intangible and tangible elements of the Bedouin social structure. It is also associated with cultural patrimony and an inherited way of life with few or no modern amenities. Modern houses, on the other hand, are built from relatively durable materials, have facilities such as piped water, sewage disposal and electricity, and are believed to reflect a modern urbanised life style.

Figure 4. The Tent from the front in Aljaffer in south of Jordan. Photograph: Author.

The concept of the Bedouin traditional tent is very complex. It has intangible properties which represent a cultural tradition and social values. The values of 'honour', 'decency', 'dignity' and 'respect' are conceptualised in terms of various abstract notions associated with the tent.

The concept of Bedouin vernacular housing heritage in Jordan

The research is designed to provide a more comprehensive understanding of the types of domestic structure and to elaborate both the tangible and intangible contexts of this mobile dwelling. In anthropological theory, the notion of 'domestic group' acquired a certain prominence towards the end of the last century. The publication of a series of studies dedicated explicitly to the subject dates from that period (Goody 1973, 1969, Schlegel and Eloul 1988). Here I use the term 'extended family' to describe three-generation households as a domestic Bedouin group. In such households, the role of the family as an agency for supporting and respecting the older generation is articulated within the Bedouin culture. The elderly who often live with their sons and their families are a sign of cultural identity, which is formed from the contribution of many generations. The Bedouin extended family has functioned as a source of political and social support throughout Arab history in general, and has played a particular role in symbolising the cultural and religious values of the concept of the family in Jordan. Loyalty to the extended family is counted on, and it is the basis for many aspects of social conduct characterised by formalised kinship to apical grandparent and loyalty to the family.

Family loyalty is viewed by the Bedouin as a positive value that ensures good behaviour and honesty among family members. The social position of one's extended family is considered to be a consistent fact (Glazer 1999) whereas in Western countries an individual may rise in society through education or attainment of wealth and then obtain an achieved status. One's status in Jordanian Bedouin society is determined by the position of one's extended family, hence is an ascribed status that is considered relatively fixed. Individual behaviour is much constrained by the desire not to bring shame upon one's family. In the Bedouin villages, the family is the fundamental social unit on which the individual's life is focused. A Bedouin family is a unit based on concepts of 'blood' (*addam*'), 'honour' (*ash'sharaf*) and 'responsibility' (*almasoliah*'). The concept of honour is a constant preoccupation of individuals which is inherited from the family and has to be constantly asserted and vindicated (Chatty 1990). Honour is a word applied to the whole network of one's kindred in the Bedouin extended family. A family in the Badia is referred to by several terms. The term 'family', *a'ila*, is derived from the Arabic verb *aala*, 'to provide for', 'to depend on' or 'to support'; it usually denotes the extended family anchored by a stable core of intangible values (Al-Sekhaneh 2005). In the Bedouin system every individual in the tribe has strong emotions related to his area generally and to his household (*bait* or *dar*) particularly. The expression *bait ash-shaar* 'the house of hair', is employed to denote the tent including its tangible and intangible properties. *Bait* may also refer to a nuclear or extended family. The term '*aa'ila* also refers to relatives who belong to the same lineage. In the Jordanian Badia, the term *dar* alludes to an agnatic lineage, a patrilineal descent group whose members can trace their relatives' *aqaarib* to a common ancestor (*jadd*). Aqaarib from *qaraabah*, 'closeness'), literally means 'near ones' and expresses one of the values of Bedouin culture. It applies to a narrower set of relatives within the *ahl*. The Bedouin saying goes 'I and my brother against my cousin, I and my cousin against the stranger' (*ana wakhoi ala ebin ammi, wana wben ammi ala elghareeb*).

Qaraabah is woven with kinship ties. In this sense, *qaraabah* regulates all interactions of a member within the community, being the centre of loyalty based on the patrilineal group. *Qaraabah* is a term that expresses interests and beliefs, and provides security, norms and emotions generated by the cultural structure. It rules the people's way of life, both as individual persons in the household and as a social group in the tribe. Patrilineal descent ideology considered as

Tangible and Intangible Properties of the Tent

having been established by Arabian ancestors is the key organising principle of such lineages. Thus group membership, group structure and leadership, are founded on the principle of patrilineal descent ideology only (Shryock 1997).

Intangible property in the Badia culture has spatial and temporal elements which correlate with beliefs in the Bedouin cultural system. The ecosystem is an association between the intangible and tangible in both the spatial and temporal domains. It is an association that specifies the values of one thing that are connected to a system in both cultural and natural heritage. The ecosystem is an interaction in all aspects of Bedouin culture. This entanglement generates the behaviour that defines the role of each object in the cultural system. Now I try to connect the previous theoretical input to tangible property in the Bedouin culture. I will analyse the word '*bait*' which refers to the space surrounding the tent or stone house. This domain is determined in the following manner. A strong man throws the stick used for grinding coffee out of the tent's entrance, and measures the distance thus attained as the radius of the circle surrounding the tent territory.

Internally the tent is divided into two separate parts. The tent dividers vary from region to region and tribe to tribe. They consist of cloth partitions called *qati'I*, which are usually decorated. This main divider is extended outside the front of the tent and separates the female (*mahram*) from the male domain (*maqad*) or (*rubaa*) which means one quarter. The most extensively ornamented *qati'i* faces the men's and guests' sitting room, the *maqad*. The *qati'i* are very large. They can be more than eight metres long and two or three metres high. The *qati'i* is placed across the narrow width of the tent's interior to give the women privacy (*sutra*) as they work and visit inside or outdoors. If they wish, the family may swing over the outer portion of the tent's main divider at a right angle to cover the front opening as a protection against rain, wind or sandstorms (Manor-Binyamini 2011, Marx 1987). The size of the tent depends on the importance of the family, but is at least seven and a half metres long. It is supported by two tent poles connected by the main divider. An important personage, such as a tribal *sheikh*, will have a more imposing dwelling, made of about six broad strips (*shqaq*), each about twenty metres long, supported by four tent poles. When the strips of cloth are sewn together, they form one long rectangle. This is then raised and supported by tent poles, known as *umdan albeit*. There are three types of *umdan albait*: the front poles called *almoqaddam*, the mid poles called *alwaset* and the back called *aldafea*. In the male part there are also two types of poles. The one in the front of tent is *amami* and the other one in the back is *alkaser*, which are connected with tent ropes, *atnab*, to keep the sides taut. For the Jordanian tribes, the left part of the tent is *mahram*, which is reserved for family members and visiting women. It is occupied by the women of the house and no men but the husband and the spouse or closest relatives gain access to it. 'The tent is woven by the women and the tribe is knitted by the men'. It constitutes a shielded space that offers protection to those who stay within it. Hence, one of the worst crimes in the Bedouin society of Jordan is to 'blacken a man's face'(*sawwada wajhaho*) by breaking 'the law of the tent' (*haqq el-bait*), i.e. by injuring a person who is shielded by its protection (Al-Sekhaneh 2005).

The northern section of the tent (*maqad*) is reserved for men and children older than six years of age. No woman may enter this section unless she is past child-bearing age. An important matron may occasionally enter for a limited time; small girls may enter only to serve the men's food and drinks. A stranger, however, will generally enter the *maqad* when accompanied by a close relative of the owner. Nowadays shortly after coffee has been served, the guest will be urged to reveal the purpose of his visit. Guests sit in the *maqad* with their backs turned towards the main divider, so that they will not accidentally see a woman through the holes. But when guests arrive in the absence of the owner of the tent, and no other men are present, the wife will assume her husband's role and entertain the guests in the *maqad* section of the tent. To preclude possible defamation, she must raise the walls of tent (*raffa* or *rwaq*), so that everything going on inside the tent can be seen from outside. One of the more curious characteristics is the south-western wall, which has a series of column bases and is mostly open to prevent any kind of suspicion. These features add up to a very specific house form, a type derived from the 'black' tent used by Arab tribes.

Although houses are more complex in their tangible components, the structural model and the intangible properties of the tent have mainly been retained. The Bedouin house is organised with respect to two sets of functions. The first one concerns the internal household functions, i.e. sleeping, cooking and sitting; and the second refers to the external household functions, i.e. those pertaining to the family as it interacts with the larger community, as when receiving visitors. These two sets of functions separate the house into two distinct parts, the *mahram* and the *maqad*, respectively. The tent is oriented in a south-north direction and the entrances of both sections are directed to the east. The entrance, however, of most houses in the first stage of transition was also oriented towards the east. The direction of the *qibla* in Mecca determines the orientation of the sleeping mats in the tent or the house. This study shows

Figure 5. Overlapping structures between tent and house in Aljaffer. Photograph: Author.

that a clear continuity in building design and spatial configuration between tent and modern houses can be discerned. When I have studied the spatial and temporal phenomena of the tent I see there is an entanglement of the past with the present generation in both intangible and tangible concepts. The word intangible appeals to me as it generates the meaning of the tangible properties. If we talk of a tent, or a stone house we do not talk about its material components. Instead we actually talk about the meanings that are embedded in the building and the symbols beyond it.

Bedouin houses thus are an integrated part of traditional Bedouin society in both its intangible and its tangible parts. This continuity is clearly expressed in the fact that people inhabiting a modern house erect a tent in the yard of their houses as shown in Figure 5 above; this signifies and symbolises loyalty to Bedouin values. Only this 'old' form of housing valorises the 'new form'. This is concisely expressed in the Bedouin saying, that 'we need the tent; he who does not have an old [tent] does not have a new [house]' (Al-Sekhaneh 2005). Bedouin housing, however, is a dynamic phenomenon affected by changes in Bedouin culture. The building methods of the houses, their materials, techniques and hygienic aspects, have evolved over the years without affecting the sense of security and a protective layout provided for the women. In that sense the structure of the tent is still sustainable. The house structure remains basically like that of the tent, although the size may be increased and the interior may

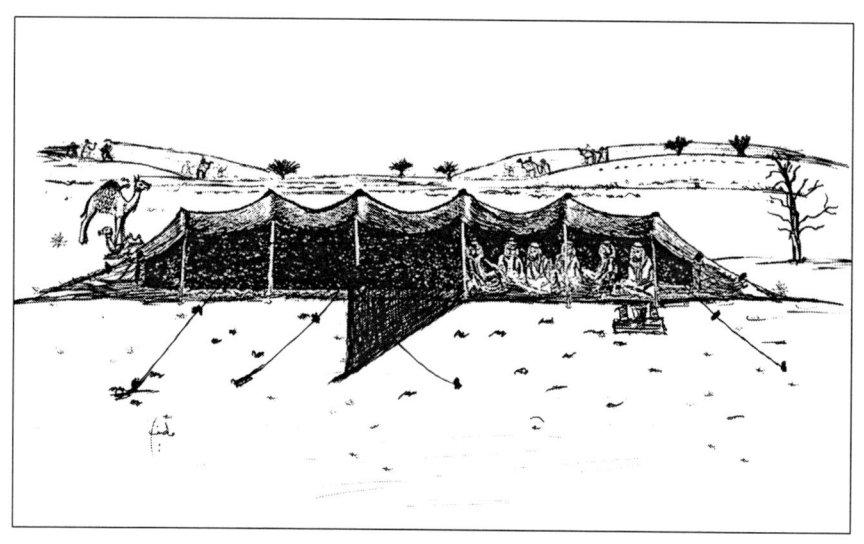

Figure 6. The domain of the tent (drawn by the author).

be sub-divided into more than one space. The law of the tent or modern house is based upon four pillars: honour, dignity, decency and respect.

When a visitor comes toward the tent he is obliged to walk towards the *maqad* before entering the domain's border to avoid the *mahram* part. If a visitor does not know this rule he must first walk towards the centre of the tent, until he recognises the coffee stove standing in front of the right side of the *maqad*. Then he must change direction towards the *maqad* (see Figure 6).

The model of a house in this area in Aljaffer is found to be almost principally identical to Jordanian Bedouin tents. Today, traditional and modern housing are physically referred to as opposites, but comply with the same cultural norms, which are deeply rooted in the traditional Bedouin culture. All the buildings in the Bedouin area of Jordan were once built with a local traditional system which took into account of the four pillars to protect the privacy of women. Modern housing is based on the same pillars.

A significant aspect of the Bedouin farming and herding society is the seasonal mobility of the household. During the winter the tents and the households are gathered in the village settlement of the community. During the growing season people move out to their fields, which are generally referred to as the 'lands'. People stay there for the whole growing season to keep an eye

Tangible and Intangible Properties of the Tent

Figure 7. The stages of stone house development, taking a tent as a model in Aljaffer. Photograph: Author.

Figure 8. The development of the modern tent in Aljaffer. Photograph: Author.

on the fields, which are often situated far from the village. If there are cattle, they are kept the whole year at the places outside the village where pasture is available in the *hema* ('land under protection') the reserved land of the tribe (*wajha ashaeriah*).

Bedouin housing is adapted for the responsibilities of reproduction and production of traditional farming and pasturing activities achieved regularly over the year. Thus the layouts of the dwelling and the different arrangements within it have both functional and social purposes (Griesi 2011). The process of conserving both culture and nature is significant for the solidarity of the Bedouin future. The natural heritage of the arid region in Jordan cannot be clearly and distinctly understood without the cultural heritage of the area.

To provide a suitable dwelling was a part of the subsistence economy, because the Bedouin economy is based on livestock and traditional building methods which require no capital expenditure at all. Materials (soil, straws and grass) are collected from communal tribal land. The household itself constructs the dwelling and in such a way that no advanced tools are needed. The strength and capacity of human labour is sufficient. Rapid changes in all sectors of society include living conditions in Bedouin areas and as more people get involved in the modern economy, the traditional methods of building will be improved. Changes have in fact already taken place. Modern materials are used along with traditional ones and new ideas for the layout of the whole yard and the houses are being implemented.

An important factor is the attitude of the Bedouins themselves toward social change. During my fieldwork I was introduced to some of these views. In the villages, at *majlis-al-Sheikh* meetings and during interviews with household members, the response to my study was positive with very few exceptions. It was generally felt that it was important to document traditional housing as it belongs to the Bedouin culture. If it was not recorded, it might be totally forgotten and the more indigenous examples may soon be gone.

At the same time, modern types of houses are considered to be desirable among those who are able to afford them. Another way of assessing people's attitudes is to see how they design their houses or tents and yards or domains when they make use of modern materials. It is evident that many of the traditional ideas are still alive and practiced. Even modern housing (built with modern materials) has inherited these traditional elements.

The traditional layout of a Bedouin dwelling is not a plan based on infrastructure or the concept of central squares and other physical features. Instead it reflects the social structure of the tribe, consisting of households, family groups and their own land (Griesi 2011).

Most people stay in the village during the winter, from November to April. Winter is the time for resting after ploughing and harvesting; it is the time for festivities such as weddings and for meeting of friends and relatives after the period on the lands. It is also the time for building new houses and maintaining the old ones. Schoolchildren stay in the village the whole year.

They are alone or looked after by grandparents or somebody with a regular job in the Bedouin area.

Lands or the ploughing fields are outside the village, sometimes a considerable distance away, up to a hundred kilometres or more. The cattle-post may be even further away. The settlements at the lands and cattle-posts are spread out. Related families may live fairly closely to each other and members of a ward often have their lands in the same area.

The access to services is much more limited when people stay at the lands or the cattle-post. At the lands people have to rely on rainwater or long journeys to collect water from an often poor source. At the cattle-post water can generally be obtained from the borehole for cattle. They are herded by the husband and the boys of the family (when they have no school), who stay for long periods at the cattle-post. Though most Bedouin households have cattle, the differences in holdings are considerable. The houses at the cattle-post mainly provide sleeping and cooking facilities.

The concept of Bedouin housing has traditional then technical, as well as economic, significance. Bedouin housing is an integrated part of the traditional society based on subsistence through farming and herding. Bedouin housing provides the necessary buildings and structures for different actions linked to farming and herding and social life within a Bedouin culture.

References

Abu-Lughod, L. 1999. *Veiled Sentiments: Honor and Poetry in a Bedouin Society*. Stanford: University of California Press.

Al-Sekhaneh, W. 2016. 'Bedouin kinship relations in Jordan: An examination of Beni Khalid kinship terminology and family organisation'. *Parts and Wholes* 27: 87.

Al-Sekhaneh, W. 2005. *The Bedouin of Northern Jordan: Kinship, Cosmology, and Ritual Exchange*. Berlin: Wissenschaftlicher Verlag.

Anderson, B.S. *Nationalist Voices in Jordan: The Street and the State*. Austin: University of Texas Press.

Chatty, D. 2013. *From Camel to Truck: The Bedouin in the Modern World*, 2nd Edition. Cambridge: The White Horse Press.

Chatty, D. 1990. 'The current situation of the Bedouin in Syria, Jordan and Saudi Arabia and their prospects for the future'. In C. Salzman and J.G. Galaty (eds). *Nomads in a Changing World*. Naples: Istituto universitario orientale. pp. 123–38.

Chatty, D. and M. Colchester (eds). 2002.*Conservation and Mobile Indigenous Peoples: Displacement, Forced Settlement, and Sustainable Development*. New York: Berghahn Books

Churchill, N. 2006. 'Dignifying carnival: The politics of heritage recognition in Puebla, Mexico'. *International Journal of Cultural Property* 13: 1–24.

Glazer, N. 1999. 'Two Cheers for Asian Values'. *The National Interest*: 27–34.

Goody, J. 1973. *Bridewealth and Dowry*. CUP Archive.

Goody, J. 1969. 'Inheritance, property, and marriage in Africa and Eurasia'. *Sociology* 3: 55–76.

Griesi, E. 2011. *Bdoul Vertikal: Die Höhle Versus Das Mehrgeschoss-Haus: Architektur, Identität, Räumliche Neuorganisation Eines Beduinenstammes*. Münster: LIT Verlag.

Oxford Business Group. 2011. *The Report: Jordan 2011*. Oxford Business Group.

IBP. 2012. *Jordan Country Study Guide Volume 1 Strategic Information and Developments* International Business Publications USA.

Katakura, M. 1973. 'Some social aspects of Bedouin settlements in Wadi Fatima, Saudi Arabia'. *Orient* 9: 67–108.

Layne, L. 1994. *Home and Homeland: The Dialogics of Tribal and National Identities in Jordan* Princeton: Princeton University Press.

Manor-Binyamini, I. 2011. 'Mothers of children with developmental disorders in the Bedouin community in Israel: Family functioning, caregiver burden, and coping abilities'. *Journal of Autism and Developmental Disorders* 41: 610–17.

Marx, E. 1987. 'Relations between spouses among the Negev Bedouin'. *Ethnos* 52: 156–79.

Massad, J.A. 2001. *Colonial Effects: The Making of National Identity in Jordan*. New York: Columbia University Press.

Murray, G.W. 1923. 'The Ababda'. *Journal of the Anthropological Institute of Great Britain and Ireland*: 417–23.

Ruggles, D. F. and H. Silverman (eds). 2009. *Intangible Heritage Embodied*, New York: Springer Science and Business Media.

Schlegel, A. and R. Eloul. 1988. 'Marriage transactions: Labor, property, status'. *American Anthropologist* 90: 291–309.

Shryock, A. 1997. *Nationalism and the Genealogical Imagination: Oral History and Textual Authority in Tribal Jordan*. Berkeley: Univerisity of California Press.

Silverman, H. 2011. 'Contested cultural heritage: A selective historiography'. In H. Silverman (ed.) *Contested Cultural Heritage*. New York: Springer. pp. 1–49.

Stevens, A. 1997. *Conservation through Cultural Survival: Indigenous Peoples and Protected Areas*. Washington, DC: Island Press.

Stewart, F.H. 1990. 'Schuld and Haftung in Bedouin law'. *Zeitschrift der Savigny-Stiftung für Rechtsgeschichte. Germanistische Abteilung* 107: 393–407.

Thomas, M. 2003. 'Bedouin tribes and the Imperial intelligence services in Syria, Iraq and Transjordan in the 1920s'. *Journal of Contemporary History* 38: 539–61.

Watkins, J. 2014. 'Seeking justice: Tribal dispute resolution and societal transformation in Jordan'. *International Journal of Middle East Studies* 46: 31–49.

Wilson, M.C. 1990. *King Abdullah, Britain and the Making of Jordan*. Cambridge: Cambridge University Press.

Zilberman, I. 1995. 'Palestinian customary law in the Jerusalem area'. *Cath. UL Rev.* 45: 795.

INDEX

A

access (to resources and services) 2, 6, 7, 13, 14, 41–4, 45–6, 50, 54, 56–7, 61, 63–4, 66, 79, 91–3, 95, 99, 102–03, 105, 129, 134, 135, 138, 143–4, 164, 165, 178, 181–3, 194, 196–7, 213
Ad Dakhiliya 112, 114, 120, 121
aesthetics 118–19
Afghanistan 13, 14, 129–52
agent; agency 1, 3, 8, 11, 12, 25, 42, 58, 59, 61, 65, 104, 120, 165, 170
Agrawal, A. 8
Ahearn, Ariell vii, 1–15, 22
aid *see also* donor 8, 80
aimag 43–4, 56–8, 60, 61
Alawite 75–7, 81, 86–7
Al Batinah 112, 114, 120, 121, 122
Aleppo 74, 77, 78, 79, 81
anthropocene 23–5
Arab viii, 3, 12, 71–90, 109, 118–21, 202, 203, 205, 208
Arabian desert 5
Arabian oryx 10, 110, 112, 123–24
Aravalli mountains 177
architecture 14, 201, 203
Asia 2–4, 5, 136
    Central 4, 24
    East 4, 5
    Inner 1, 4, 21, 22
    South 1
al-Assad, Bashar 12, 71–90
al-Assad, Hafez 71, 73–4, 76–7, 83, 85–7
assets (financial) 45–7, 76, 99, 100, 148
authoritarianism 71, 76
Avram, M. 169
Awasthi, Nisthasri vii, 13, 153–76

B

Badain Jaran desert 4
Badia 12, 73, 78, 200–14
bait 203, 206–07
Baival, B. 42, 54

Baluchistan 131–2, 137–8, 140–42, 144
Bayar, N. 31–2
Bedouin 12, 14, 73, 200–14
belcheer 17–20, 33–5
Bhotia 157–9, 163–4
bird 12, 61, 79, 80
Bocco, Riccardo 3, 9
Borchigud, W. 33
border 13, 14, 31, 61, 129–52, 163, 170, 200, 210
boundary 1, 3, 11, 13, 14, 95, 117, 131, 136, 138, 140, 143, 148, 161, 181–3, 185, 186
Brara, R. 178
Brinkmann, Katja 115
buffalo 183, 187, 189, 190, 194, 197
Bulag, U.E. 20, 32
Bumochir, D. vii, 11, 17–40
al-Busaidi, M. 110

C

camel 4, 48, 49, 135, 136, 138
camp 18, 54–6, 60, 61, 64, 171
capacity building 51, 104, 124
carbon (emissions) 6, 24
carpet 130, 138, 148
cashmere 48, 130
cattle 4, 48, 75, 83, 109, 136, 138, 163, 180, 187, 189, 190, 194, 197, 211, 213
ceremony 12, 65, 168, 170, 177
Chakrabarty, D. 24
Chatty, Dawn 10, 12, 123–4
children *see also* young people 6, 7, 75, 78, 162, 169, 170, 173, 187, 208, 212
China 4, 5, 8, 11–13, 17–40, 50, 91–108, 130, 149, 165
Chinggis Khan 26, 29
city 12, 75, 76, 77, 78, 80, 81, 83, 84, 86, 87, 112, 122, 148, 159, 169, 172, 182
civilisation 23, 29–32, 35–6
climate change 3, 4, 5, 8, 21, 26, 27, 50, 92, 145, 172, 190, 192, 194

Index

Cohn, B.S. 123
collectivism 8, 25, 27, 41, 45, 46, 47, 53, 75, 95, 102, 129, 133, 159, 164, 179, 182
commodity; commodification 13, 41, 43, 50, 54–6, 64–5
commons 5, 9, 11, 12, 25–7, 30, 45, 179, 182–4, 189
communism 31, 34
community 1–3, 6–9, 11, 13–14, 22, 25–8, 32, 43–4, 48, 51, 53–4, 57, 59, 60, 63–5, 72, 76, 82, 87, 91, 95, 101, 111, 112, 116, 118, 124, 130–4, 136, 144, 153–4, 157–60, 162–6, 169–74, 177–99, 206, 208, 210
conflict 12, 2029, 33, 55, 58, 61, 64, 66, 83, 85, 130, 133, 144, 180, 181, 185, 189, 191
conservation 1, 2, 6, 8, 10, 12, 14, 28, 30, 31, 41–3, 45–6, 50–1, 54, 58, 60–1, 64, 65, 78–9, 91, 109–28, 136, 156, 160, 166, 171, 173–4, 178, 188, 195, 202
construction (of ideas) 20, 21, 23, 27–9, 31–2, 34–6, 43, 54, 58, 64, 65, 111, 156–8, 160, 161, 171, 172–4, 202
corruption 76, 78, 85
cow *see* cattle
credit 12–13, 74, 86, 91–108
Crutzen, P. 24
cultivation 6, 10, 11, 17, 20, 109, 110, 114, 130, 147, 154, 162, 166, 170–1, 178, 180, 196–7
custodial land use; custodianship 12, 28, 63, 136

D

Dagvadorj, D. 30
dairy products 80, 96, 98, 101
Damascus 74, 77, 78, 81
Dana Declaration 2
Darma valley 13, 153, 155–7, 159, 161–2, 167, 169, 173
debt 13, 93, 98, 101–04
Deed Mongol 11, 17–18, 20, 33–4
degradation (of land) 2, 5, 8–11, 13, 19, 21–8, 42, 44, 50–1, 53, 58, 59, 65, 144, 147, 160, 177, 183, 191
deity 63, 168, 170, 177, 178, 182, 184
democracy 2, 29–30
desertification 5–6, 27, 50, 80, 82
determinism, environmental 9, 27
devbani 177, 180–1, 189
development (economic) 2–3, 6, 8–10, 12–13, 21, 25–8, 30, 33, 46, 50–1, 53, 58, 66, 71, 77–80, 87, 91–3, 95, 101, 103–05, 124, 154, 160–1, 164–7, 170, 172–4, 184
Dickhoefer, U. 116
discourse 2, 3, 8, 9, 11, 13, 20–3, 27–8, 32, 35–6, 43–4, 46, 51, 64, 111, 159–60, 172, 184
discrimination 2, 6, 63–4, 156
disease (of livestock) 134–5, 147, 182
displacement 78, 87, 148, 172
donor *see also* aid 27, 35, 43, 51, 53, 72
drought 5, 12, 22, 57, 74, 78–82, 86–7, 135, 145, 181, 189, 190
Druze 72, 74, 83, 86
Dukhan, Haian vii, 12, 71–90
Dulam, S. 30
Dumont, L. 111
Durand line 13, 130–2, 136–43, 148
Dyer, Caroline 6
dzud *see* zud

E

economy; economic *see also* socioeconomic 2, 3, 8–12, 23, 29–30, 34, 41, 43, 44, 46,47, 53, 60, 64, 65, 71, 74, 75, 78, 82, 85, 86, 91, 104, 105, 114, 117, 118, 121, 122, 130, 133, 135,148, 153, 154, 157, 159, 162–4, 168, 170, 178–80, 184, 194–5, 212–13
ecosystem 2, 4–6, 28, 43, 92, 115–17, 124, 147, 164, 202, 207
education *see also* school 6–7, 13, 31, 33, 78, 134, 135, 158, 163, 168–70, 206
Eickelman, Dale 123
Elbegdorj, Ts. 29

Index

Empson, R. 11
entitlement 45–6, 157, 194
Ericksen, Annika 53
erosion 5, 50
ethnicity; ethnic 11, 17, 32–3, 54, 56, 83, 86, 120, 131, 133, 144, 147, 154, 157, 158
ethnography 2, 11, 13, 14, 153, 159, 160, 188, 202
Evans-Pritchard, E.E. 154
eviction *see also* displacement 7, 80

F

FAO 9, 73, 55, 95
fence 17–19, 33
fire 5, 6, 166
Fletcher, R. 156
flood 5, 74, 86
fodder 11, 17, 19, 74, 78, 80, 86, 87, 93, 136, 138, 145, 147, 178, 180, 187, 188, 190, 192, 193, 197
folklore 179, 181
forage 129, 135, 145
forest 4, 11, 41, 43, 61, 156, 157, 162–7, 171–2, 174, 177–200
Forest Department of India 11, 160, 162, 164, 165, 172, 174, 177,183, 184, 188, 191, 195–7
Foucault, Michel 156
framework (conceptual) 2, 9, 43, 45, 51, 54, 92, 104, 133, 155, 157
fuel 61, 80, 81, 99, 136, 138, 164, 165, 178, 180, 184, 189, 190

G

gazelle 59–61
goat 4, 48, 82, 114–16, 136, 138, 156, 185–7, 194, 197, 203
Gobi Desert 4, 43
Gongbuzeren viii, 12–13, 91–108
governance 3, 8, 13, 26, 133, 135, 174

government 1, 3, 6–13, 17, 19–24, 30, 32–4, 41, 43, 46–8, 50–1, 53, 58–62, 64–6, 71–6, 80, 82–7, 91, 92, 94, 95, 97, 98, 103–05, 117, 130–5, 143, 144, 148, 153, 156, 158, 161–5, 171–4, 180, 184, 196–8, 200, 202
grazing *see also* overgrazing 4–6, 9–10, 12, 17, 24–5, 54, 57, 60, 79–80, 83, 85, 95, 99, 102–03, 109–10, 116–17, 125, 129–30, 135–8, 141, 143–5, 147–9, 154, 157, 162–5, 177, 180, 184–7, 189–90, 193, 197
Green Gold Project 26, 50
guest *see also* hospitality 207–08
Guha, R. 178
Gujar 179–80
Gujar, B.R. 179

H

Hahn, Allison viii, 1–16
Hajar mountains 112, 115
Hakim, B.S. 110
Hannam, Ian 9, 24
Harasiis 9, 12
Hardin, Garret 9, 25–6, 28
harm, environmental 11, 21, 23–9, 164, 167, 172
Harrell, S. 32
ḥāwzat 14
health
 human 78, 81, 99, 134, 135, 170, 171
 livestock 103, 135, 145, 168, 189
hema 109–12, 211
herb *see also* plant 154, 163–6, 170, 173, 178, 183, 189
heritage 14, 201–03, 205, 207, 212
Himalayas 153–76
Hindu 122, 158
Homs 76, 78, 79, 81
honour 14, 84, 110, 124, 135, 202, 205, 206, 210
horse 4, 48, 52, 57, 101, 148, 162
hospital 6, 74, 86
hospitality 135

Index

house; housing 7, 14, 81–2, 164, 171, 192, 201, 203–05, 207–13
Humphrey, Caroline 11, 21–3, 63
hunting 13, 19, 41, 42, 44, 51, 56, 58–61, 63
husbandry 1, 3, 46–8, 51, 115, 163
hydroelectricity 13, 161, 167

I

Ibāḍism 110, 114, 115, 117, 119–21
Ichinkhorloo, Byambabaatar viii, 13, 41–70
identity 9, 11, 13, 17–40, 41–70, 110, 118, 134, 154, 156–61, 171–4, 202–05
ideology 9, 28, 60, 72, 82, 178, 206, 207
illegality 13, 41, 556, 58–61, 85, 166, 173
IMF 9, 74
imperialism 178
India 5, 6, 8, 11, 13, 131, 133, 153–76, 177–200
indigenous (people) 2, 14, 130, 180, 202
   knowledge *see also* traditional ecological knowledge 28, 29, 109–28, 172, 178
Indus River 130, 131, 136, 138, 142, 148
industry; industrial 14, 24, 32, 46, 104, 114, 122, 154, 164, 196, 197
inequality 43, 46, 48, 50, 64, 66
infrastructure 10, 13, 78, 134, 167, 212
insecurity 10, 13, 144
institution 2, 6, 8, 24, 46, 51, 54, 58–60, 65–6, 73, 77, 92–3, 95–6, 103–05, 135, 179, 182–4, 188, 194, 196–7
intangibility 14, 200–14
interview 2, 43, 44, 53, 59–61, 63, 71, 73, 75, 77, 94, 95, 97–8, 101, 116, 125, 159–60, 162, 167, 188–9, 212
investment 10, 30, 42, 74, 77, 80, 86, 93, 99, 100–04, 117, 118, 195, 197
Iran 5, 130, 141
Iraq 5, 79, 83–4, 200, 203
Islam 109–10, 118, 202
IUCN 10, 73, 79

J

Jabal Akdhar 14, 109–28
Jiang Rong 20

Jodha, N. 178
Jordan 5, 14, 200–14

K

Khan, A. 31, 34
khural 44, 56, 64
Khyber Pakhtunkhwa 138, 140, 144
Kilcullen, D. 81
Klein, J.A. 8
Krätli, Saverio 6
Kuchi 13, 14, 129–53
kuncha 154, 162–3, 167
Kurd 71, 74, 82–4, 86

L

Landen, R.G. 120, 121
land mine 134
language 3, 7, 20, 102, 104, 172
law 9, 10, 24, 34, 35, 55, 57, 82, 85, 86, 109, 110, 117, 133, 134, 166, 167, 198, 202–03, 208, 210
Leach, Melissa 45
legislation *see* law
legitimacy 12, 42–3, 45, 53, 57–9, 61, 63–6, 110, 173
Li Keqiang 33
liberalisation *see also* neoliberalism 12, 49, 75, 82, 87
literacy 135
livelihood 2–4, 7–8, 10, 11, 13–14, 22, 26, 28, 33, 41, 46, 50, 54, 64, 78, 80, 87, 92, 95, 96, 101, 104, 105, 117, 129, 130–1, 134–6, 144, 153, 156–7, 160–1, 164–6, 168, 171–4, 178, 181, 182, 188–91, 194–5
logging 41, 58, 61, 186
loyalty 120, 200, 205–06, 209
Lund, C. 45, 58

M

mahram 207, 208, 210
management (of land, resources) 2, 6, 8–9, 24–5, 27–8, 45–7, 50–1, 53, 56, 58, 60, 65, 91, 92, 95, 100, 105, 115, 117, 118, 124, 134, 164, 171, 172, 177–99

Index

maqad 204, 207–08, 210
marginalisation 6, 13, 87, 92, 103, 105, 144
market 7, 8, 13, 29–30, 41, 45, 47, 53–4, 60, 80, 91–108, 140, 145, 148, 149, 164, 165, 168, 170, 178, 181
marmot 59–60
al Mazrui, Salah viii, 14, 109–28
McCabe, J.T. 111–12
McCarthy, J. 45, 53
Mearns, R. 45
meat 14, 61, 80, 104, 114, 153, 156, 163
media 8, 73, 76, 80, 172
  social 33, 34
medicine *see also* herb 53, 135, 154, 164–6, 173, 180–2, 189–90, 192, 194, 197
Meena 179–80, 190
micro-finance 91
Middle East 1, 3, 9, 78, 80, 86, 203
Middleton, N. 4, 6
migration (human) *see also* displacement; transhumance 14, 78, 81, 87, 119, 129, 130, 135, 137–41, 143, 154, 156, 162, 168, 174, 189, 190, 196, 197
Miles, S.B. 120, 123
military 73, 79, 83, 86, 133, 143, 161
mining 10, 30, 41–4, 50, 51, 53, 54, 58–61, 64, 65, 143, 196
misconception (about nomadic pastoralists) 1–3, 6–11
mobility corridor 140–1, 143, 147
modernity; modernisation 3, 6, 29, 77, 87, 117
Mongolia 1, 4, 5, 7–9, 11–14, 17–70, 93, 130
motorcycle 18, 59, 78, 101
mountain 4, 14, 19, 20, 56, 57, 60, 109–28, 130, 135, 143
al Mughārī, Saʿīd bin Alī 118–19
Muscat 112, 12, 122, 124
musk deer 161
mutton 129, 140, 148
Myadar, O. 35

N

neoliberalism 13, 47–8, 53, 64, 66, 156
Nepal 163, 165
network, social 3, 9, 12, 13, 41, 43, 45–6, 54, 57, 61, 64, 71, 74, 85, 86, 147, 206
NGO 5, 21, 25, 27, 36, 91, 120, 188
non-equilibrium model 5
Nongbri, T. 164
nutag 13, 33, 42, 43, 46, 53–66

O

official 3, 6, 7, 10, 20, 22, 24, 44, 45, 61, 76, 85, 95, 101, 123, 130, 162, 164, 166, 184
oil 74–5
Oman 1, 10, 12, 14, 109–28
oran 11, 177–99,
Ostrom, Elinor 25–7
otherness 31, 42–3, 54, 56, 59, 63, 64, 73
otor 57, 64
overgrazing 21, 25, 50–1, 80, 153
ownership *see also* property 12, 25, 26, 28, 42, 45, 48, 63, 65, 82, 117, 118, 124, 188, 195

P

Pakhtun 129–35, 138, 140, 143
Pakistan 5, 13–14, 129–52
Palmyra 75, 78, 79, 81
participant-observation 2, 43, 160
pasture 7–10, 13, 14, 17, 19–21, 23–7, 32, 41–3, 45, 46, 48, 50–1, 53–5, 57–9, 61, 64–5, 80, 85, 95, 102, 109, 116, 129, 130134, 143–4, 147, 154, 156–7, 164, 166, 168, 171, 179, 187, 189, 190, 195, 197, 211
patronage 12, 71, 74, 76, 77, 85, 86
Patzelt, Annette 111
Peterson, John 120
plant *see also* herb 6, 19, 53, 111, 115, 119, 124–5, 135, 154, 165, 178, 180–2, 187, 189–90, 193–4, 197

Index

policy; policymaking 1–3, 5–11, 21–7, 30, 32–3, 35, 41, 46–8, 71–5, 77, 82, 85, 87, 135, 148, 153–4, 156–7, 159–60, 163–5, 168, 172–4, 178, 184
politics 1, 8, 11–13, 21, 23, 28–9, 31–2, 35, 45, 657, 64–5, 77, 85, 118, 122, 130, 133, 136, 148, 156–7, 159, 161, 164, 179, 184, 188–9, 194, 203, 205
populism 71, 75
poverty 27, 33, 47–8, 74, 78–83, 87, 91–3, 105, 144, 158, 163, 190
privatisation 6, 9, 25, 26, 28, 34–5, 41, 45–7, 50–1, 53, 71, 82, 95
property 42–3, 45–7, 53, 82–3, 134, 169, 171, 179, 203, 207
Punjab 136, 138, 144

Q

Qaidam Basin 17–20
Qinghai
  Lake 17
  Province 11, 17, 18, 26, 33
Qinghai–Tibet Plateau 91, 93, 104, 105

R

Rabari 6
Rae, J. 117
ur Rahim, Inam ix, 13–14, 129–52
rain 5, 60, 74, 86, 114–15, 130, 138, 143, 180, 187, 189, 192–3, 195, 197, 207, 213
Rajasthan 11, 177–99
rangeland 4, 5, 9, 10, 12–13, 24, 26–8, 48, 53, 59, 91, 95, 99, 100, 102–05, 110, 115, 117, 118, 134, 143, 153
  household contract system 13, 99, 105
remoteness 6, 135
resilience 3, 5, 8, 21, 54, 134, 159, 160, 173, 181

resources *see also* access; management 2, 3, 9–13, 19, 21, 23–5, 27–30, 34, 41–7, 50–1, 53–6, 58–61, 63–6, 74, 75, 78, 80, 92–3, 105, 110, 111, 129, 130, 134, 136, 143, 147, 148, 156, 163–6, 171–2, 177–99, 202
Ricoeur, Paul 157
rights *see also* access; tenure 2, 12, 13, 45, 51, 53–5, 57–8, 60, 63–4, 77, 83, 118, 134, 162, 164, 166, 171, 173, 180, 184–5
risk 1–3, 10–13, 21, 25, 27, 91–3, 102, 145, 166, 167
ritual 12, 168, 170–1, 178, 182
road 17, 18, 134, 161, 162, 165, 167–8, 170–1, 173
Rosenblatt, N. 81
Rung 13, 153–76
rural 3, 8, 12–13, 33, 42–3, 45–6, 54, 64–5, 71, 74–9, 86–7, 91–3, 101, 104, 162, 179, 190, 193, 195–6
Russia 34, 50, 131, 132

S

Sabloff, Paula L.W. 29
sacredness 178–9, 182, 188
sadhu 178, 182, 183
sanitation 82
Sariska Tiger Reserve 177–8, 182–3, 187
Saudi Arabia 5, 115, 200, 203
Schlecht, E. 116
school *see also* education 6–7, 74, 75, 86, 169–70, 173, 212, 213
scientist 5, 19, 20, 23, 35, 116, 119, 120
season; seasonality 5, 53–4, 93, 95, 101–05, 115, 129, 130, 134, 136–8, 145, 153, 154, 156, 163, 165, 187, 189, 193, 197, 210
sedentarisation; sedentary 3, 6, 9, 23, 31, 33, 35, 114, 118, 129, 130, 134–5, 157, 164, 170
al Sekhaneh, Wassef vii, 14, 200-14
Sen, Amartya 45

Index

settlement; settled *see also* sedentarisation 3, 7, 9, 11, 13, 81, 119, 130, 136, 146, 154, 170, 171, 180, 200, 203
shame 135, 206
shrine 178, 189
Sichuan 12, 94
Sikor, T. 45, 58
Singh, Aman ix, 11, 177–99
Sivaramakrishnan, K. 178
Skeet, Ian 120–1
Sneath, David 21–3, 28, 45, 46, 64, 93
socialism 41, 45–7, 53–4, 60, 131
socioeconomic 1, 9, 65, 87
socio-technical 46, 65
soil 5, 20, 50, 212
Soviet 31, 132, 140
spirit; spiritual 11–12, 42, 56, 58, 60, 63, 65, 168, 177, 180, 182, 196–7
Starr, Stephen 78
state 2, 3, 5–8, 10–14, 19, 22, 23, 26, 32, 34, 35, 41, 45, 48, 49, 51, 53, 54, 61, 71–6, 82, 85, 87, 95, 105, 117, 122, 123, 131, 133–4, 153, 154, 156–8, 160, 161, 163–5, 168, 172–4, 179, 189, 196, 200, 202, 203
Sternberg, Troy ix
Stoler, A.L. 123
subsidy 48, 80, 87, 98
subsistence 46–8, 50, 104, 118, 122, 148, 153, 163, 212, 213
suburb 12, 76, 78, 81, 87
Suchman, M.C. 58
sum 43–4, 46, 51, 56–63
Sunni 75–7, 87, 121, 131
survey 2, 44, 48, 58–61, 63, 119, 188–9, 191
sustainability 3, 8–11, 20–5, 27, 28–9, 30, 36, 63, 91, 124, 134, 136, 147, 160, 165, 168, 172, 178, 180, 192, 209
Swift, Jeremy 104
Syria 5, 12, 71–90, 117, 200, 203

T

Taklamakan Desert 4

Taliban 132, 134, 143
tax 47–8, 95, 143
temperature 5, 114, 119
tent 14, 81, 144, 200–14
tenure 3, 10, 12, 14, 117, 136, 144, 148
Tibet 1, 20, 156, 161, 163–4
tourism 26, 35, 95, 98, 101, 102, 104, 117, 164, 166, 172
trade 76, 104, 114, 117, 122, 138, 148, 153–4, 163–6, 168, 170–1, 173, 180
tradition 2, 7, 8–10, 12–14, 27–9, 42, 46, 53–4, 57, 61, 65, 76, 79, 80, 81, 85, 86, 91, 109–11, 114, 116–20, 121–2, 125, 130–1, 134, 135, 143–5, 147, 154, 158, 162–5, 168, 170–4, 178–81, 183–5, 188, 193–7, 202–05, 209–13
traditional ecological knowledge 178
transhumance 13, 130, 153–76
transport 10, 13, 53, 101, 135, 136, 138, 163, 168
tree 19, 59, 118, 171–2, 177, 180–2, 185–90, 192–3
trespass 11, 83, 110, 184, 197–8
tribe 12, 71–90, 110, 111, 114–18, 121, 124, 129–31, 133–5, 137–8, 143, 157, 161, 180 200, 202–03, 206–08, 211–12
truck 101, 143
Tsetsentsolmon, B. 31

U

Ulaanbaatar 56
UNEP 10
UNESCO 9, 202
urban 3, 22, 26, 32–3, 35, 41, 43, 46, 53, 56, 65, 71, 75, 77, 78, 95, 148, 204
'urf 109–10, 117

V

values 12, 14, 58, 103, 120, 135, 156, 157, 186, 188, 202–09
vegetation 4, 5, 56, 115–16, 147, 154, 180, 187, 190, 195–7
veterinary medicine 75, 86, 92, 135, 188–9

Index

W

Wadi Dana Nature Preserve 2
war 3, 35, 118, 130–4, 143, 144, 148, 163
water *see also* rain 5, 10, 24, 41, 42, 50, 53, 54, 57–60, 65, 74, 80, 82, 86, 95, 111, 177, 180, 187, 188, 190–1, 194–5, 204, 213
Weik von Mossner, Alexa 25
well 47, 58, 74, 78, 80, 86, 180
wetland 61, 95
Wilkinson, John 112, 117, 120–2
Williams, D.M. 20–1, 23, 27, 28
women 92, 135, 170, 173, 181, 185, 188, 203, 207–10
wool 48, 49, 153, 154, 156, 163–4
World Health Organization 9

Y

yak 4, 96, 101, 104, 156, 162, 168
Yeh, Emily 7
Younes, H.A. 110
young people; youth *see also* children 13, 57, 60, 73, 77, 78, 81, 153, 162, 165, 166, 168–70, 173, 189

Z

Zahran, M.A. 110
zud 5, 27, 48, 51, 53, 58